Law of Attraction: The Tithing Testimony

Experienced by: Michelle Finlayson
Co-Inspired by: Brian, Aidan and Dreana Finlayson

Dedication:

I dedicate this book to Me. I learn more and more to love me each day. I am forgiving me for all of my perceived failures. I am starting to see the Gem that I truly am!

This book is also for my babies! Aidan and Dreana, you mean the world to me. The moment your existence began, my life has only gotten better each and every moment. You are a true blessing, and I am the luckiest mommy ever! Thank you for choosing me. Thank you for loving me, and letting me love you! Thank you both for always being You.

Brian, you are an amazing husband. Thank you for knowing who I was before I did!

I love you Cleo, Chevy, Dodger, Anabel, Rose, Jack, Fate, Snowflake, Angel, Thunder, Dufus, SGM Fin, the Cat who is still nameless, and Mykah!

Mom, you never get thanked. Thank you for loving us as much as you do!

Jerry, I am thankful for you.

Dad, I love you.

Sandy, you are awesome.

Chad you are the best brother one could ever ask for.

Denae, Blayke and Declan, this book is dedicated to you as well, because you all are awesome, and I am blessed by You.

Rhonda Byrnes, you have opened my eyes. You are my mentor, and I am blessed to know you.

To all you readers: Do you know how long I have wanted to write to you? This is how special you are! Thank you for being in my world.

Contents
Acknowledgments

Law of Attraction:
The Tithing Testimony

Experienced by: Michelle Finlayson
Co-Inspired by: Brian, Aidan and Dreana
Finlayson

Introduction:
Why I wrote this book

Allow me to introduce myself. I am a woman who has been inspired my whole life. I am one of those who try and have tried everything. One who works with no pay; I do it only for the opportunity to hang out with a great mentor. I am one who goes to college, only because it was fun. I am one with the guts to tear down a house (for remodeling) with no instruction manual telling me how to fix it. I am the one who holds large dreams and just 'knows' they are possible. I am a dreamer. I am a glass half-full gal. I always knew there was more and had difficulty settling for anything less.

     I felt and still feel this way; my downfall was I needed everyone's approval in my endeavors. Instead of the support, I was told over and over to be 'normal.' They thought my dreams were too big, they thought they were too much effort when there were other 'normal' things I should be doing. They told me I was a mom and I needed to start growing up. My desires were large, though as I accomplished many of them; they all felt empty as I wasn't receiving the support from the ones I mostly wanted it from. I fell a lot, I got up a lot, and I succeeded a lot. Though none of it meant anything if I didn't receive the, "Good job," or "I believe in you," from my family.

     I guess I just always knew 'I' would happen. I kept lifting my head back up when someone I loved forgot to encourage and believe in me. I hoped that one day I would get my successes and also feel like a success. The only way I figured I could feel like that success was to finally get, "I'm proud of you." All I could do in the meantime was continue to follow my dreams and hope my miracle of finally being approved by my family would eventually happen.

     Continuing, I was introduced to the book, "The Secret" by a friend. I read the entire book and learned that the way I had always been, was considered normal to many! I started to realize that all of my daydreams were the normal process for the life I had always "Seen." Rhonda Byrnes, (without knowing) taught me that it was okay to be me. She taught me I could help better the world with me being me. I could do this when I stopped believing my daydreams were a waste of time; and allowed them to come through. She taught me that the dreamers are the ones waking up the world. She taught me that, "What I do" is my gift. She taught me I should love me enough to see my contribution in this world. I read her books like some read the Bible. I took years to practice what she said, and a lot of my 'dreams' started to become believable.

This has brought me to today. As I have practiced over the years, I have had this inherent need to share as Rhonda shared with me. What she teaches is absolute truth! Magic is real; God (or whomever you call your higher power) is real! Miracles still happen! Life is here for you. You are life. When you access this power, life becomes really good!

My journey has brought us to our book. All those years I wrote everything and anything down; keeping all my thoughts stacked in large storage bins. I loved and love to write. As I wrote down all my learned info and inspired ideas, the collection bins began overfilling. I was finding my courage to be me again. I grew and grew, and one day I was led to tithing. Tithing helped me accomplish my achievements and helped me accept the love from my family. Immediately, once I tithed, I saw many miracles begin to happen. I knew it was finally time to bring my writings to you. I decided to test God on what he said in Malachi 3 in the Bible. (International Bible Society, 1984) I tithed and documented it down. I wanted to know if this was true. I wanted to know if this could be true for me. I made a diary; I tested God.

As they say, when you are finally ready, "Mountains will move for you!" My mountain has been a consistent dialog in a short amount of time. Writing this book has been so much fun and so much 'In the flow.' It has been therapy for me, as all of me can finally be acceptable to our world. I wrote this down for you and am documenting it for me.

One last note; all my life I have been trying to get rich; and now it is happening. I am becoming the definition of wealth as I am learning to let go. As I let go, God takes over, and what He has come up with is utterly amazing. It is a feeling of bliss, of being taken care of, of learning I am worthy. I am worth what it is I desire. This feeling is like no other feeling.

What I have mostly learned from this writing is that it was me all along who is supposed to be proud. I am the one that matters, and when I become proud of me, so does everyone else. Thank you for being with me on my journey!

As always, Michelle

Chapter 1:
The Journey Begins
19 September 2013, Thursday

Tithing came into my life one day when I learned of a prosperity class that was going to be given at church. This was synchronistic, because for the last few weeks I had been asking God to find me an affordable way to receive energetic clearings from Christie Marie Sheldon. God instead answered my request through a course I could afford.

At first, week after week during church, they would talk about the class and I would think, "This is something for me to do in the future." I filed it. I held it in my awareness for a later time. Then as the weeks neared for the class to begin, the message seemed to be speaking only to me. First it was church, and then one Sunday evening I received a call asking me personally to join the class. At the time of the call I had plenty of projects going on. It felt completely right to say to the woman, "No, not at this time."

The next Sunday we did not go to that church. Instead I still had been looking at other churches; looking for the best fit. This church was great, though it was not like the Tennessee church I came from. I was searching for Tennessee in Colorado, still. At this new church I tithed ten percent of my income which consisted of change I found and the change from my twenty dollars a day I received from Brian (my husband) to buy our groceries.

I had come so far in my decision over the years about tithing. And I was finally comfortable giving back to God 'my' (money I collected that was always considered extra) ten percent. Though messing with Brian's income was out of the question; because that was 100 percent accounted for. We lived month to month with all of our investments and bills. We had lots of obligations with paying everyone back, so the thought of also giving money away seemed far-fetched! It was not like I was being greedy and wanting the money for all the good stuff; I was strapped with paying everyone back. My old debts took priority over any new; or so I thought at the time.

This week we could see everything our current journey had led us to. Our journey had led us to really giving up, really surrendering to all our past and living only from the present moment and the 'new' from here on out! It felt good to just live! We also went to a barbeque. We were finally doing it. We loved having the choice of church, loving our home, and loving our new friends. We finally separated ourselves so much; we jumped off the cliff from everything and everyone we knew.

We started really living! Living day by day and seeing the blessings unfold in Life. We were happy. The kids went back to school on Tuesday, they loved it. Brian was on his second week back to work, he loved it! I was getting used to the idea of being home with no 'real' job.

This whole 'no job' thing was difficult for me; though I allowed myself to learn what was being taught. This gave me the opportunity to find value in me. My job was "Me" and it came with a to-do-list of learning to find significance in all my dreams and all my interests. I had permission from the bills (Brian took care of the bills so I never saw my 'lack' from not having a job) and my husband supported my new role. I was the only one who had to learn to be okay with it. I knew this, so every day I practiced breathing and letting myself learn to accept all of this. Every day I learned more, I learned to trust more and more; and soon I would learn to accept this. During that time, I maintained the house, prepared dinner, made my own bread, and was always available for my children and all their school activities. The family ran smoothly as I practiced.

Each day I also made video blogs on YouTube and continued to write.
Another significant accomplishment was that I started working out. I began realizing each day how awesome it was to have a free gym via my husband's job. Because our bills were so strapped, a gym membership would have made me feel guilty. So every time I drove to the free gym I got to be really happy! I would realize over and over that I manifested this! I intended to be on this active duty post; I intended it and I got it. Things like this, the simple things, are what eventually brought me to where I am today. And today I am good.

We also were excited to get back to being around a whole bunch of soldiers. Brian and I met on active duty years ago, and when we left the Army and moved back to Wisconsin, we found ourselves missing the comradery. We missed the connections from all the friends, and the same lifestyles we experienced when we were both in the Army together.

Also, In Wisconsin, (years later) Brian decided to go back into the service as a Reservist and then, later he took a full time AGR position. AGR means he worked as an Active duty Soldier for the Reserves. He counseled many different reserve units. In Wisconsin he had a really good job; though he was one of the only army people in the area. Each day I would beg him to take his uniform off prior to us going out, because he would constantly get stopped as people would want to thank him for his service. People began treating him as if he was a celebrity. We were thankful for the gifts, though also began to feel like we couldn't go anywhere where he was not noticed.

Needless to say, we were excited to live the army life again with other soldiers, this time where it was normal to walk around in ACU's! I enjoyed the Army life because (to me) it brought back family and community (which I was striving for.) I also wanted prosperity. I wanted to have the consciousness of a multi-millionaire while also 'in' the Army. I know and adore the Law of Attraction, so I did what I know works; we threw this large request to God as an intention. We affirmed that we would be wealthy, make friends, be happy, call this new place our home, and also have high vibrational people to hang out with.

As intentions go, we are enjoying everything. We love it. It all came true so far. We have the home we were striving for. The kids are loving school, they feel popular and have fun and excel in their academics. The soldiers we hang out with are all high ranking and have a business mindset. We are involved with church and school. We volunteer and are a member of our community. I enjoy my days doing what I love and the people I love enjoy theirs. My dogs are happy, safe and accepted. My house is clean and my overall consciousness to wealth has shifted toward the better. How this all came about; I can tell you are only manifested intentions. I have no answers besides that, it just did.

To clarify, there was a lot on my part to grow into. Again I started working out. I was learning to be comfortable staying home and continuing my Vlog's and my writings. I also allowed myself to grocery shop. This is significant because of our current money situation; I hated to be the one at the cash register. I began overcoming this fear with allowing my husband to give me 20 dollars in cash each day so I had a 'no fail' plan to become friends with the cash register again. I was making ground in this area; I was growing.

I also started reclaiming the paper work of the household. I began managing the paper work required to become foster parents. I also started setting up doctor appointments. This is all significant because when I began, I felt, I was at rock bottom; in turn I had detached from every responsibility except my children. Brian had been in charge of everything, and now I was allowing myself again to try; to reclaim a sense of worth. I was allowing myself to rise. So when I found myself on the phone transferring our doctor status from Wisconsin to Colorado; I was feeling pretty damn good about myself!

Continuing, I then put up an ad asking to babysit babies! I was getting more comfortable being a stay at home mom! I was getting really good at accepting "Me!" I have wanted a baby for a while and was overly excited as we waited for a foster baby to come into our life.

Still I was getting anxious and figured babies would get here quicker if I could occupy myself with other people's children. I put the ad up and soon received a call and an interview to babysit a nine week old baby boy.

Oh things were getting so good! Sunday, the next week, I decided we were going back to our original church. Possibly this decision was so easy because I had allowed myself to try something new the week prior. Something shifted over the weekend and I found myself yearning for our original church. Funny, how that works, huh.

That morning I counted all of my money and prepared 10 percent for the tithe at church. I also went the next step. After I counted the ten percent, I also counted ten percent again for the next week, because God says to give your, "First Fruits." I put that bag in the cupboard and decided, any extra money the week would bring, would be added to the initial bag. I was feeling pretty good. And of course because I was, "In the flow" I received a call from a friend to watch her little girl for the evening! I was ecstatic. I get my one year old and a paycheck! How much better does that get?

In church, later that morning, the Prosperity class is talked about again. And this time I heard God screaming, "Do this!"
After the service I told Brian that I thought I needed the class, and he was very supportive. I talked to the lady about joining and said we will bring the 55 dollars (the cost of the class) on Thursday. It was funny what happened next. She looked at me 'all serious' and said, "You know this class requires you to tithe ten percent?" I said, "Yeah, I am okay with that, I do that already." Remember my income was always tithed. Even though I did my part in tithing, I still felt her comment as I was not tithing on Brian's.

I then remembered the cash in my wallet from counting both tithes earlier that morning. I counted the bills and realized I had 56 dollars! I do not know how my change from my 20's turned into that much, but it did. And to top it off, I had a dollar bill that I had written a "Million" on that I never would spend. That was my special dollar. Even though I have that dollar at all times, I make a conscious effort that it stays in my wallet. With those figures, I had 55 dollars, and that was the exact amount of the class! I ran up to her and said, "You are never going to believe this!" And she said, "Nope happens all the time!" What happens all the time is the synchronicity of when the time is right, the resources are always available. Many times it is considered crazy and/or miraculous.

There is actually a story on "The Secret" (under their website TheSecret.tv and if you choose the tab "secret stories" you can find similar stories) where a woman was losing her home and had to make the decision on a weekly basis if it was her or her dog who was going to eat. She chooses her dog. It came to a point where her electricity bill was going to be shut off. She knew, "The Secret" at this point and started to affirm that God (or universe or whomever brings you comfort) was going to fix this! One of her 'signs' that she asked to be shown at times when she needed confirmation were balloons.

This specific afternoon she sat out on her porch which faced a park. Two people were sitting with balloons on their chairs. She thought it was just a coincidence. Next she had an inspired idea to go to the bank and take the credit card she had (which she never used) and pull out the 200 dollars (which was on the card) for the electric bill. She drives down this long windy road and sees two (not one!) mailboxes with balloons tied to them. She again thinks it is just a coincidence; "A birthday party must be happening in the neighborhood" are her thoughts. She then gets to the bank and a newer teller (only a few days on the job) takes care of her transaction. Because she is new, she is slower with the transaction. The teller is on the telephone confirming the girl's money status when the girl looks in her purse and sees two one-hundred dollar bills. This woman was losing her electricity; do you really think she would have forgotten that she had two one-hundred dollar bills in her purse? She then cancels the transaction with the teller; and turns around to see the manager come out of his office with a bouquet of balloons! This time, she did not think it was a coincidence and trusted that God came through! (Byrnes, 2007-2014)

Back to our story, with another significant point; the 55 dollars I had in my wallet was 'my money.' I purchased this class with my money! This was the only money I had! I gave it all because I thought this class was worth my all! I wanted change so much that I was going all in.

Later in the day, we were home. The kids went to play. Brian went downstairs to watch the Packer game. I listened to the first chapter of the prosperity Cd's (the material for the prosperity class.) As I listened more and more, I kept getting the feeling that we should tithe ten percent of Brian's income also. I was getting really upset at my thoughts and was overjoyed when my little friend knocked at the door. It was time to babysit and the CD's and all of my wavering thoughts were getting a break!

We had a good time babysitting and soon her mom was here to take her home. Her mom wanted to give me twenty dollars. Mind you, I charge four dollars an hour and my little friend was only here for two of them. She explained that she pays her daycare ten dollars an hour and she also wanted to pay me ten dollars an hour. I told her "No," I couldn't receive it, and I asked her to only pay me four dollars an hour. She agreed and later gave Dreana (my daughter) the other 10 because she 'helped.'
After she left I was mad at myself. Here I am making all of these financial breakthroughs by letting myself participate in the class, and I still could not receive more money. Right then I said to God, "Show me" because I wasn't letting myself shift. I needed His help.

In hindsight, as I write this, I am starting to get it. It reminds me of when I finally learned how to lose weight. I had been excelling in my first few weeks of a weight loss program (this was right after my son was born) and someone asked if I was pregnant. Here I am actually consistently doing it, losing 2.5 pounds a week, and instead of getting a "Good job," I hear, "What's wrong with you."

But you see, just because I finally knew how to do it; my life was not perfect; instead my journey finally got to begin. So yes I finally was doing it, I finally was tithing 'my, (not my husband's) First Fruits,' though still I was not yet perfect with this, I had only just begun. All of this stuff, all of the stuck stuff, finally gets to come up. I now get to look at it all and begin unraveling its perceived hold.

This part sucks, don't get me wrong, but if it is coming up, this means it has nowhere to go but to go Away! Prior to it going away, it has to be identified and worked through so an opening can be shown for its exit! In hindsight, I asked for all of the crying this week, all of the uncomfortable 'change;' because I asked God to change me. I asked for help because I did not know how to help myself.

Continuing with the next week, Brian went to Georgia for three days for work; and prior to him going he purchased all the groceries for the time he would be gone. We did not have to spend any money the entire time he was away. I was able to fill my wallet again with the ten dollars I made from babysitting. I tithed one dollar, and guess which dollar I finally had the courage to part with? Yep, my special 'one million' dollar bill was the bill of choice. I was letting go, I was beginning to trust God with my finances!

Each day that Brian was away I considered tithing on his income. I Googled tithing testimonies on YouTube and watched many videos, I watched a lot more than many, I watched tons!

I cried and yelled at God a lot. I screamed, "I do not know how this is possible? All of the money we have is accounted for." I screamed, "Are you kidding me?" Each time I screamed and/or cried, more and more layers came off. I was freeing myself. I was starting to accept that if I did not know, God did. And if God did not know, I had to know that truth as well, even if 'that truth' was wrong. I had to know if tithing would save me. I had to know if God would save me. It was hard because if I was not saved I had nowhere else to turn. Tithing was my last resort; God was my last resort. I hoped God was real, but if He wasn't, I was letting myself see the truth anyway.

I finally got to acceptance and I asked, "If I am to do this can you please talk to Brian for me about our decision?" Then out of nowhere I received a Facebook posting from Brian. He took a picture of a penny sitting in a flower (not on the ground, in a flower!) and he said in the post, "Maybe it doesn't grow on trees, but in a flower?" I laughed, cried, and thanked God. It was as if Brian's soul was saying, "This will be okay." Brian may not have known what was going on, but his conscious did. Continuing on with my acceptance, I told Brian (that evening) we were going to tithe ten percent of his income. I explained to him that I did not know if tithing was going to work; but it felt right and we were going to try. And all he said was, "Okay."

The evening continued and soon I gained the courage to look at the bank account; I had not done this in two years. I noticed there was seven thousand dollars there, relieved at the amount; I glanced (very quickly) at the deposit from the first of the month. I wrote ten percent of that deposit and put it in my 'money bag' that I had created the past Sunday. I was thankful we 'had enough.' It seemed it was easy to give, at least this time. The only reason this was easy was because I know (from doing the bills two years ago) that Brian makes about $4,000 per month. I had no clue what was coming in and out, but anything over four thousand seemed like an overabundance.

All I had to do that day was actually look at the balance and write the check. I wrote a check for $228.69.
I then started thinking about our rental income. Really, we were not receiving much rental income. Basically we (in the past) paid our mortgages and then were reimbursed by the renters. The amount over was never really significant. But our focus was always on, "This will be great in thirty years." This was fine until this past year when everything messed up. We had a renter in one of our houses that cost us 'tens of thousands' of dollars and a lot of head-ache. That property (so far) had been a loss. Though, somehow we were able to manage.

Side note, talking about how God takes care of you, always, prior to any rental problems our bills were stretched. We always had 'enough' but never any room to do anything super-special. About this same time was when I started a huge 'growth period.' I could not take this "day to day," this "having our paycheck only make it month to month" anymore. My dreams as a kid and continuing from then had always been to be rich. I did not want to be super woman or a doctor. I wanted to be an author and rich. Since then (around this time frame) my dreams of 'being rich' turned into wealth. My definition of wealth is more than 'enough money,' more than 'enough love,' and more than 'enough health,' more than enough everything you could possible dream for! Wealth is life, wealth is love.

I did not seem to know how to get to this definition. I decided to ask God to help show me. During that time, I handed all the bills to Brian and learned to trust him. He was so detached from the money, that I figured he could just pay them, instead of me moaning and pouting about how unfair it all was. I have no-clue how he did it. I went to Tennessee for a year with my dogs and my kids and the bills got paid, somehow we could afford the gas trips from Wisconsin to Tennessee monthly. Somehow we could still afford Christmas. Somehow we could afford the beginning of the rental mess.

Now when I say God always takes care of you, I can guarantee you we did not have any money for my extras last year. Though, last year still happened. And so now, yes we were taken care of without tithing. Though, I think, tithing is a deeper level of trust with God. And we are all taken care of no matter what. Though, by being obedient to God with our finances, He shows us more prosperity. Tithing is asking to learn how to trust more and to be shown the instructional manual of how to grow from where we are and where we want to be.

Now, back to me considering our income from the renters; remember we were not receiving much in income; it was really just reimbursement with a little extra. Though little as it was, it was still income, right? So here again I argued with God. Our budget was exact. How can I tithe on rental income when it was pretty much exact? And anything over was going to a tithe? What's the point?

Also that extra, that 'anything over' was and is what we bought groceries with. And to top it off, not only (last year) did we have major problems with that renter, we also had a renter that owed us five months of rent and refused to give us our money. And then, all of our properties went vacant at the same time. We have five of them; can you imagine all of those mortgages not getting reimbursed?

And then we had to for the first time, pay a property manager because we now live in Colorado, instead of Wisconsin where the properties reside. And then, we have to come up with all of their security deposits because they all are moving out at the same time. And then one of the properties has a lady who refuses to move out. Like really? And then we had to evict another tenant, so they (according to law) got a few months free rent also! Great system for landlords, huh! How we did this all and managed so far, I do not know. God has taken care of us. He kept us afloat!

To cover some of this downfall, Brian's mom loaned us three thousand dollars. This was supposed to be paid back by me getting my real-estate license. I had to get down on my hands and knees and beg my brother for the money for licensing. He said, "Yes." So as I humbled myself, at least I received a positive result.

Weeks later he said he was not going to give me the money. No hope of salvation from our mess, all we could do was keep moving forward. And amidst all of this, I decided to tithe. I know it makes zero logical since, but this was my decision. But since I could not figure it out myself, I turned to God.

God told me to tithe. Okay, so you know how I tithed that first paycheck, shocked we actually could do it comfortably, then God told me to tithe on the one rent check I finally received. Finally one rental is rented, four are still not. I did some more crying and saw another deposit of 730 dollars. I buckled down and wrote a check for seventy-three dollars and put it in my tithing bag. Though, remember we had seven thousand dollars, so this hurt, but still seemed okay. I then heard God say, "There's more."

I receive $255.00 dollars per month for a disability from the Army. Every month that $255.00 dollars is great and needed for our budget. God told me to write a check for twenty-five dollars to give to Him. Again we had seven thousand dollars, so, I guess this could be okay. All of that is $327.19; our tithe was getting paid. Remember all of my financial issues; $327.19 is huge to give away. Though currently, in this moment, it seemed like it was doable. I did not, and still do not know if it is doable forever, though here, in this now, it is.

The day passed and Thursday evening was here, it was class night! Throughout the week, I cried a lot, and finally accepted I was doing this. I was excited to finally allow myself to tithe.

I get to church and the class is cancelled.
We were having a flood and everyone needed to hurry up and make it back home.

Side note: In this class they usually let you sign up for the first two weeks. It is a twelve week course. When I signed up, it was the second week sign up. I listened to the CD's for week one, and I was going to class two of the course. Now, this Thursday coming up, is the 'Real' second class.

As I was driving home that evening, I was mad. I told God that I was finally there, and I did not know if I could have the courage to do it next week. Then I laughed at the irony of the whole thing. I was finally 'ready,' and then I got stopped from Giving. Then I started to think about Abraham from the Bible. (International Bible Society, 1984) Remember, he was told to sacrifice his son on the Alter. I am sure his week (then) was a lot like mine. Finally he accepts it, and God says he does not have to actually do it! Because you know what they say, "If you give, you will be given back." So what's the point?

And if you do not give, you are cursed. (Referenced from Malachi 3) (International Bible Society, 1984) When you do not give, you have money troubles; your car and computer break down. When you give, your bills are miraculously paid and then you also become prosperous. I know; though, these are the rules.

I came home, confused, though thankful. And just kept breathing and asking for continual guidance and courage for the next week.

. . . .

Chapter 2
Taking the Leap

The next day (Friday) at six A.M., I saw an ad for a mom wanting a babysitter for the coming Saturday. For some reason, I 'knew' she would answer early in the morning. I called, and I got the job. Excited, knowing I am going to be forty dollars richer!

Side note: The mom with the nine week old called this week and decided she wanted to be home with her baby. I did not get that job. I had to keep breathing and reminding myself that that specific mom was not my source of income.

So when the new lady said yes at 6 A.M., I was feeling very prosperous and very thankful!
Later that morning I went to the gym, and had an awesome run. I was feeling thankful for my 'almost tithing,' for my 'almost forty dollars.' I was feeling clear. I felt like I was in the flow, and no problems were in my future!

I get home and checked the ads again; I do this hoping to expand my current prosperity. If I can get myself a Saturday job, I can also get myself a baby! I soon saw an ad from a mother looking for babysitting for her baby! How much better does all of this get! I am excited, though this mom will only pay 200 dollars instead of 400 a week (which I should charge,) so here began my conversation with God. I'm like, "God, she has a baby," and God's like, "Yeah, but she is only paying half of what you want to be worth."

As I am arguing with God, I receive a phone call. A mom (who saw my ad offering babysitting) had two older kids and wanted to know if I could watch them on Saturday. I could not believe my luck; of course I said yes! Now I have 80 dollars coming Saturday evening! There were no babies (only a toddler,) though the money was good! I tithed my eight dollars and prepared for Saturday.

This all happened on Friday the 13th! My Vlog that day was about what a lucky Friday the 13th it was!
....

Saturday came, and I can tell you all these children were a lot different than I thought it was going to be. I had my first experience with a lot of kids. I am becoming a foster mom and my goal is to have eight kiddos. Currently, what I want is not what I wanted in the beginning. As time flows, my goals have changed throughout the process. In the beginning, I wanted some babies, some teen pregnant moms, another five year old girl, another eight year old boy, and some autistic kids. I wanted both fostering and adoption.

This was the general goal, and since then, the idea of babysitting came into my head. All the kiddos I am wanting are all doable now that I have babysitting and fostering as options.

Also the space of the house and seats in the car are determining factors that have helped critique my decisions.

My current goal so far is: I am moving out of my oversized, gorgeous office downstairs, into the laundry room. That room can hold two teenage moms and their two babies. The room is very private and large. I also want another four or five year old girl to bunk with my five and a half year old princess. I would also like another seven or eight year old boy and my nine year old son to share a room.

That makes two moms, two babies, my two kids, and the two older ones which all equal up to eight! The foster agency (Colorado) says that is the max! The current plan allows for the current space in the house. It also allows for the four younger ones to have space in our current vehicles. And my current plan assumes the teens are going to want their time away from the family. They also will either come with cars or be eligible to start gaining their cars pretty soon.

I am also assuming, in their case (the pregnant moms) (because foster kids usually have to go to public school) that they will get the option of home school. With this plan, they will be able to do their sleeping, we all know during pregnancy the majority is spent in dream land. It will also give me an opportunity to go to the gym at five A.M. whenever I want (even if Brian is not here.) Reason being, I will have two more adults in the house. It will give them time to do their studies and give them time to work. When they work they get the opportunity to tithe (and this I get to teach them!) and see just how far their paychecks get to go to get them their cars, future apartments, college and a good step on life.

I get my babies from my two teens and I also want to babysit two more throughout the day. I can either leave the two babysat babies with the teens or bring them along to pick up Dreana and her sister from school. The two boys can walk home. And Voila! I have room in my car!

Initially I wanted ten kids because that is what the Wisconsin foster agency said, Colorado said eight. With my current plan, I can still have ten! I love the teens because I feel I can be a great mentor to them. I love babies, who wouldn't? And it is a huge goal of mine to give a sister and a brother to my two!

Yes, I want this many children! Crazy, but this is my dream! Moving forward that is my current goal; I also have the intention to own the home I currently am renting, as well as to have myself a Denali!

I have been on my spiritual journey for a few years. I have seen many miracles and much growth. I have decided I really do enjoy a big, loving, happy family. I enjoy traveling. I enjoy the idea of speaking to millions about this awesome universe, God, higher self (which ever terminology brings you the most truth) and I enjoy my writings. I also was unsure if I liked property because it made me rich or if I had a real passion for it. Oh and I do; I really enjoy property! I have my five houses. I want lots of apartment buildings, some duplexes, and some business ventures. I am sure as time continues I will have many more goals.

Prior to the home we currently live in, I 'just' lived in a house that I bought then moved out and purchased another one to replace it. All of these houses were just that, houses, investments. This is the first home I love! Isn't that funny how it works like that! All of the money I have spent on houses, and the one I call home, the one which is my favorite, is owned by someone else!

Hence I have an intention to own this home and then dig out the hilled driveway, and tear down the one car garage (that currently exists.) After that, the garage spot will be lowered to the same level as the lower level. We can put a three car garage there and on top of it (the top will now be the same level as our second floor) we can add extra house. I can leave the lower level bedroom (huge, the size of a living room) for the teens, assuring their continued privacy. It is almost like they have their own apartment. I can also move my office out of the laundry room into a brand new bedroom upstairs. The extra hallway will be off from my dining room, offering easy access to the other two bedrooms and an extra bathroom!

This is all good because (as foster children) babies can only stay in the parents' room until they are a year and a half. When they are older than a year and a half, I am not going to want them to bunk with kids six and seven years of age. And if the babies are different sexes, a boy and a girl, they are going to need separate bedrooms. So there you have it, my remodel intention!

My teens are probably going to be going to college when they graduate high school; this ensures reason for me to plan for their little ones! There is a good chance that I am going to need to make room for their babies while they are studying for a short time; here is our reason for getting them their own rooms. How all of this comes together, I am not sure yet, my role is to make my intentions and trust their outcome! This or something much greater!

Currently our home is owned by our landlord. One of my intentions is for him to sell this house to us as well as (when he retires from property management) his other properties.

None of this has been talked about with him; it is just talked about with God. We shall see how and if that is 'God's highest plan' for all parties involved.

Also the Denali! The reason for the Denali is because it is pretty. I need a larger vehicle to have my large family as well as their friends. I actually hated the fact of giving up my beautiful jeep, but I wanted my large family more. I came to terms with giving up my jeep, so the search for a large vehicle began.

I found the Denali. Now I just wait for it to come to me. I bought my jeep about two years ago, so obviously if I traded it, there would be negative equity. Also I have no idea what our credit score is for trading. And a Denali is twenty to thirty thousand more than my jeep, and you already know what our financials look like. I have no clue about the house and houses and Denali, though these are my current intentions! I do have a very strong feeling that they are coming soon! I do not know how it all comes together, though I have a feeling it is.

For the current time I see things as they are. I also see how things are unfolding. I know it is all working, even though I do not see how the end result shows up. I see that my current tithe is possible! My current Jeep (with 'shifts' with the driving of kids) is do-able, and my current house can accommodate! For now, everything we have is 'enough,' we have plenty. I also see our preferences have a say as well, and I see them finally being heard! Our job now is to wait, trust and watch how it all unfolds!

Now back to my Saturday. This day I had a lot of kids, all between five and ten years old. And then three neighborhood kids, and a one year old! I ran 24/7. I fixed this fight, cleaned this mess, fed this kid, and then held a one year old the entire time! This was a lot more work then I assumed! I still want a large family, though, now I understand more of what a large family consists of, lots of people and lots of needs.

As the day continues we get a phone call from my husband's buddy, Richard. He says he just was asked to tour with a popular country music singer! This is huge, what an enormous, unexpected blessing in his life. And then Richard asked Brian, if Brian would tour with him. How it would work is the country star does a tour to all of the military, so he goes overseas to do concerts for the troops! Richard asked the military general (in charge of this project) if he can have a military guy (my husband) come along. With this current plan, my husband would be able to go on tour with him. He would also be able to hang out with his best friend for quite some time! I would have my teens to have some adults in the house. I have been writing all my life; though Brian has been writing poems all his. His poems have been turning into Richard's songs.

And to top it off; Brian would be able to do this under the 'job,' the Army! I mean seriously! Would I have been able to come up with this! This is all God!

Here is another story that happened. As I was going through another layer of the tithing, Brian comes home for lunch and tells me someone called 'out of the blue' and asked if we would sell one of our properties! The property she asked about is the one we had the most problems with. She wanted it because it is the house next to hers and she wants a double lot.

Oh my goodness, if you would have asked me last year, I would have said, "No;" not until I receive a large profit! Though now, sure! Take it! It is all currently too much! I told Brian whatever he thinks a good price is to sell the property, to go for it, though no matter what, I am taking ten percent of the sale price and giving it to God. Because if He can actually help with this property, then I can give Him back what is His; His ten percent.

With this, that property could be done, over. I can give to God. My grandparents could be paid off (they bought the property for me) and (currently we are not making our 'reimbursement' from it) so we would have that much more in our budget to pay our tithes! And there are also some property taxes due (from last year) that are more than welcome to go away! Oh, this would be lovely! This or something much better! I now receive all the blessings due to me!

I tell you all of this because I want you to see what was presented so far, even though we have not even tithed yet! And I wanted you to see how 'my circle' has also prospered from me not tithing yet. They say when you clear, everyone around you also becomes clear!

Another thing to mention is that our country music star and my property have not yet come together; though they were offered. I guess being offered these large things is amazing in themselves! If we are feeling this good from 'just the offers,' can you imagine what it feels like to have them accomplished?

Another thing, I asked Richard last night what it felt like to have people singing his songs, and having an agent ask him to tour. He said, "Very amazing and super natural." I then asked him what he thought shifted all of this for him. He told me he thinks because he followed through on his decision to stop drinking 31 days ago.

I thought about that a lot last night. My decision to really tithe, I think, is shifting me and my beliefs. I think there is so much more that I cannot currently comprehend, and by this act of very large faith, I feel like I will never be able to look back. Richard, thank you for your comment last night; it really grounded me more in my decision.

Saturday came and went.

....

Sunday was here and we were told not to tithe in church, just at the class. This was imperative because at the end of our twelve weeks, if our lives did not change, our tithing was to be refunded. And by tithing at the class, the money could be documented. We were told to 'bless' the offering basket as it passed at church. On the way to church I was okay with this. Also on the way to church, I noticed all the loose change in my husband's cup holder. I collected it, counted it, and then pulled ten percent out. The ninety percent went into my change purse, and the ten percent went into an extra envelope sitting in my purse (I decided to give this to the church.) That amount was only like thirty cents. Though, do you know how awesome it was to give that thirty cents to church, and realize I was three dollars more rich! Unexpected blessings are everywhere. Enjoy what you have and you will receive more!

Sunday night I was breezing through Craigslist and I saw an ad for Surrogate Moms. This ad jumped out at me. My story goes like this. After my daughter was born my husband had a vasectomy. A year later at Christmas, I realized I wanted another baby. For years I begged my husband's body to grow back. My intention was, "God can do this." During those four years I tested positive twice on pregnancy tests. My doctor thought I was crazy, and she asked me if I was cheating on my husband. It was almost as if I could get, but not stay pregnant. After those years, I finally gave up, and am now on my journey to being a foster mom. It is funny when you finally accept, how things change.

So I wanted a baby. I am now getting my babies from the foster agency. The Surrogate agency has moms who want a baby, and they can get a baby from me. I figure as I am 'full' (because I am already getting what I want, my foster babies) it will be easier (then it would have been in the past) to hand over the baby in my belly after nine months. It appears as if it is all a win/win for everyone!

I replied to the ad and moments later (on a Sunday night!) she replied back to me. Talk about being in the flow! She sent some questions for me to consider, such as would I consider an abortion if something went wrong, would I carry multiples, would I carry for gays or singles. I answered her questions, and then added my requests. I added my family, including my two kids, will help interview the prospective couple. I will do this if I can at least send birthday cards and Christmas cards each year; my way of keeping in contact without overbearing the new family. And my third requirement was/is financial. On her ad she said we (surrogate moms) would get paid 16 to 40 thousand for the pregnancy and the process.

I felt my response was 'In the flow' and accurate when I typed my last prerequisite. I said what I thought was a reflection of my growing financial frequency. I said, "I will only do this for a couple willing to pay forty thousand dollars." The forty thousand (I chose) was because the top of her range was forty thousand, and my family only gives the best and expects only the best.

I never heard from her again. I am not sure if that is the process of weeding her and her vibration out so another agency can come in, or if I am trying to raise my financial frequency in the wrong way. Either way I am not judging myself, I am just watching to see if or how being a Surrogate Mom unfolds. This or something much better!

I thought about surrogacy. I know I truly want to do it. It is a definite desire. The reasons are: One, I get to experience pregnancy again. I never thought I would. (Funny how that sentence came out, maybe it is the reason I never did 'stay' pregnant in the past.) I also know what it feels like when your dreams come true, it would be awesome to be a part of someone else's dreams. It is also funny timing that when the ad popped out at me, it was when I was already full with the plans of being a foster mom. The foster agency answers my desires with their babies; and I can answer someone else's desires as I am able to carry what they cannot. I do not 'need' to keep (of course I may not need them, though I am blessed by them and they are blessed by me) the baby that would come out of me. It becomes much easier to hand off the little guy or gal to a mom who has been praying for years for them.

And yes I know I would be sad when our nine months were over. Though only 49 percent of me would be sad; while the other 51 percent of me would be filled with lots of good emotion as I get to see mom and baby finally come together. It was perfect timing when this ad presented itself! The reason I tell you this story, is because all of this is being presented to me now. And I am hoping for it all, but also watching how it unfolds. God says, (In the Bible under Malachi 3, paraphrased) that He will open the gates of Heaven and pour down so many blessings, that there will be too much abundance to handle! I am watching; I am curious if this is what He was talking about. (International Bible Society, 1984)

Monday morning was here and I prepared for my run. I was grumpy. I think my vibration was circled around the tithing. I ran, and I ran. It was neat because the gym was packed with a lot of soldiers, and when I was running I was doing it in alignment with them all. There was something to that experience, it was really cool. I was running with them, it was like we were in a race, or a marathon.

I was with them all; it was as if we were outside amongst millions of cheerleaders. It felt more surreal then what we were seeing with our physical eyes. It was not 'just' the treadmills; it was this awesome 'altered reality.' This was an awesome morning!

Because the gym was packed, I jumped off the treadmill (when my thirty minutes were finished) with no cool down. I had to offer my treadmill quickly to the next guy. I was then, within moments, in my chilled vehicle. My face was still red when I arrived home.

The gym was awesome, and when I was home my vibration reverted back to cranky. My kids had the day off of school, as they slept, I scrubbed my house.

The night before a friend had called and said her baby had a fever. She told me the daycare would not have her being sick. She asked if I would stay on standby for Monday if she could not go to daycare. Monday morning came and she went to daycare. Though funny, hours later while I was vacuuming, I missed her phone call. Her daughter had a rash and had to be picked up. Because I missed the call, the mom had to make other arrangements. So as you can see, my cranky vibration was affecting my day! I knew all of this; though I was still stuck and did not know when I was going to be unstuck!

This is such a large point, when we know we are stuck; we just need to recognize, and accept it. Because when you are stuck, you are stuck. Though to eventually get unstuck I chant to myself, "This too shall pass." I remind myself over and over that I am okay for feeling stuck. Obviously I would prefer something different, though currently, I'm stuck being stuck. So instead of trying to get unstuck (which is impossible because trying to get unstuck helps you focus more on being stuck) I accept being stuck, and remind myself that sooner than later it's going to shift. What I mean by this is we need to accept our bad day, jealous moods, and feelings of failure. When we do not, we never move through them. Always accept how you're feeling now, and be ok with it; and know that you will soon shift. When we do not accept the current feelings, this is when we find ourselves in a six month depression. What is better, 24 hours of a bad mood or six months of a deep depression?

All in all, that day I did my part, my part was to move. The underlying vibration for the day was off; I moved and accepted this as I also knew I was getting much closer to this passing and my next day would inevitably be here.

Tuesday was the first day (for the week) back to school for my kiddos. I took them to school and enjoyed having the house to myself.

My vibrations from the day prior were continuing to stick to the current day; so I did what I know works. I moved. I listened to lots of tithing testimonies and repeated over and over, "What would it take for me to believe this can happen for me."

As my vibration was moving, more sticky stuff came. My husband texted and wanted me to send a check for eleven hundred dollars for a security deposit from a renter moving out. To this point, I told my husband we were tithing; though I never told him how much. After that text message, I turned the testimonies on again and this time I turned the volume up louder! I asked God for some proof that He was going to hook me up and show me tithing miracles were also for me, instead of only for everyone else. I said, "God, I'm not talking about twenty dollars here, you GOTTA come big." I reminded Him that He promised in Malachi 3 to prosper me. (International Bible Society, 1984)

Lunch time was soon here and so were more triggers; my husband brought up the rent check again. I finally could not take it anymore! I explained to him everything I was learning on my research on tithing and through my research, tithing should work. All we had to do was trust it a little more. All we had to do was be a little more patient. He said, "Okay." He supported me in our new adventure.

I showed him the checks I wrote for God, and he again said, "Okay." He was good with what I had done! My relief was overwhelming. Then we were prompted to look at the account and noticed, so far, we had plenty for the tithe checks, rent checks, and money going out for bills. My confidence grew even more. I happily wrote the rent check and danced to the mailbox. We were okay and we were going to be okay.

During that same lunch was when Brian told me about more phone calls with the person wanting to buy the rental. I thought it was hilarious, because thirty minutes prior I had just let God know I was expecting something huge from Him. How much huger could that have been? The rest of the afternoon came and went into the evening.
....
Wednesday I ran again. It was a good run, though my body took it harder than usual. I expected some overabundance in the mail Tuesday and Wednesday; nothing was what I received.

What I did notice was that our cable company from Wisconsin (this summer) kept charging us (per month) as if we were still using their service. That afternoon I noticed it, my husband called to let them know of their error. Soon he called back and told me to expect a refund in the amount of 111.11 dollars as a refund from the company. Crazy number, huh!

I also began moving my and my husband's office into the laundry room to prepare space for our teen moms!

As each layer of the tithing unfolded, I finally was at the question of 'gross income' verses 'net income' tithing. Finally I did it, I asked Brian for his gross pay numbers. I then wrote out the check for the extra one hundred and thirty-six dollars and some change that also was allocated from my checkbook.

So there you have it! I was caught up with God! I wrote all the checks. I kissed and blessed my tithing bag and begged God to give me the courage to actually give it. The rest of that day I kept being reminded to breathe and trust.

Minutes prior to getting my kiddos; my girlfriend calls to tell me she received an unexpected check of five hundred dollars in the mail. At first I was excited for her, because I am clearing, so everyone else around me is supposed to be clearing, and apparently they are! Then I got jealous! I am the one 'intending' to tithe. Where is my prosperity? Where is my five-hundred dollar check? I accepted my jealous feelings, and reminded myself to breathe and move. I then get my kiddos and learn they brought home an opportunity to raise money for the school. Hmm, I am looking for my money and God instead wants me to collect money for the kiddos' school. I laugh and let God know He is hilarious.

I also end up with a neighborhood kid all evening because his mom had to go to the emergency room. I watched all of this, more opportunities for me to give! I feel I am supposed to be doing some receiving; nope not yet! This is getting hilarious. The evening brought cheerleading for my daughter. Great, except we were in the wrong building for a quarter of the practice! I talked to God and asked, "What the heck!" The evening then turns into night.

The majority of my feelings are really not mad, just watching what all of this turns into. It is like the beginning of a movie. You are really not mad or happy, just real curious how it unfolds and patiently waiting for the prosperous punch line.

....

Thursday was our big day; our 'real' tithing day! I woke up at five A.M. thankful it was not a run day. My body was still recuperating from the day before. My husband was out of the house by 5:45 A.M. for his run. I had the morning to myself knowing full well that this was the big day.

I prepared the kiddos' lunch and breakfast and soon it was time for school. Soon I was back home, alone and now engulfed with a new idea! The idea that came floating into my head was to write this whole experience down! What a test this could be, to see if tithing works!

If this works, what a testimony it could be! How much better would the world be to see proof that all of this works; and how cool would all of this be; if it works for me!

I then wrote and wrote. My husband did not come home for lunch because he was out of town. I eventually showered and wrote some more. I kept being surprised at the clock each time I checked. All of this just kept coming out of me. I never got to the laundry or picking up the house. I had to stop myself at 2:10 because it was time for the kiddos. I then organized all of my writings and put them away. I also had this overwhelming urge to Vlog about the day even though I was short on time.

My Vlog was about all of the clearings and releasing I was feeling. In the Vlog I mentioned how terrified, yet excited I was that we were four hours out from the tithe. I had always wanted to write and Vlog during my journey, and I always wanted to show the 'In the moment' vulnerability. Here I was speaking of it; the whole world got to see me scared out of my mind, but continuing to move forward. It was incredibly terrifying, though it was also rewarding and liberating.

The time came to pick up my geniuses; we were soon home with no homework for the evening. They instead requested to go door knocking for their fundraiser. We head out and the two of them make a deal; Aidan knocks and Dreana talks. To my surprise, my daughter was ecstatic and in total agreement with the deal. She is five, though I tell you she is a natural 'sales woman.' We begin to door knock and I soon witness my Dreana standing patiently at the door. Our participant opens the door and says, "How can I help you?" Dreana calmly and so sweetly says, "Can I have some money!"

Ha, ha, that response had these people donating their life savings! She bounced through the neighborhood, door to door, donation to donation. We have decided she is going to make "Girl Scout of the year" when she sells her cookies. She is a natural!

We were later home when we heard a knock at the door. It was Aidan's friend asking if we wanted to donate to the same fundraiser. The thoughts that ran through my head were, "No, we just donated our time to the school; there is no need to donate money. We are supposed to be getting money for ourselves not finding ways to give more away!" Though my son did not follow suit, instead gratefully gave one dollar of his $13.50 to his friend's collection. After my son's donation, the two continued to door knock for the friend's envelope.

And you do realize this is supposed to be a competition. The competition consists of the child who collects the most money is the one to win a prize at the end.

So as Aidan is collecting money for his friend, helping him get closer to the winning prize, he seems to be A-Okay while I am flipping out! Aidan instead cared about the fun the two were having, and had his heart in the correct place; while he showed me where mine should have been. I thought a lot about that. I was grateful to receive such a large lesson from my son. This is what it's supposed to be. We are all one. All the money collected goes to the same school. There is no need for competition. My son knew this; it was me who had the problem.

It was now time! Nervous, I excitedly drove to church. I kept telling myself to breathe and trust. I get there and there is about thirty adults sitting in a big circle. They are laughing and giggling. Good so far, a high vibrational group I found myself in! The leaders then begin our class and asked for testimonies from the previous week.

Testimonies come in as a cash find of 450 dollars from our first member! Another woman being told, "It's covered" as she was about to pay for an oil change. Another woman received fifteen hours of free babysitting from her day care. That same woman works agency, so she gets called in each morning if there is work for her. She received a call every day of that week! She also was taken out to eat by her boss! There were more; my newest intention is to take notes next week!

My time came for a testimony. My testimonies consisted of the small stuff that came my way during the week. We received a free case of beer and a Panera gift card. Of course I tithed two dollars for the beer and $1.50 for the gift card.

I then spoke about the large stuff. I talked about Richard and his music and Danielle's 500 dollars! As I was finishing up I let the group know I had been waiting for my extra-large prosperity (for the week) which was the possible sale of my rental!

We soon were quiet as the fifty minute CD started to teach us our lesson for the day. Later it was break time. Here I went outside for a smoke, no kidding, but the door locked behind me! I asked God about that. No response, though I thought it was ironic that I was locked out of the prosperity circle! I am sure further guidance will come with that as our writings flourish into the future. Funny how that seems to be the answer sometimes, though the last answer we prefer; we tend to want to know now and shun away from the 'waiting period' it sometimes takes. After break we finished up the CD and were led into discussion.

A woman commented about her realizing she despised wealthy people. She felt like her prosperity was blocked because she did not want to be like 'those' wealthy people. Another lady commented that she used to feel that way also. Years ago she used to do the payroll for wealthy people.

She explained that these people were giving, generous and loving. From that experience she learned wealthy people were close to her heart! I quickly seconded that comment. I told them of my experiences with wealthy people were the same. I now think the wealthier you are, the closer to God you are. I feel the only way you can get wealthy is to let go and let God! I feel this way because, to receive so much money there has to be some magic involved. And my definition of magic is God.

This is where my struggle has been and is still. I (currently) feel that if I do not make forty thousand dollars a month, I feel I am not as close to God as I want to be. This is what I am working with still! This is what I have been working with for the last two years. And I think it is funny how it all came to me through tithing. They say; if you want help with your finances, give them to God. This whole time I have been asking God to raise my financial frequency, though I would not give my finances to Him. So here we are now.

Continuing on, I want to give some testimonies of the rich, the wealthy people I know. Last year when I was living in Tennessee, I was driving to Indiana for Thanksgiving. My husband was also driving from Wisconsin to meet us; Indiana was the halfway point and also where Richard (my husband's best friend) lives. There I was, the night before Thanksgiving, broke down on the highway. I was broke down with a newer jeep, three hours from Indiana, and nine from my husband.

The ironic part of this story is that I always buy newer cars because I prefer to spend money on a car that consistently works, instead of saving money by learning how to be my own mechanic! So you can understand my shock when my car broke! This never happens to me. Secondly, I am three hours from anyone I know. I have a car full of luggage, a BB-gun, three dogs and two kiddos. We are all scared, confused and praying for guidance and help. And all of this is ten o'clock at night, the night before Thanksgiving. No mechanics around.

I get my car to start again and end up having to pull over at the next exit which happens to be dark and in the middle of no-where. I call my husband and he says he is on his way to Kentucky (where I am stalled,) nine hours away and this is all he could do. He told me to call my brother. I am crying calling my brother, asking him if there is something I can do; he is a mechanic, owner of his own shop. Basically the car over heated and should not be started until the pump, or whatever it was, was replaced. During all of this, a car showed up. We had been stalled on one of those exists that tended to get zero traffic, in the middle of nowhere. Nobody came here because (as I learned) this is not a safe area and not really a used area. That is, nobody except this random stranger and his teenage daughter.

As all of these ironies continue, our stranger is on the phone with my brother and then my husband. These conversations consisted of him handing over his social security number, blood type, resume, and first born child to prove he was worthy of saving me!

I mean here was my angel being interrogated by the men in my life to ensure his help was safe. I am just watching all of this, still in shock, freaked out and hoping for the best. It turns out he knows mechanic work and ensures me my car was definitely broke. He offers to take my family, dogs, and a gun to his house for the night.

Here I am crying so hard because I do not know the answer. Should I hang out in my cold, dark jeep all night or chance my family with this stranger and his teenage daughter? During this evaluation in my head, our stranger sat there so sweet and patient. He knew I was scared and we soon decided to allow him to scoop us up to safety.

We get to his gorgeous, expensive country property home. He offers for my three dogs to hang with his in the garage for the night. We laid Dreana down on his leather couch and he makes sure to turn the TV on for some background noise to help assist with her dreams. He informs my wide awake son of his PS3 system and games upstairs; he lets him know he has free rein to play, play, play! During our conversation he learns Aidan is a drummer. He tells me he has this brand-new drum set he was about to donate to a thrift store. He offered to give it to us. We had been affirming for a new drum set for months!

He then stays up three quarters of the night talking with me about all the miracles in his life. He and his wife were in the middle of a divorce and this was his first holiday without her. I think the win for him (in this situation) was he had some company for his first holiday without his wife. He then explained that the only reason he was on that dark, empty exit (that evening) was because at the last minute his daughter's boyfriend wanted to go home. So he drove the boyfriend home and happened to be around to save us.

He then talked about how generous he had been lately. He had just bought a new phone for a random lady. She had been in the same store with him and he overheard her mention her cell phone broke and she had no money. Our mechanic felt pretty awesome to get to be her angel. He said it felt so good to give to her and to show his daughter the true meaning of the holidays.

He later said, a few months prior, he had donated sixty thousand dollars to his church for them to build a new building. He said it was the craziest thing, all of a sudden all of his bills kept being returned to him as paid!

His electric bill returned explaining someone in the community paid and his money was not accepted! Seriously what company do you know just doesn't credit your balance. Instead his came back with an explanation! Oh how I loved that night. So special, the time spent with him.

In the meantime, my husband drove to Richard's and picked up a trailer and then drove all night to Kentucky. The next morning (Thanksgiving Day) my dear friend asked us for our order as he offered to pay for Mc Donald's. Then when my son woke up, he took our BB gun and stood out on the front porch to shoot targets with my boy! My son had a blast! He then left me with his daughter, as he went and picked up his Thanksgiving dinner for him and his kiddos. He was awesome in everything instead of the title, chef. Thanksgiving was take-out for his family! Oh his daughter is so beautiful. We talked about everything! They are such a sweet family!

Around nine A.M. Richard and Brian make it to Kentucky and we were ready to be saved again. We loaded my car on the trailer and all piled up in Brian's truck headed back to Indiana for some belated Thanksgiving!

I have to let you know I forgot this man's and his daughter's name. I am sure we could find their house again, but their phone number is nowhere to be found. I have remembered that week every day since. They were a true inspiration and I would love to see them again. If you, the reader, are him or if you know of this story, please contact me so I can tell you in person how much this family changed my life that day! Thank you.

Here is a description of our angel. He is a construction worker and fosters 8-10 autistic children. His mother owns the foster agency in Kentucky. He and his mother live in the same neighborhood; they live in Magnolia, KY on Old Gas Works RD. He has two teenage daughters; one who paints her finger nails every day and a twelve year old son that loves four wheelers. Again I am so thankful for how you helped us! You were our angel last year and I have retold all of your generosity probably a million times since them. Thank you from the bottom of my heart.

Later we get to Indiana and Richard, Brian, and plenty of their mechanic friends fix my car. I still have the filter, or whatever it was that broke, hanging from my rear view mirror as a reminder of how blessed I truly am!

As the weekend ended, my husband and Richard headed back toward Wisconsin, (Richard had a treatment on the way, as well as my husband had work.) I had to stay because my car needed one more part that was arriving via mail later that week. The kids and I were offered the house as an exchange to babysit George, Richard's dog!

The mechanic friends fixed my car and also Richard's plumbing as his bathroom pipes also decided to explode that week! Oh it was a crazy week, not to mention our last day was filled with my boy sick with the flu cuddled next to the cold kitchen floor. Crazy it was, though also filled with a perfect example of generosity. We headed back to Tennessee with many grateful memories. We were and are so thankful to you all.
Here is only one testimony of rich/wealthy people I know. Later I may tell more. Though as you can see, this is why I think the wealthier you are, the more giving and kind you also are.

Finishing up with the events of our tithing class; the group then passed around the tithing basket. My tithe was filled with $7.52 in change, $148 in cash and checks for $427.19, $327.19, and $136.13 for a total tithe of $1,046.03. I did it, I gave my tithe!

The class, before long, divided into teams, becoming small groups of prayer partners. We all grouped up and did our meet and greets. Our leader than mentioned if anyone tithed cash, the people should meet with her to get it documented. As our class ended I made my way to her office and helped her count my large bag of loose change.

I soon drove home, still scared, but what was I to do? I just said, "God, okay, I'm done. I did my part, you're on now."
At home Brian was excited to tell me about his day. He and his co-workers had gone to a job fair (that afternoon) to talk with troops and ask employers to hire their transitioning soldiers. He loves his job. He is like a school girl when you ask him how his day went. He talked about how the three others were referring to him as NCO in charge. He was telling me about the fun car ride they took as they headed out of town, the jokes between them, and the employers they conjured up to do future presentations for all the soldiers. He talked about cheerleading with my daughter (they attended for the evening.) He also spoke how he was an awesome mentor for her when the class finished. He would have talked all night if the evening hours weren't chanting for sleep!

He never asked about my class. I was thankful for that; because I still did not know what I was feeling, thinking or expecting. All I was doing was breathing and hoping for some miracles to start showing up.

Chapter 3
Things are getting better!

The next morning (Friday) at 0430 I awoke and decided not to run. Instead I took my dog on a walk through the neighborhood and listened to an audio about prosperity.

Our host was from the radio show, "Awakening to Abundance," and our interviewee was Karim Hajee. Karim spoke about our attention to lack instead of abundance. He used the example of a person not making their desired income; they tend to use the words, "It is because of the economy." He says, "Do not focus on what is missing, instead focus on ways to better budget, ways to make extra money." (Hajee, 2014)

The things spoken about in the interview, I already knew. Though when we know something, there are layers of it that we continue to learn as we hear it more. This day I heard, "Accept only the truth and give no energy to what is currently being shown." This statement has been in my awareness for a long time, and today it found its way into my heart. I got it. Such as me, I have already tithed; I cannot do anything about that now. Accept it (the now) and focus on what the now brings next. I wonder what God's got in store for me. And of course some fears come up such as, "What am I going to do if this does not pan out?" I cannot do anything about that now, the money is already out. Almost like 'who cares' if something does not pan out, do something about it then. Because as of now, all that could be done is done. Quit living in the past. The past is done!

Worrying about the past and being excited in the moment are two emotions that cannot exist together. A decision has to be made, you are either worried or you are living. You either wear the red dress or the blue; you cannot wear both. Make a decision; are we living or worrying. The decisions you made in the past has already been made. The past already happened. You cannot go back; you cannot change what happened; accept it and live in today. Life has moved on since the decisions you made. Those decisions are done; there is no relevance in going in the past and reliving what has already happened. You live in the now, not in the past. The past is done. You made the best decisions you could at the time. In the past, that was the best you could come up with. And now that you are wiser, you wish you would have made better decisions. You only know there were better decisions to be made, because you learned from the decisions you made then. Back then you did not know what you know now. The past had to happen, so today could happen. You may be mad at today; but today is exactly where you need to be to get to tomorrow! Life unfolds for us, but it cannot unfold, if it has nothing to unfold from.

My tithing is done, now my focus is on what's next. I continue to grow; I recognize my growth. As I live this more and more each day, it becomes habit, it becomes a subconscious belief. Practice makes perfect. Continuing on with our interview, he asked us to push ourselves away from the words, "I don't know what to do," and repeat over and over, "I may not know what to do, but God, my higher self, whom ever…does." (Hajee, 2014)

Here is how you let go! I have been practicing with this a lot today. As I hear my fears, I talk to them and say, "It's okay, we might not know how, but God does; we can let this go now."

This worked for me when I was going to Wisconsin for Christmas last year. (My husband moved out of our house, rented it and moved into and managed an apartment building.) When we were there (Wisconsin) for October (2013,) the kids, dogs and I stayed at my mom's house. That was nice, but I would have preferred some privacy. As I was making plans for Christmas, I affirmed that I wanted a vacant house to stay in for the month of December (2013.) At this time, I did have a girlfriend who managed properties, so there was a chance that this would happen; though the chance appeared small. I still affirmed it; however I was also okay with just staying at my mom's. It wasn't preferred; in the most perfect world it would have been nice to get a house to ourselves. Since this was such a crazy request; I did not think much about it. But when I did, I told myself to stop, because if this was supposed to happen; it would.

Guess what, my mom called a week later, and offered me her vacant house for the month. I had completely forgotten about hers! She moved out of her house into a new one. The year prior it was rented with 'bad' renters. At the time, that house was vacant but on the market. Out of the blue, my mom decided to rent the house and not sell it; and it was currently vacant. She offered it to us! This was awesome.

Another quick story to affirm this point was also when I was in Tennessee. I was thirty minutes from Nashville. Country music singers were everyday life there. When February was approaching, we were making plans for my birthday. I had made a goofy request and said I wanted to go to a barn party and hang out all night with a country music singer. I wanted kids to be welcome and I wanted to spend the night so I could have some beer. Now yes, I was next to Nashville, but I did not know any country music singers. I knew it was a goofy request; I would be okay if I did not receive it; but it would have been cool if I did! I let it go, and went on with the month considering what to do for my birthday.

A couple days later, my husband called and asked if we wanted to meet in Indiana for my birthday, this way it would only be a six and a half hour drive for the both of us.

It felt right, so I said sure! I soon realized that Richard is a Country music singer! We get to spend the night at his house all week! My kids are always welcome, as well as my three dogs. It is always a blast, we party 24/7! Talk about this affirmation coming true! Though I did not consciously realize it at the time. Remember your wishes always come true; they come true in ways that may be different than what you assumed they would come as, though they always come true. Just have the belief and courage to dream your big dreams!

I remembered both of those stories today as I kept reminding myself that if I do not know, I am positive God does. I affirm this, and let it ground more and more until I believe it as truth. And truth always shows up. Know that you may not know, but God does. Then ask to be shown the answer. You will be shown if you ask. Focus not on why this is happening; instead focus on how I can do this.

Speaking of God knows all; did you know your subconscious operates like Google? Just like an internet search, if you want to see cars you do not ask, "Why are you not showing me pictures of cars?" Instead you type in, "Pictures of cars." If you want something, then ask the right questions. You do not ask, "Why did my boss fire me?" Instead ask, "What are the lessons I am learning from me being fired; how can I grow from this." Ask, "Did I get fired because I need to be open for the next achievement in my life?" "If this is the case, can you inform me on what it is I am changing into?" "Can you help prepare me for what I am changing into?" "Can you keep encouraging me and letting me know that I am on the right track, so this growing period is efficient and smooth?" "What can I do right now to help trust what it is I am growing into?" "Can you please help me trust that the resources and people needed for my new growth are on the way?"

The last point our speaker brought up was the subject of letting go. The three rules to live by are:
1.   To know what we want.
2.   To have the courage to ask for it.
3.   To trust enough to receive what it is we want.
How he uses number three is he tells his mind, "No, my subconscious mind is working on it! There is no need to dialog about the process, we do not know, God does. Our job is to let God figure it out; our job is to get out of the way. What can I do to get out of the way in this moment?" (Hajee, 2014). Such a statement! What a way to let go! Command it. I personally would say, "Shh; don't worry; God's got this!"

Later in the day, I picked up my children and prepared for Brian's return for the evening.

We had Dreana's big game that night where she was going to be cheerleading with the big, teenage cheerleaders! Brian was preparing for the game by looking up the registration and game schedule to see when we were supposed to arrive. Brian started laughing. Apparently the players (that we were to be cheering for) lost all the games so far for the season; the scores were three games of 60ish to zero. Dreana was cheering for the team with the consistent score of zero.

I watched this, wondering why our team was the losing team. He then said, "Can you imagine what the coach of the opposing team was telling the players, "Don't worry, score what you want, this is a definite win for us." Then Brian declares, "Talk about the underdog." Then I got it. The reason this bugged me so much was because I always believed I was the underdog. Yes I achieved a lot, but each task was so hard because I never felt like anyone was supporting me. Instead, I always felt like I was being cut down when I was trying my hardest to move forward.

Even today I was talking to my mom about the preferred foster kids I was hoping for. And my mom says, "How are you going to feed all of these kids." I snapped back and said, "Can you ever say, 'Wow that sounds exciting?'" Her response was, "Yes, that does." Maybe my current growth is about learning how to stand up for what I want to hear, what I believe. I also am realizing that when I do, I get the response I want. Just like Dreana when she asked for what she wanted, "Can I have some money?" Maybe I need to be okay with asking for what I really want, and stating what I really believe. We really do learn many lessons from the tiniest of people.

All in all, I affirmed our team was going to win! The underdogs were going to come out on top. I sent lots of love and blessings their way. When we were at the game they scored! The first score of the season! We did not stay till the end, only till half time when Dreana's cheerleading ended. Without seeing the final score, I have faith it was a good game! Dreana enjoyed the heck out of cheering for the game. Also, Aidan's girlfriend was a cheerleader. Both kids enjoyed their evening!

I did not receive any blessings in the mail Friday. I tell you this to dialog all of my expectations, good and bad of financial abundance. Though, my hope and growing belief is still here. I guess one day at a time. What did happen was a conversation with Brian about finances. A few weeks ago, one of the properties was cleaned up and prepared for a renter, and it came with an unexpected two thousand dollar bill. This sucked, but what are you going to do? The clean-up crew sent a letter stating payments were accepted instead of the whole bill all at once.

They emailed yesterday reminding us of our bill.

Brian nicely emailed back reminding them of their option for payments and again letting them know we were expecting a five hundred dollar bill and upset and confused with the unexpected expenses. He was honest; letting them know we trusted them, and expected the best, though that bill was not what we expected as the 'best.'

All we can do about this is watch. If I had a billion dollars I am sure that I could fix all of these bills and financial messes. Though currently I do not. I need to trust that there is a plan and it is going to keep us afloat while all is being worked out. Trusting God more and believing He was/is changing this around for us, is all we can do. All we have to do was believe and keep breathing in each moment, and let that moment turn into the next. It is easy to get wrapped up in the 'what ifs' when thoughts of the future come about; though there is no point to that. Paying attention to the current, and safety in the moment is the only hope.

....

Saturday came and I found the perfect outfit for my day. I found a pink skirt that I have had for years, though have not been able to fit in. I looked amazing in it! For the last few years, I affirmed that I would lose my extra weight, though to also do it as a life style instead of a diet. About a month ago I decided it was finally time. How this worked for me, I cut 90 percent of my bread out of my diet. This worked, where the majority of my diet is healthy, though I can still have a little 'bad' here and there. I lost ten pounds in the last month. I tried on my skirt, and it fit! How much better does that get.

I also talked with my mom that morning and told her what a good sales woman my daughter was. My mom said that she expected Dreana would rock with her sales because I have been teaching her (for the last five years) how to respect money. She said Dreana has been so comfortable with the subject and treats it as her best friend; so of course asking for more was an easy task!

This made me feel good. I have always felt alone with my studies and choices for life. And a lot of the time, I felt like I must have been a failure because no one ever let me know I was doing well. This comment from her was my sticker for the day! It was a little bit of love that said, "Yes, you are doing good, look at your achievements through your daughter's excelling relationship with money!" My day was starting off beautiful!

Continuing on with that comment, I also received another one Thursday. Brian told me that I was the glue that held the family together! Now I have got to tell you, I have been asking for these beautiful 'love notes' for some time now.

I have been striving for value, wanting to know how I contribute, I asked God to show me proof. And as intentions go, I am getting some pretty awesome confirmations!

Later in the morning I noticed the neighbor not having as great a day as I. She looked frustrated; so I invited her four kiddos over to play. The neighbor was so thankful and enjoyed her break. It was nice to notice how I can help, and to also be thanked so sweetly! It was a win-win. I had six kids, whom were all surprisingly calm! All were occupied with quiet activities. The neighbor received her break, and I did not have to lose because of it.

The day was starting out pretty good. Brian received a free oil change for his truck. He also told me of his increased BAH (money the Army gives you for housing and food) we were to be getting. We talked of the promotion board coming up where we were expecting his rank to change from E7 to E8.

I also listened to the movie, "The Secret." The comment that resonated with me was the comment about keeping new ideas to yourself. This spoke to me, I have been excited about this book and want to hurry up and share it! Though as I get excited to read to Brian, I keep getting told, "No, not yet." I have to embody these entries a little more; I have to share them with me. And soon Brian and the rest of the world will be able to enjoy.

That evening Brian played his guitar. I love when he does this because it is so meditative when I get to listen. There is something to the vibrations of music; and I am lucky to have a musician in the house. As he played; I typed. Thank you for that! I am affirming that I am going to get his music on a CD so I can listen to it over and over throughout the day, not only while I type; But all day.

We also got to see 'girlfriend of the week' on Skype with Richard! He is such a ladies man, and I am affirming he soon will find his 'one!' I later was on Facebook and saw a girlfriend from the past. I have a lot of triggers with her and have kept my distance for as long as I could. Though, we all know that the answer in life is to 'balance.' She had posted something that resonated with me so I 'liked' her comment. That was huge for me. When we go through our clearings, as we forgive, we end up in the middle. It does not mean that we choose to enjoy our everyday lives with people we no longer connect with; it just means we don't hate the idea of it anymore. We are allowed and supposed to move on and grow through friendships and connections, though the goal is to be ok running into them once a year.

I think throughout my tithing, I am also going to be doing some forgiving.

I have wanted to forgive a lot of my past for a long time; I logically know the benefits of forgiveness. Though I have had some trouble with it. I have been affirming for quite some time that God will show me. All I can do is let that go and let Him take over. Because of it I have a 'knowing' that emotions are moving through me. And I look forward to the day when I can really say, "I do not think I have those issues anymore." They were only brought into my life, at that moment, to show me what I would not see within myself. I decided for years to hate them; and now I only see them as blessings that brought me to me.

Deepak Chopra was interviewed by Oprah one day. She asked him about this subject. He said for the last few years he could honestly say he had not had any 'issue' with anyone. He said it was an accomplishment and he could see his growth. She reminded him that that was not what he used to think or be; he smiled and said, "I agree." In his younger years he was learning how, and now, call it wisdom, call it age, he feels he has finally mastered it! Now friends, this is the definition of a true master.

I also chit chatted on Facebook with another 'old' friend. She asked what I was up to and I told her I was writing a book. It was so funny to tell her that. This book is embodying itself into me. I feel it. It feels so right. Finally I feel like an author. I feel myself number one on the NY best sellers list!

The other day I was writing, I then went outside for a break. I stood at my deck looking over the day. It felt so amazing. I thought to myself, "This is what someone who writes books feels like!" I felt and feel so productive and so 'on purpose.' For that moment, I felt as if I had been writing books my whole life. I felt like people knew me as a writer. It felt so real and amazing! Thank you for that!

I think my current blessings from tithing are my writings. I have been writing ever since I started. These words are pouring out of me and I am so excited to get back to it when I take a break. It feels amazing! My visualizations are getting stronger. I feel like I am clearing so much. I feel like this story has been stuck in me for so long and now it finally has an outlet. It also is helping me not worry about the 'what if's'; I am too busy writing! It truly is a blessing.

My most recent intention is to meet my publisher. I would like to receive an advance. I think if I receive an advance it would help me feel more wanted. It might mean that my publisher cares about me and already knows I write good books. I would be good enough to get an advance. I know the lesson here is to already know I am good enough, though this is where I am currently at. I also really want to be on the New York best-selling list, and to be published by Hay House Publishing.

Hay House is my dream publisher; many of my favorite authors are publisher here. I would like to experience their world. I truly am expecting dramatic results from my tithing. And when I don't see them as I am expecting, I keep breathing and try to move through the frustration.

I hope my message is imperative to the world. I feel Rhonda Byrnes's message was. She taught the whole world. Her message was very simple and got the whole world to know a different way of life. Because people heard her message, they were able to take it further and learn more. She was able to grab the attention of everybody. This is what I adore about her. I would like to get the attention of everybody. I would like everyone to know that God will take care of you, if you want Him to. If everyone can just get that simple message, it will bring comfort to all; and some will continue their lessons with further research; but at least all will get to know God. Each religion can see the results. Just like each religion could see Rhonda's message. Each religion speaks the same message. Each religion contains God or a definition of God. The message is always truth. The message is if you trust God with your finances; your finances will flourish. You will flourish.

Another insight also came, my brother came streaming through my thoughts. I had an urge to call him; though I did not know why. As I was about to call him, I was not feeling too good about it. All of a sudden, I realized why he popped in my head. I had him in my head because he was thinking of me. Just because he was in my head does not necessarily mean it is because I was thinking of him. Instead it meant he was thinking of me, and that is all I needed to know. We have to remember we are connective beings. I did not have to do anything in that moment except understand it was him, not me.

The night ended on an awesome note!

....

I started my Sunday morning listening to another audio. The interviewer here was Debra Ponamon from the radio show, "Your life without limits." Our speaker was Victor Da Pointe. Victor spoke of commanding your thoughts. (This interview was a live interview and there is no recording). This was significant for me because I am currently working on stopping my continuous, routine, daily thoughts. I loved what he said. He said, "Just command your thoughts." When you hear them, tell them to go away. When we get wrapped up in our thoughts, we do not realize it is a recording we are listening to, the same old recording we have been listening to for years. We think they are real, but they are not. I tell you this from the bottom of my heart; try to take note of your thoughts. You will soon realize what it is I know. You think they are real because you 'hear' them.

But truly they are not. They are not in the now. They are the same thoughts you have thought over and over for a very long time. If you want something different to come into your life, then it would be good to stop that recording and command and direct your life!

Try this, stop for a minute and remember what your thoughts were every day for the past week during breakfast. They are the same as they have been for eons of breakfasts. Do this for your thoughts at lunch and prior to bed. They are still the same. 90 percent of your thoughts are the same day in and day out. When you realize this you can play with it. When you 'hear' your thoughts, you can learn to stop them. You can delete them.

Each part of our spiritual journey is a challenge for growth. We do not change overnight. Deleting and stopping these residual thoughts is what I have been working on for some time. Many techniques are out there to help. Such as when you wake up, the first thing you can do is to start writing or speaking a gratitude list. Now mind you, a good practice would be to put a reminder note by your coffee maker to do this. Reasoning is 90 percent of your habits are the same each day. If you do not 'remind' yourself to do this, then your normal programing will take over. It is the same when you commit to working out. Having a work out partner keeps you committed. They are your reminder note.

What Victor said was, when you 'hear' these same old messages coming in, start making a habit of commanding them to stop and delete. You could make a reminder for this too. I put many reminders in pen on my hand. This reminder note never goes away! It helps, because when I get caught in these continuous messages and think they are real; I look down at my hand and am reminded to make a choice to think this thought or not. This goes along with what I have been saying about 'breathing.' I have trained myself to 'just breathe' as an automatic response. I had that written on my hand for a while, before my programming made it truth. Now it is lodged as a self-imposed aide to help when I need it.

Again, I loved what he said; I have added this to my hand! Also he spoke about the continuous chant of the word, "Source." This is a great thing to chant while you are cooking dinner, or getting mad, or doing anything! The more you affirm this, the more you realize you do have the ability to be any you, you want to be.

Just try it for a minute. "I am source. Source. Source. Source. Source. Source. Source. Source." Do you see how this can get you into an instant meditative flow? Meditation does not have to be a certain sitting position or chanting. Meditation only means shutting the mind off. Most people know how to meditate, though do not recognize its definition.

Meditation is when you are 'lost' in a song, when you are playing your guitar, when you are exercising. These are all forms of meditation. The key to meditation is to know what it is and apply it to benefit any circumstance. A good example is when you are really mad and you need to get out of that energy before you do something you do not want to do. When I am here, I tell myself to breathe ten thousand times; or I start singing my favorite song (in my head) over and over. Chanting, "Source" works as well.

We can induce meditation wherever and whenever we choose. It just takes practice. Each day we learn and embody more of whom we choose to be. As long as we have designated our preference and keep our eyes on the end goal; life will unfold in our favor.

Monday morning I woke up late, missing my run. I was irritated, though accepted it, and chanted all day to find the bigger and better in the day. I sent my kiddos off to school and filled much of my time with writing. When Brian came home for lunch I asked him to help move the large pieces of furniture out of the office; I wanted to start emptying it for our teens when they get here. To my surprise he said, "Yes!" We moved the desks and book shelves out and he headed back to work.

That afternoon I wrote some more. The things going through my head were still the continual battle of the money. Would the money come through? All I could do was keep breathing. I walked to get the kids from school. The walk did us all good; we released stuck energy, caught up on school news and prepared for an awesome evening.

After homework Dreana went to play in her room and Aidan wanted to play his video game. I took the time to refill the book cases and started cleaning up the mess Brian and I made from moving the office. Aidan and Dreana's friends came over later and everyone was chill and happy! Brian came home and we spent the rest of the evening organizing our new office.

At one point, I was sitting outside with Brian, feeling as if it all already happened (having all the new foster kids) and we had our first night off. Almost as if all the kids (my kids, foster kids, teenagers) were at their friends' house and we finally had the house to ourselves. I was feeling how peaceful and quiet it was. How clean and organized life appeared. It was really neat. This, what I did, was a meditation. When (even though it has not happened yet) you can feel what it feels like when it is happening. The movie, "The Secret," mentions this. They have you go through a visualization of driving your favorite car. When you are feeling the drive, when currently no car exists, this is when your dream becomes inevitable.

That is what I felt like. I felt as if all my dreams were inevitable. What a feeling!

As our evening continued, Brian was talking with Richard. We had asked Church if Richard could perform there the Sunday that he will be in Colorado. This is an intention that might be coming about. Ever since I began going to the Unity Church in Tennessee, and I saw all the musical talent up on stage; I affirmed one day I would see Richard up there. And at Church this past Sunday, I had an overwhelming need to ask the details and to inquire about Richard. So as of now, emails are beginning, and it is one step closer to seeing Richard perform in my church!

I also was on the phone with Danielle. I was telling her about how my mom was giving me compliments about my daughter. I also told her how uncomfortable I was that Dreana wanted to be in Girl Scouts. The reason I was upset was because they want her to go camping and wear brown. Now, I love camping, though in a retreat setting! I like it all set up and what we are to do is relax and be happy. I do not find the thrill in setting up sites and touching worms. And my daughter is such a girly girl. She has been dressing in high heels and wearing pearls since she entered my womb! I was a little upset that she picked Girl Scouts. Ahhh!

I attempted to talk her out of it and of course she is just as adamant as I am. She told me she wanted to do it, and she was positive we would only have to go camping once! Earlier when I was talking with my mom about this stuff, she reminded me of when I was little. She said that the cafeteria ladies were not wearing gloves when they served our food, so I had the whole school boycott hot lunch! She encouraged me to continue to go forward with Girl Scouts, and maybe, I could teach Dreana to get the girls to Boycott the brown and get new pink uniforms!

As I told my friend these stories she offered her perspective. She said, "Isn't it funny that you and your mom are getting along as you talk about how much you disagree with the subject of your daughters." I laughed so hard, I got what she was saying. It's almost like those moms sitting outside grade school all giggling and connecting, as the subject matter is about the teacher not being good enough, and/or the school is not doing the right thing, or how the kids looked goofy as they fell down on the basketball court! Everyone is in high vibration as long as the subject matter is something to be upset with.

Mom and I were having that same high vibration, as I was making fun of my daughter's interests, and she was remembering how she was making fun of her daughter's interests.

I then remembered when I was a kid; I had a love note passed to me when the teacher caught us.

She demanded for the letter to be given to her to teach the class the lesson that notes are not to be passed in school. I would not give the letter up; I ate it. My reasons were I was feeling the little boys embarrassment as the words from his heart were about to appear as a speech in front of the class. I could and would not let this happen! To me, this was wrong! This was more wrong then the wrongful act of passing notes in class. It was one of those decisions. Just like our high school grade calls for us to dissect a rat, hmm, do I get an A or do I save the animal? The ones where you can see everyone's view point; but you have to go with the 'best' answer, even though all answers are somewhat correct and simultaneously incorrect. To me, his embarrassment was a little more wrong than the law of the class room. I got in trouble at school, but figured at home I would be safe. I assumed my mom would have applauded me for standing up for my values. Nope, instead I had to choose from not going to my friend's house for the weekend or not playing my basketball game. I have repressed that for years! How could my mom not see that I was doing the right thing? I did what I felt was right.

Amidst my convo with my girlfriend, I came to realize maybe my mom really did not find the attraction in boycotts. Maybe she thought they were goofy and a waste of time. The same feelings I feel about Girl Scouts! But you know what; I did not find boycotting goofy and a waste of time. And I am sure Dreana feels the same about Girl Scouts.

Danielle offered some words of advice. She said, "You know you do not have to go with her (my daughter), you can drop her off for her activity." Here is when I said, "But what I want is to be with her in her activities." She then told me a story about her. Her son flies remote control airplanes. Airplanes are not Danielle's 'thing'; her thing is to watch her son's face light up when he's doing his 'thing!' We do not have to like everything everyone is doing. Instead we can like that they like it. And that is what you come to the event for. To see the excitement in someone doing what they love, and you share the excitement by watching it. Meaning, Dreana is in charge of her days, I do not have to ensure her fun by ensuring I first know how to have fun with it first. All I have to do is show up and watch her unfold. I do not have to touch worms; I can watch her. I do not have to set up tents; I can watch her giggle as her and her girlfriends figure it out. Life is good.
....
Moving onto Tuesday, Today! Oh my goodness today has been cool! As I am writing and waiting for Brian to come home; I received this random phone call. The call was about one of our properties in Wisconsin that we used to live in. We became friends with the neighbors here. The phone call came from a brother of one of the neighbors.

They are moving to the area and want to live next to their sister. The sister googled my name and phone number, and had him call me. His questions were about how to rent the property.

I had a lovely conversation with him, and gave him my husband's information. I informed him the property manager takes care of the properties. I gave his number to my husband and it is the start of wonderful blessings. What I want to say about all of this is a lot! First, God always works when it is a win-win. Sometimes we do not see it as that when we are not 'winning;' though lessons in life are also considered 'winnings.' The person designated to give you your lessons are learning as well as you are. Yes, all of our five properties became vacant all at the same time. Though, look at this situation. Isn't it ironic that this property became vacant the exact time that this brother was moving to the area? Is that not so cool for them! And the win for us; when the property management company interviews this guy, our property will be rented right away! This one will only take a few days to fill instead of two months! Oh yea, this is cool!

And of course how random the phone call was. His sister was an acquaintance whom had no idea if I still owned that property. As her brother said, she had to do some Sherlock Holmes to find me! She was led, as we all are!

Next, in my day I received a big ole fat No-show! I had an appointment with a mom for babysitting. Now, you think I should or would be upset with this; though I wasn't. I was thrilled, because I really didn't think this mom and I were going to be a good fit. And life went perfectly as we didn't even have to meet!

I also had this awesome affirmation come through for me! The reason I called this mom was because I was getting frustrated and desperate. I stopped caring about what I wanted and was going to babysit who ever would call. Well today I started over. No, I do not want to babysit anybody; I am going to babysit a set of twins from the hours of 9-5! And the mom of these two twins is going to pay me 50 dollars a day! I know these prices are normal, though I seemed to be attracting the other moms who want me to work for a lot less. And I almost gave in; now I see my error. I am waiting for only this. I am not taking second best. I know what I want and I am letting it in now.

Continuing with my morning, my car overheated. Goofy! I laughed and first took it as a sign for me; I was looking for ways that I was 'overheating.' What part of me was trying to push through? Maybe it was the babysitting. Actually, I think it was the amount of trust I was not giving to God for my finances. I was pushing too hard.

After these thoughts I started to laugh, and wondered if this was God's plan in getting me my Denali! This also brought up the memory of last week when we received a flyer in the mail for the dealership. In it they said they want us to bring the car in because some of the cars have a default. Maybe the default is going to bring me to my Denali. No clue, just excitedly waiting for it to unfold!

Brian came home for lunch and made us tasty scrambled eggs. It was one of those lunches you could have eaten for hours, not because you were hungry, but because it was that good! As we ate, he was telling me about work.

A side note to explain this story. My husband and three others were handpicked for their current position at work. This job is a new job for the army. They had to all be the 'best' because it was such a task to get the job 'up and running.' All four of them are great NCO's, and all of them are the same rank. Though, my husband has the least time in service in their rank. In easier terms, he is kind of like the young guy in an older guy's position. Kind of like the freshman playing in the senior guys' basketball. Ironically when they needed a team lead; he was designated. Today he said he had his first meeting with one of the other guys. One of the guys had a suggestion for the team, so went to Brian to get his approval. That was cool all on its own. Brian felt good with his new leadership role. And then the meeting went even further when this guy told Brian that he thinks Brian is a really good choice for team lead. He told my husband that of the four of them, Brian really seemed to have his head on his shoulders and presented himself really well. Also this guy could easily see Brian as getting promoted to Master Sergeant very soon. He told him he possessed all the qualities and leadership skills that are displayed in other Master Sergeants. So aww, Brian got a big ole compliment today!

And speaking of that, here is another story from a few days ago. Apparently, there was another guy my husband knew from a previous class he went to. They were both E7's and this guy (whom also excels quickly) told Brian that he was sure Brian would be the first in the two of them to receive E8. He also said that if by chance he got it first, Brian would be in line to get it next! Well the other day, Brian found out this guy received his E8. What happened with him was that he was in an E8 position but was not receiving his rank, so he left active duty and stayed reserve. In his reserve status he received his E8. Immediately when Brian saw this guy getting his E8; his belief skyrocketed! Talk about the power of words. What you speak; you believe! What you believe; You ARE!

During lunch we also had visitors from the electric company.

The other day when I was at the store, my neighbor made sure to tell me some men in hard hats had been at the house. First, I thought that was goofy because lots of people knock on your door; though this time my neighbor just had to let me know! I look on my door and there is a note stating the men were from the electric company and they may need to get in my back yard (which is fenced) to do some electric stuff. I had a feeling then, as I do now, that there is something to that. Though, then and now I do not get it.

Brian called the company to figure out what was going on. They said they already got what they needed but would contact us if they needed us again. Well today they show up unexpectedly! All they did was get access to our back yard and pull some wires, dig a hole; which all seemed pretty normal. Though I still have a feeling that something is coming out of it all. Actually right now the only thing I can voice is maybe it was a representation of me. As I tithe, I am now connecting with God on the financial level. So maybe my neighbor was excited to tell me about the men at my door because his soul was letting me know that I am finally 'plugged in' and I should expect lots of cool stuff! Because since then, lots of cool things have been happening.

Next what happened was Brian missed a call from the Wisconsin police department. I think there was a reason for him missing the call, I am sure that part will unfold itself. Brian called them back to find out that one of the rentals received a complaint from a neighbor, stating the yard has not been mowed in quite a long time. So good.., bad, actually it was good. It was good because I got my update I was looking for. Our renter moved out. Oh yea! This renter gave us so much trouble and then refused to move out after her lease. She had to be evicted after her lease. Hearing the news that she was out was awesome! Brian told me the management company decided to take her to court for all the money she owed us. So yes we had lots of bad with her, but we were ready to just let her and her memory go. The management company stood up and took over and is now getting us what we deserve. This is cool!

Next Brian called the management company and told them about the police complaint. And you know what they said? Oh this is great; they said they actually had planned on mowing the grass that afternoon! I am talking like, yep, everything is taken care of. As if they presumed this was to happen and were already energetically on it!

It is funny, the way I see all the problems last year as being very ironic and out of our control. It was the breaking point. It was God telling me, "Are you done yet; how much more are you willing to take?" If, I think I can handle more, He's going to make things even more silly and ridiculous!

For example, with that same property last year, the renter kept causing problems, then not paying rent, then not paying her water bill. We said, "Just go, don't worry about your bills, just please leave!" She instead took us to court for her not paying her water bill and the judge agreed with her! It was crazy. Then to top it off, she got a lawyer and then asked Brian to pay for her lawyer fees. I mean.. like right! The most ridiculous stuff. It is almost funny, God's like, "I had to make things crazier and crazier until you finally believed I am doing this!" Now I feel like everything is reversing and all of that money and more is coming back in the most super natural ways. Thank you God! Thanks for getting me to this point! Crazy as it was, the journey is kind of funny, now in hindsight.

Later in the evening, Brian came home with a determination to finish nine SGT major courses totaling 88 hours' worth of study. He wanted to finish all of this in less than a week. This kept him in front of a computer all evening! Aidan hung out with his buddy and Dreana and I headed off to Girl Scouts. It was funny because I was against Girl Scouts; though we signed up because Dreana really wanted it. And I figured I would learn and accept my differences with it. I am so glad I went. The leader was awesome. She really had a way with the girls. I enjoyed all the mom conversations. The moms who were there verses the moms who were at the orientation, were people I would choose to hang out with. They are all successful and driven people. They are all intelligent, nice and awesome. Oh, these are a group of women I can see connecting with on a personal and professional basis!

Dreana had so much fun. She giggled a lot and told her leader that her favorite activity is eating! Lol, this is probably why she is so fit, because what you love, loves you! This is why she can eat Doritos and still have her 'girlish' figure; the Doritos transfer themselves to a self-induced, healthy meal when they come around my daughter!

We came home and had a late dinner of Mac and Cheese. The kiddos were then off to bed; and so was I.

....

Wednesday was here and I did not work out. Today my excuse was I was lazy! As everyone was running late, I began to affirm that Brian would take Dreana to school. Guess what happened; as I was getting her in my car, Brian asked to take her.

I cleaned and picked up the house; then showered. I soon got the great idea to tell stories of all the synchronicities that have happened to me. I love proving the Law of Attraction! This is significant, because it is something I have always affirmed. When Aidan was a baby; Brian was in Iraq. My brother bought me a video camera and taught me how to use it.

I made video after video of Aidan, me and all the dogs to share with Brian while he was overseas. The cool thing about this is I have a forever record of Aidan when he was little, and I learned that I really do enjoy making videos.

Years later, when the awareness of me writing my books started to come; I remembered how much fun I had with those videos. One day I pulled out the camera and decided I was going to make an audio book of all the miracles that have happened in my life via using the Law of Attraction. This day a really cool memory was manifested. I am always practicing small intentions on a daily, weekly basis. I do this because when I allow the small things to come into my life, it helps affirm the large things are possible. Yes, I affirm to be a New York best-selling author, I also affirm to have people buy me lunch! With that said, that day I affirmed that I would see a girl with a ladybug shirt or something to do with ladybugs walk by my yard. As the morning went by, my daughter came running out the side door crying because a book fell on her. I asked her what she was talking about; what book? She ran in the house to get it for me. She brings me the book titled, "The Ladybug Girl book!" I tell you, when you make an intention; it comes true!

This story is an example of how we grow into our intentions. I have wanted to be an author since I was a kid, and now is when I am prepared for my intention. Eight years ago was when I was introduced to using a video camera, and now is when I see how to get messages of truth to the world. The process always begins with a learned interest and then lots of growth of, "Yea, I am good at this; I can do this!"

That day I recorded a lot of videos. There were a lot of synchronistic stories that happened in my life because I practiced, "The Secret." It took me all day. It was one story after another! Each Vlog was filled with a story that happened to me; they referenced what could happen when someone intends their big dreams! The emphasis was on knowing what you want, then asking for it, and then letting it go and letting God handle the how!

Here is one story that happened to me. The rest are found on You Tube under Michelle Finlayson. This story was from when I was a Realtor a few years ago. I had a lender friend; we used to share leads for new clients. If I received a client that did not have financing, I would suggest my lender and when he found a client who was not working with a Realtor, he would suggest me. We had many clients between us; we were a great team.

One afternoon close to the holidays, a time where there was less people purchasing houses, I sat on phone duty.

I was having a great month (even though it was the holidays) that I keep intending I would sell more! Phone duty is the Real-estate office's 'free' secretary. This is where we Realtors volunteer to sit at the front desk and answer any person's question if they call. Our benefit is when the caller does not have a realtor; they become our new client. Phone duty was a great way to pick up new leads. There were only a few Realtors in the office. The only reason they were there was wrapping up old business until the holiday was over. I was on phone duty and A-Okay with it! I had been busying the quiet time (because no one was calling about Real-estate) talking with my lender. He was also at his office. I told him I wanted someone to come into the office, needing a lender and a Realtor. He laughed and said, "Whatever!" He just asked to let him know when I was leaving the office for the day.

I kid you not what happened next! This very attractive man walked in! He tells me that he needs to find a Realtor to help him purchase a house within the next week. What is really neat about this story is that, no one ever 'walks' into the office looking for a Realtor. Most people have an agent, or meet them on the phone while they are driving around calling Real-estate signs. No one just 'walks in!' Especially a young guy who knows how to use the internet! Possibly you will see an older guy, but never younger. To top it off, he was gorgeous; win-win for me! So you can tell my excitement at the time! I am married, but attractive men are attractive men! I asked him why he just 'walked in', his response was priceless. He said, "When you need something done, it is best to do it yourself, and make sure it is done right!" His story was, he had just sold his house the week prior and now needed a new house to put all his stuff in! He needed this done fast and he didn't want to wait; we started right away.

After our gorgeous client left, I quickly called my lender friend. He was shocked, surprised and full of smiles. I found our new client a house within a week, he closed within 3 weeks (usually closing was 5 weeks out) and my lender friend was his lender! It was a win-win for us all!

Here is one of those really neat, synchronistic stories! Remember, I had an intention, I asked for it, and I let it go. The reason it was easy for me to let it go was because I thought it was a tad far-fetched; there was no need to stress over it. I also was in the flow. I was having a good phone convo and was happy to be there. When we are in the flow we should just ask for the biggest and the best, because at that point we are filled with good feelings and feelings of goofiness. We are already 'full' with the happiness of life.

When we make requests in this state, it does not matter if they come true; instead it is just too cool if they do! This is when the magic happens.

Before I knew it, it was time to get my kiddos. We were home and hurried with homework so we could make it to the babysitters. We planned to drop them off at four because the babysitter had to drive to Denver for her daughter's track meet. The plan was for me to drive the kids to her house then back to meet my husband, do dinner (date night!), and then go to our CPR class.

All of this did not work out! My flow seemed to be anxious that afternoon. My GPS stopped working, and I was lost on the way to the babysitter's house. I was late dropping them off. (At this point I knew my vibration shifted so I continued to ask for it to rise.) I then finally made it home and it was five o'clock. I realized the class started at 5:30 not 6:30, so Brian and I rushed to make it on time. Well of course, the traffic was crowded and we did not make it till 6pm. We get to the class and there is no one there. We searched and searched the building and finally find it! Remember this whole time I kept telling myself to breathe and raise my vibration! We get there and they let us in.

The class was supposed to go to 9:30; instead the class condensed itself until only 7! We had some good times at the class and then lots of unexpected alone time after. We could not pick the kids up early because they were in Denver. Brian and I went to dinner and had a very good time. The meal was free because Brian had been gifted a 15 dollar card a few days prior. Our meal came to $15.01 and the lady at the register paid our one cent! We were feeling good, and had a very good, free dinner! After, we had an hour to spare; we went to the grocery store without kids! It was a great night. We then picked up the kiddos and watched them fall asleep in the car. So cute my kids are!

Later I talked with Danielle. She told me she was asked to do a wedding for a T.V. show. My goodness, the twist of events! Side note: she is a wedding officiate. She was conflicted with this opportunity because the purpose of the show was to see if people would still marry while simultaneously the cast of the show created many marital challenges for the couples. The show was popular because they get people who want to be married, and then try to break them up, to see who actually still gets married in the end.

This opportunity was completely unexpected for her! Also it was a great way to publicize her name and her business. Though, the values of the show did not match with hers, she ended up declining.

I thought about this a lot and also tried to get her to think more about it. It reminded me of Girl Scouts. I started being against the organization even though my daughter really wanted to go.

I made myself see what I could learn about myself by checking it out. I wanted to know if my reluctance for her going was because Girl Scouts was bad or if it was only my triggers that were bad. What I learned was that it was my stuff that needed to be cleared and once I owned up to that, it became a win-win. Dreana got to have her Girl Scouts and I was able to support it!

I wondered if Danielle needed to do the weddings for the T.V. show so she could learn to detach from her clients. She comes to her weddings with many blessings for the couples' future, though it is not her 'job' to need them to stay together forever. Their future life is theirs, not a reflection of what Danielle needs from them. It is her job to marry them and let them enjoy their current commitment. Her job is to let them go after the wedding. It is our job to always let go when our job completes.

I think we all get wrapped up in this. Our job is us. It is not our children or our company. All we can do is live in a high vibration each day and let God do the rest. This happened over the weekend at my house. Aidan wanted to go out to eat and I did not. I told him to put 'going out to eat' on his goal board and let it come to him. He complained a lot and I almost gave in, thinking I had to be the source of his happiness. We all know when we want something, when we are in this needy spot, the thing does not come. We have to find happiness first, and then all things come to us.

Thursday was here! This was our next big day; it was our third class of our prosperity course. This day I skipped my work out. I instead brought the kids to school and uploaded more video blog's of my synchronistic stories. The house was a mess and it seemed a lot of stuff was piling up. I had not written in two days and was feeling behind. I also had more stories I wanted to record for the video blog's. I was a little frustrated that four baskets of laundry were still sitting in my living room. But what could I do? I knew it would all be handled when it was time. I concentrated on the current project, and that was the Video blog's!

Around one o'clock, I received a random phone call. This phone call was someone asking about my debt. I listened to their offer and found out that they wanted to take all of my debt and give me an easy monthly payment to finally pay it off. Oh goodness, this was exactly what I was affirming! I had no idea how it would come together because we had so much debt. I did not think we would qualify for a debt consolidation. I listened, hoping it was true, and hoping he would hurry up with his explanation because I had to get my daughter from school. I eventually ended the conversation with a promise to call him back.

After school, I talked with him again, we scheduled another time for him to call when I had all of my credit information ready. I had lots of hope and relief for my future!

That evening I explained the services provided by the company to my husband. At this point, I did not know our budget, but I knew anything would help. I just kept going with what Jack Canfield said in, "The Secret," (paraphrased) he said, "Take life the same way we drive a car at night. The head lights allow us only to see the next two hundred feet; each 200 feet eventually gets us to Las Vegas." I followed the next two hundred feet and told my husband we are doing this, and I am positive the budget will figure itself out!

That evening was filled with a quick dinner, quick explanations and hugs and kisses good night. I went off to class and Brian helped the kiddos into bed. He used his time in front of the computer doing more Army courses! I was in a great mood driving to church. I was excited that all of these good things were coming my way. I was feeling taken care of.

Side note: do you want to know what happened with my money so far?? I had to make a decision to basically pay the bills or to tithe. I chose to tithe. Many of my bills come out as automatic payments, I was worried because I figured the tithing check would bounce or we would have a negative balance in our account. I had difficulty even looking at the account. It was Wednesday that I had a feeling to look at the account. The only withdrawals were my check I wrote to the renters for their security deposit (that I was guided to write,) and the three tithing checks. I do not know what happened with the rest of the automatic withdrawals that were supposed to come out. I am telling you, God hooks you up!

I get to church about a half hour early and help set up the chairs. I am feeling good. My vibration is sky rocketed! We soon sit down and the teacher asks for any testimonies. I raise my hand and tell them about how taken care of I feel! The next lady describes the same feelings. Last week all we could talk about were the 'things' coming our way, and this week all we could talk about was how good we felt. We are growing!

At this time a woman walked in, late for class. She set the security alarms off! This did not happen because she opened a door when she was not supposed to; this happened as she walked into our room. Her presence walking into the class set the whole alarm system off! It was funny because everyone was trying to figure out what happened and how to stop it. They eventually had to call the security person and ask them to come to the church. I looked over at the woman as she was beaming with a very high vibration; I mentioned to her that it was her, her vibration that set the alarms off!

It is the same philosophy as when you know you have lots of energy going through you, and your light bulb bursts. Her energy was bursting excitement into our class!

A few examples that were told of prosperity, I will share now. I decided to write down their testimonies this time! There was a woman who told us of how she made our homework of saying, "I am prosperous" (200 times a day) easier. She made the affirmations into a song. The song she chose was, "Santa Clause is coming to town." Instead of the song's words, she sang, "I am prosperous" over and over with the same melody. The reason for the song is that we want to say, "I am prosperous" 100 times in the morning and 100 times in the evening. Now this is great, but remembering to do it is a task until it hits your subconscious as a habit. A good technique is to leave yourself reminder notes and to find the same spots or occurrences in your life where the habit can be formed. Suggestions could be in a song, or at the gym, or in the car, or a ritual right before bed. Notes reminding yourself of your new habit are great until the habit becomes a habit!

You know what; I just want to say how thankful and full of gratitude I am feeling right now! I am literally living the life of my dreams. I am home; writing! That is all that is on the schedule right now! I am actually writing this book, excited as heck that this is actually happening! Thank you for being with me!

Another woman told of a random call she received the day before. She had an application on the website, "Monster" years ago. She now is working her current job, which she enjoys, however still continues to affirm all bigger and better. Out of the Blue, she received a call saying someone found her application on the website and wanted to know if she would be interested in a position as Marketing Director! This job pays way more than she is currently making and it also comes with a pretty cool Job title! Her interview was the next day. I loved listening to her tell her story; she was in such astonishment. She was just so surprised that this was offered to her. She did not go looking for this job; this job came to her! It is a beautiful example of how our lives could be lived with ease. All we have to do is just be, all will come to us. We are to be happy and full. When we know what we want, this or something much better, we can have the courage to ask for it, let go and let God. God delivers.

Another guy is currently studying to be a spiritual counselor and a minister. When I first met him in the class (last week) he seemed to be very uncomfortable and unsure of himself. He was doing what we all were doing; he followed the rules by paying tithes and trusting God. Over the week he also received a random phone call.

Someone had dropped his name into a hat (at an event) for a director of a specific school to call him. He did not know anyone who would have done this; the school was in a different state. His story is so cute. He said the school was expensive, though the training is exactly what he had been affirming. The director also said that people that graduate from this class, on average, end up with twenty clients, all paying 200 dollars a session. This is an action from the universe! His prosperity is being received from knowing exactly what training he needs to be at. Blessings come in all disguises! Oh, I really love this class!

Our final testimony came from the teacher. She told us that the attendance at church (last Sunday) was very low; due to a retreat most of the congregation was at. I can attest to this, I was there and there were maybe twenty people in the second service. The offering was very small. The minister was thankful for our tithes as they filled in the perceived lack. This made me feel awesome! When we give, we are always hoping that the people receiving it really appreciate it. Our minister did. This made me feel awesome and assured we were doing the 'right' thing. As the money goes out of our hands, it is God who designates the needs in our world. All we have to do is feel good when we are giving and the receiving will go to the right place; always!

The class was fun. There is a lot more comfort between the participants; lots of laughs and connections were made. I also went on break and did not get locked out this time! After break we finished up with the CD and then blessed our tithes before we gave them. This week I gave eleven cents and felt amazing that this was my contribution! It does not matter how much you give, it matters how you give; and I am positive my eleven cents turned into a million bucks!

Wrapping up our time together, we all went into our groups. We were to speak our affirmations and prayers to the group and have everyone repeat them back to us. My prayer was, "I now trust God, within me, to show me how to receive my advance for my book prior to my mom coming to visit on October 11th 2013!" After I spoke, each member of our group, one at a time, grabbed my hand and repeated to me, "The source within me, now shows me how to receive my advance for my book prior to my mom coming on October 11, 2013." Let me tell you, I was almost in tears; and I am as I write this. It felt so authentic, that I was good, that my group would say this for me. I felt and feel so blessed to have this. Thank you!

The rest of the group told us their affirmations. I said to one member, "Divine consciousness within and without manifests good within your life." To another I spoke, "God within you helps you receive the perfect prosperous teaching job!" Blessings to you both, blessings to us all!

As I was heading out I told someone how we received a free oil change. The week prior she told us of her free oil change. She then told me her friend died this week. She was thankful to experience how beautiful and peaceful it was. This woman, who died, knew she was going to, and accepted it. The week of her passing, she spent many hours of one-on-one time with her dearest friends. After her funeral, the ten friends went to lunch to celebrate this beautiful woman.

She also told of all of the generosity. The lunch they went to was paid for by her sister. She also explained that the brother of the lady, whom passed away, flew for the first time from Germany (for the funeral;) this was an accomplishment. The woman, who passed, was a very wealthy lady, and all of her money was going to her brothers and sisters. As she told me all of this, you could see the gratitude in her as she explained how everyone was being taken care of. This is what I am talking about! As I listened to all of this, I could tell that our whole beings were filled with gratitude and this is what life is.

I continued by saying how happy I had been all week, even for the 'bad' stuff. I described how my newer jeep had over heated at the gym and how my response was laughter and full of questions to God, wondering if this was how He was getting me my Denali! She then said in the beginning (of our class) she 'knew' this (the tithing) would probably work because people talk about it all the time. Though, she has been shocked and surprised that this really is working for her. How ironic, all of our good came the second we started tithing. I really liked that. When I began the class, I had the same concerns. I am experiencing the same stuff. When someone other than me told me she did not believe in the beginning, and she is utterly amazed at the results, it was a connection. It was a connection of two people experiencing the same bliss together. It was confirmation. We are all one, we are all normal, we all fall and we all rise together. We are never as alone as we feel at times. We are one and all loved, we are all love.

As I walked out the door, I thanked our teacher. I am thankful I came. I am thankful I am here. I was not going to come; now I see I couldn't have spent my Thursday evenings any better. What a connection my comment made. I talked with them (husband and wife) for a good twenty minutes telling stories of how we all came to Unity. I told the story of my first experience. When I was in Wisconsin years ago I had learned of Catherine Ponder. And through reading her books, I was led to her website, and then led to this church called Unity.

I soon googled what this church was, and found out I completely resonated with it! I wanted to go so bad, but thought I would be caught by my family if I did (Yes I am 32 years old, not 8, though was still terrified of being caught!) Christmas Eve (that year) I went to my mom's house for Christmas. My family then came home and Brian and I tucked the kiddos in bed, preparing their dreams with Santa's arrival. I soon left Brian with his peace and quiet and headed off to the midnight service at my first Unity experience! I kid you not, during the service my purse split in half. I am watching this, freaking out and not knowing what to do. I then was sick; I feared I was going to puke during the meditation where there was nothing but silence. I was dizzy, and started to see lots of ants on the carpet! I was losing it! I did not know if my family was right and I was in the 'devil's' place or if my body was freaking out because I was trying to ditch my old beliefs. I did not know the answer, but I kept going with it and breathing. I knew eventually my answer would come. I am so thankful that I went and tried Unity again, this time in Tennessee, and then of course, I am enjoying Unity in Colorado.

I was later driving home from church. I had the music blaring. I was filled with gratitude an absolute belief that my dreams of wealth and a New York Best-selling author were on the way. I was feeling bliss. I had tears of happiness pouring down my face. I felt taken care of and encouraged and wanted.

I was then home feeling really good. My good vibes must have transferred to Brian because he was smiling as he told me about his day at work and his evening. I then told him about my evening. I felt goofy telling him I cried all the way home, though when I finally did, it felt so good to be honest. I told him how I felt and I wanted him to go to the next prosperity class. I said the financials were the same if he was there or not, because I was tithing for the two of us. I explained the blessings were the same, because the blessings were coming to our family. Though the gratitude I felt was from experiencing the class, and I wanted him to feel that too.

My intention is that each time the class comes up, (multiple times per year) I am going to tithe more and more. The next class, I am tithing 20 percent, and I probably will write a book about that as well! And next time Brian is coming to class with me!

Goodnight to a beautiful Thursday!

Chapter 4
Things are clearing!

Good morning Friday!
I spent the early hours in the gym and then was home to get the kids off to school. I was soon home and a little nervous about collecting the credit card bills for the finance guy. As I delayed doing this, I found some unfolded laundry. I figured if I accomplished a smaller 'mess;' I would gain courage for the bigger one. Finally I had to move forward and trust that God was in charge. He would hold my hand as I made my call and as I plunged through the rest. I then called the finance guy. I admitted my debt. He then collected all the info he needed from me, and scheduled a finalization appointment for me on Monday. With the phone call done, I felt relief. It all was very easy. My affirmations, of my disappearing debt, were happening.

During the day we were also without electricity. The electric company had turned off the power for the whole neighborhood because they were switching to a different service. I thought my stuff and the power company, correlated. Because there was no power, I wondered if my decision with the debt company was correct. Was God unplugging Himself from me because I still was not getting it, or was I regenerating (getting bigger and better service) because I finally was listening? All I currently know, is the debt company feels right. Currently the feeling is right and we will go from here! I affirmed this help, I now get to trust that these steps turn into the next ones, and the steps I am making are in the right direction. If God could hook me up with a phone call from a company saying, "Help is on the way," then He also could hook us up with how to continue to get help. I am breathing, I am trusting, and I am prosperous. God knows what He is doing. I did my part, now I watch and trust as it unfolds.

I then started to think about all the things we still needed to purchase. This was the last weekend we could use our credit cards; my safety net was about to disappear. I made a list of everything I needed. I then checked all the remaining balances of the cards. I was nervous about using the cards after I said I wouldn't, though I was nervous how we were going to make it if we didn't. I asked God if it was okay that I make some purchases. I had needs and it felt right to have them, though I wanted clarification, hoping to not 'mess up' and only make correct decisions from here on out.

My list included registering Dreana for Girl Scouts, Girl Scout and Cub Scout uniforms, an oil change for me, food, Aidan's birthday cake and gifts, new brakes, Dreana's bed, a thermostat for my car, cigarettes and gas. We also had the Vet on the list, though I wasn't sure of any vet open over the weekend; we took this off the list and trusted a new answer would come later.

Before I knew it, it was time for me to go to school. The kids had a 'Fund run' for their volunteer event. That was a blast. I got to help keep score as they ran lap after lap. Dreana is usually lazy and will not run; today she did. I think she was motivated by her peers and the aspect of competition! After her race, her class went back inside, I said goodbye and then waited for Aidan's class to begin their run. His class did not come. They ran earlier in the day; I had no clue. I felt bad about missing Aidan's race. I assumed his class (because they were third grade and Dreana was kindergarten) was after hers. My lesson this afternoon was to not assume, instead get exact details. I feel bad, though I forgive myself, and affirm to be there next time. I love you Aidan; I love you Dreana.

I used my last kid-free hour at the house. Remember we did not have any power, so I could not type this book or talk on the phone because both devices needed to be plugged in. All I could do was sit and/or read. So I did some reading and kept telling myself to breathe as I was waiting to see how all the financials were going to work out. I also patiently waited for guidance to know if I should go shopping or not.

Soon, my hour was over, I leave to go get my kiddos and Brian is parked at the school to surprise us! We all go home. I talk to Brian about my intentions with shopping and the available balances left on the cards. Each of the cards had more than 300 dollars remaining; there was more than 1000 dollars to spend. This was significant because I had given 1,000 dollars to church this month; I received it back, not how I thought, though it came back. I took this as a good sign that we were doing the right thing. We then ordered the Girl Scout registration on-line as well as the Girl Scout and Cub Scout uniforms. Then we told the kids to pack up because we had plans! They were cranky because they wanted to play, but I convinced them that they would like the events of the evening.

We soon made it to the store and took our car into their shop to get an oil change. The whole time I kept asking for confirmation that we were doing the right thing. As I was looking around the building, I see this sign with lots of 8's in it. Eights mean finances are good; I was on track, and I was currently being blessed and given a gift! Now I'm feeling even better. As we leave our car for its service, we head into the store and walk toward the toy isle.

I let the kids know that tonight is the night my boy gets to pick out his gifts, and Dreana gets hers too! (For whose ever birthday it is, they get to pick out a few toys. The other kiddo gets to pick out one toy for being the birthday sibling.)

We then get our gifts, party gift bags and the goodies that go in them and headed to get our car. The car was taking a long time. Brian was not getting the service he was expecting. His vibration was really nervous, and so I think the universe was giving him what he was 'asking' for. We then were on our way home and stopped at Subway for a dinner treat! We also stopped and filled up with gas and soon were home.

The excitement and anticipation of the evening filtered through our children. They had their toys, but they were not able to open them until Aidan's birthday party on October 12th. The kids were both excited and frustrated as they knew they had some days to wait!

We ate dinner and then Brian and Aidan headed out again. The boys went and picked out Aidan's cake and paid for it in advance. Then they headed to Home Depot to purchase some 2 by 4's to finish making Dreana's bunk bed. Later Brian comes home and says he is tired and hopefully the credit cards will work on Saturday for the grocery store, because he had no more energy for another shopping trip for the evening. We had to trust they would work, because wearing ourselves out trying to gain a safety net, really did not make much sense. There had to be a better way; here was a lesson in trust.

The evening was filled with bliss. I had very happy kiddos and I received all of what I wanted. I headed to bed for some reading. Five minutes later I was a sleep. I usually have trouble sleeping. Lately, a lot of my fears have gone away, and I have been able to sleep through the entire night.

Saturday morning:
Oh how I had waited for this day for a very long time. Today was the day of the Reiki session! I was excited to weigh myself at the gym. When I had weighed myself in the middle of last week, I had weighed in at 143.5 pounds. This was goofy, because I had expected to lose a pound or two. Nope, I pretty much stayed the same, well, I lost a half of a pound. Though, I did not get too frustrated, because I had allowed myself to have a few spoonfuls of peanut butter throughout the week. My intention this time around with losing weight was to keep it off forever! I wanted to allow myself some goodies here and there, without feeling guilty. Today I weighed in at 144. I was initially mad because I did not want to see that, though I soon became okay with it. I also knew that last night I had a sub, and subs have a lot of bread in them.

And I also was wearing a t-shirt instead of a tank top. I also worked out at 8 instead of 5. I decided to just accept it and expected awesome results the next time I weighed myself.

During my run, I was running next to a whole bunch of people in costumes. That was fun! They all decided to dress up for Halloween. My work out went quick and I headed home. I was excited about the afternoon. I looked forward to this for a long time and today was finally here. As I waited; I cleaned my house. I wanted to put the budget together, though I still was unsure of where to start. This not being complete was bugging me, though; I knew it would be okay to just sit in my frustration until I knew what to do about it.

I also received a random phone call from the leader of the prosperity class. She was wondering what my tithing of time consisted of. I told her I ran with the 'Fund run' for school and I hoped to volunteer at the soup kitchen on a weekly basis. She advised me to talk to the lady that manages the book store, at church, because she was in charge of the soup kitchen. I then had Craigslist float through my head, I decided to check and see what our urgent message was all about. I checked at the perfect time and finally got myself a free baby crib! I called Brian, he was at the grocery store, and asked him to pick it up. This was cool; I finally had my baby bed, sooner than later I would have my baby!

This whole time, as I anxiously waited, Brian was having himself a frustrated day. I think he is nervous about money and all of the changes. His morning consisted of being in the grocery line for 45 minutes, hitting every red light, and getting lost on the way to picking up the crib.

He finally was home with an overabundance of food. We had so much, we had to fit it all in an extra cupboard and fill the top of our refrigerator! It was like Christmas seeing all of this food. Thank you for this! Brian then mentioned that the crib was a drop side crib and this was not what the agency said we could have. I did not care. I said, "For now, I am going to enjoy having a crib in the house, and when it was time for the agency to check our crib, then we would get the 'right' one." Then, Brian received an idea of how to 'fix' the crib so the side would not drop down! How much better could my day get! He put my crib together. It now sits on the perfect wall of my bedroom, just waiting for a baby!

As our time was winding down and getting ready to be here, my friend called. I told her about all my good 'luck;' she was uplifted! Soon it was time to leave for Reiki! We get to church and my kids are good and hanging out quietly. It is our turn for our session. I followed orders, not knowing how all of this goes. I lay down on the bed, and they made me feel comfortable.

Three people put their hands on many different parts of my body. It felt neat. There was a lot of heat coming from their hands. I was unsure of what to expect, so I just watched, curious of results, and was excited this was finally happening. This experience I have wanted for a long time. I had manifested, and realizing this made me feel like a million bucks. The results I was hoping for were only icing on the cake. Living a dream I created was the cool part!

What I noticed so far is, my knees don't 'feel' anymore. I had always 'felt' my knees. They did not hurt, but I knew they were there; and now I do not feel that. The reason I bring this up, is because I have had knee problems for a long time, not painful, but definitely problems. My knees would sporadically buckle, sometimes I would be walking and I would almost fall. There was no real issue with them; it was just annoying that they had potential to buckle.

I also felt (at the therapy) weird, burning, and tingling in my calf and lower back. I have never felt this before. It was almost as if someone was poking those areas with a fire poker. The feeling only lasted for thirty seconds, nothing to worry about, only something I noticed. Overall, I guess, I am still watching for my results from the Reiki session; watching how my comfort level gets bigger and better as I allow myself to unfold with this new experience.

That evening we had dinner and the kids were out for a bit. Soon the kids came in and we all feel asleep. Again, I slept the entire night.

....

Sunday morning was neat; I woke up early and had the early hours to myself. I did a lot of visualization and played in my own world for a while. The kids and husband woke up. We had eggs and soon it was time for church. Again, I did not bring money for tithing because we were to reserve that money for our class.

Church left me preoccupied. I felt frustrated that I was there. It was one of those mornings where I wanted to day dream all day and had a lot of difficulty sticking with reality. Church was not bad, but being anywhere besides in my head, was what was frustrating. When the service was over, I talked to the lady about the soup kitchen; I also received a random hug from the prosperity group leader. I thought that was weird. I watched it. It seemed like I was receiving all of these blessings from everywhere, I just could not put a finger on what all of these blessings meant. Were they just nice things happening or were they leading to something I currently did not understand? Was I opening up and experiencing new relationships, new friendships? Was I becoming a member of this community? Was life loving me, and welcoming me into happiness?

I did not know, but it felt good, I appreciated it.

That day, I talked to my girlfriend as she shared some insight. She told me, I have a pattern. My pattern is that wherever I am, whatever I do, people tend to respond to me. I have a natural gift of people always wanting to be around me. They enjoy me, they feel uplifted by me, and they tell me their stories. People enjoy being around me. She told me, she thinks, I was a famous person in my past life, because people are always drawn to me.

This weekend, I also had a realization of me being a homeless person in a past life. All my life, (this life) I have always been attracted to wealth. A lot of wealthy people are attracted to me. Though a pattern, and a fear, I have had for a while is, if I mess up; I will end up homeless. This weekend, I realized, that has already happened. There is no need to worry about it happening in this life. What I have been doing with that belief, is reminding myself over and over, that this already happened. I can now let it go. Isn't it weird how realizations just come to you and a belief can just go away?

I also had another realization during the Reiki session I want to share with you. First let me tell you a quick back story, my story is with my fear in the subject of demons. All of this started when my beliefs began changing with religion, I was slowly moving away from being a Christian. This is something I have been working with for years. This is the reason I have had trouble sleeping and being alone. My past is filled with many nights of waking up, turning every light in the house on, and then begging myself to have the courage to fall back asleep. I would sit in a terrified state for hours; hoping morning would soon come.

Since the class started, I am less scared of getting my laundry by myself. I also have been sleeping through the night. I feel safe. As my realization continues, during the Reiki session, the woman puts her hands over my head and all of a sudden, I feel the terrifying feelings I feel when I wake up in the middle of the night. But this time, I know that I am in a safe spot, I am not alone in my house; I am in a room full of twenty people. I know, I am currently safe, as my husband is two beds over. I let myself engulf in this fear, knowing I am safe to feel it. I realize her hands are over my head, this fear must sit in my Crown chakra; I now understand more how to move through this fear. It is not designated to me, and the middle of the night; it is stuck in my head, and can also be felt in the middle of the day. Now that I know this, I can work with it, and finally get rid of those frightening nights.

As I write all of this down, this is my sticky point. This is my vulnerability.

And of course, as I open up this space to you, I ironically receive two text messages, as my energetic level opens up, the physical world responds. I am getting the opportunity to not face my fears and let them go. I talk myself into just breathing and trusting that God and light and love are with me.

I take a break, and check my phone. The first screen that pops up on my phone is a browser search of the animal totem, Dove. The reason I was searching this, was earlier a dove came crashing into my window. I read the post, and the words that stuck out from the message are, "I am to release all hate and revenge." Right away, I realize that I still need to forgive my brother, his wife and my previous best friend. I have been trying to do this for years. I have been trying because, I know, it is poison for me to hold on; though I have not been able to fully do it. I ask for guidance on a daily basis to take my hate and hurt from me.

Maybe, now is the time. I am going to write about this, hoping as it gets out, onto these pages, that it has an avenue to clear and stop being stuck. Years ago, I had a best friend. We grew up, and took different paths in life; but we were still close when we saw each other. We had one of those friendships that people would always say, that even though we did not see each other all the time; when we did, we could pick up as if we had been together the day before. Our relationship ended up falling apart. Prior to it crumbling, I was having a great life. When my husband went to Iraq (eight years ago) I had let a lot of old stuff go, and really enjoyed all of the new. There I was, fit, had the perfect baby, did well at work, and school, I had no debt, new investments, and more money than I needed. I was living the life of a billionaire as far as I was concerned. All was really good. I remember I used to get a lot of compliments of how happy I was even though it would appear I should be sad, because this was the same time my husband was at war.

That year came and went. As the year was ending, and I knew my husband was coming back; I was nervous that all my good would go away. I was unsure if I was going to be able to keep my happy relationship with my son, and keep the weight and T.V. off. I was nervous we would also have money problems. Well guess what? My husband came home, and of course he did not want to eat weight loss food. He wanted the T.V. and also the beer. He wanted my time, and there was a lot of learning that needed to happen in having a family of three instead of only two. The money that he was making from overseas went away, and he was working three part time, minimum wage jobs, to get us through. He seemed less concerned than me, with the maintenance of our first rental property. He seemed to want to take over what I had accomplished.

Everything fell apart. Our marriage was not happy. I started affirming (well my definition of it, I did not know it at the time) that he would go back overseas, or miraculously give us the life style that we had. I did not know any other way that our money and our happy life could come back.

What ended up happening was, months later, Brian left for his second tour. I remember that phone call like it was yesterday. They (the Army) called and wanted to talk with him; he was not home, but at work. I recognized that call, the same call I heard a year ago; my heart fell. I said to the lady, "My husband was not supposed to go back (to war;) he had to be home for at least 3 months before this call was allowed to happen." She said, "Mam, it's been 3 months and one day, please have him call me when he gets the message."

The phone call ended, and I fell to the ground; wondering what to do next. I couldn't believe this was happening again. I was mad that my good life could only exist if I had a husband overseas.

Needless to say, that second deployment was nothing like the first. This time I was mad. This time I would yell at him when I only got one day a week to talk with him. This time I wanted a divorce. This time, college did not go very well. This time all of my friends left. I remember how it started with my friends. I was going camping with them, my brother and his wife. I had to drop my son off for the weekend at my aunt's house; and I was not feeling good about it. This was the first time I dropped him off for an entire weekend.

My camping experience led me to the realization that I was no longer funny (to my friends) and my ideas were no longer intriguing (to them) because I now speak about the other side of Christianity. I also had been to college and had a lot of new knowledge that they were not accustomed to. My intention for the camping experience had been to have fun, and share with them. I was no longer the same, and they did not take to that. My friends were mean to me. They would cut me off, start arguments, go off and not invite me; it was pretty bad. It was one of those nights when your friends purposefully keep you out of the conversation. They purposefully do not invite you. They were mean. My feelings were hurt. I did not understand what was going on.

A few months later, I stopped by my brother's house unexpected; all of my friends were there and were planning on going to dinner. For years we hung out as best friends, we all went to dinner and parties together. This was the first time I was not invited. I asked to go, and they told me "No," they had reservations and there was no room for me. They also wanted a kid free evening (they did not have any children) and my toddler was not welcome. I was heartbroken.

I saw all of this going on, and I guess it just festered until I hit an all-time depression that took years to get over. I am still not fully over it, so maybe this next piece of writing is necessary and will finally get it out of me! Please bear with me and try to visualize how you will have your own conversation with the people in your lives.

This is maybe what I need to do, so here goes.

Hey you three, specifically Cletus, Chastity and Angelina, I am very hurt by what I perceived happened over the years. I think you purposely did mean things to me, spoke mean things about me. I feel like you were always talking about me. I hated those weird feelings whenever I would walk into a room and you were there. I could feel the thickness; I knew I was not wanted. I felt like I was talked about and laughed at behind my back. I felt like I was not good enough anymore. I felt like the 'dork' at school and my life was incredibly hard at the time. I also felt like I tried really hard many times to get over it. I was nice to you, hoping we could make this better. I attempted to do things for you. I tried to always be in places that you were at, so we could 'make up' accidentally. But truly, I know in my heart, that I was still hurt; I am still hurt. I guess I have tried everything I can do to just get you out of my life; because you hurt so badly.

The reason you hurt so bad, is because you hurt me when you stopped loving me. You were a big part of my life, and my life also included my future. I did not see myself in your future; I thought there was little to live for. I did not feel whole; all I wanted was to fix my broken heart. I know that I said some mean things along the way; and I am sorry for them. The reason I did was because I did not know how to act around you. I was at a loss for words, for what happened. You hurt me. I want to heal. I want to forgive you, and forgive that time of my life. My intention is to let it go. I am not letting you go, those emotions and feelings. It is not healthy for me to hold onto this, and I know you will feel better when this finally shifts. Please help me let this go. Whatever you are holding onto about me, please release me. I love you, and am sorry for the hard times. It is my intention to release all of this. I am, for the final time, asking for this to go away, from me and from you. I am asking for healing. As you feel this release, please understand it is for the best. I wish you many happy experiences and love in your life. I wish you healing as well. I wish the best for you. I wish you the best health. I wish the best for your kiddos. I wish you plenty of success in life. I wish all your dreams to find you, in a very easy and affordable way. I wish you happiness, health and wealth. I wish you forgiveness from yourself, and all others. Here are my blessings that I am sending you.

I am releasing all my hate, and revenge I have with you. I am letting you go, so you can live a happy life. I love you that much; I am releasing all of this hate and hurt. Thank you for loving me as much as you did. Your love meant the world to me, and was so great, that many strive for it. You are beautiful, worthy, and acceptable to all. You are worth all of your dreams.

Angelina, your babies are very handsome! I am proud that you have found such a great relationship with your husband. You really do find joy in having him around. I appreciated all of your sex stories. Sex is a subject that you love, and you love with your husband. I am glad you were able to have your boys; for a while there, it seemed hard for you to get pregnant. I am glad that you did, and am happy for your family. I miss you. I miss your stories. I am proud of your dental degree, and that you enjoy your work so much. I think you look awesome with your weight loss, and I am proud you have found this life style easy. I send you blessings on all your financials. You are good just how you are. And I should be thankful for you. This is how I choose to see you. Thank you for all of the lost time, it has brought me closer to appreciating who you are, and who you have taught me to be.

Cletus, I was jealous of you for a long time. Here I am the one, who had all the dreams of being a successful entrepreneur, and you were the one who did it! I am proud that you have multiple, 'tens of thousands' in your bank account. I am proud that you can purchase a car with cash. I am proud that your business has succeeded as much as it has; and will do. You are on your way to becoming the next Henry Ford! You are truly a billionaire, and I am excited that I have such a successful brother.

I wish you would have included me in your life. I felt hurt, that I was no longer your friend. I felt kicked-out. Who knows why you did this. It was probably because you did not feel good when I was around. And that was probably because I was jealous. I was hard to love, so I consciously understand why you did not want me around; though it hurt. You were my best friend that rejected me, and that feeling sucks. I want you to know, I am forgiving you. I am letting this go. I would prefer an amazing relationship with you, though now, it is okay, as I am learning how to have that amazing relationship with myself. Thank you for rejecting me, it brought me closer to me. And the more I love me, the more I can send you love. So thank you for the hard times, they have taught me an important lesson. It is the lesson to remember who I am. I love you. I am proud of you.

Let me back up for a minute. Angelina, I want to tell you, what I think you are good at. You are very beautiful. You have gorgeous features, and beautiful long, flowing hair.

You are very beautiful, open and loving. You are good with kids. You always seem to be around them, and listen with them. You made me feel like a million bucks; and this is the way you make them feel. This is why you are always invited to all of their activities. This is why you are always invited to the party. You are awesome to be around, and it shows how you care about everyone else's achievements. You take the time to make people feel beautiful on the inside, as well as the out. You are always excited about pedicures and new clothes. You love to shop, and are always making people look better than they did before you came around. You are lovable and sweet. People love you and want to give to you what you have given to them. They want to learn how to love as much as you have loved them.

Cletus you are very smart. I know you do not think you are, but you are. You have an ability to make lots of friends. People love to be around you, because you are so fun, and full of life. People enjoy your presence. And to top it off, this has served you in the business world. This is because, now people have an excuse to be around you when you fix their car. This is why their cars are so well maintained. It is you they are paying for. You are always living life to the fullest, with your day to days, your adventures in the snow, and your growing family. You love your boat, your dog, your house, your two kiddos, and your wife. You are doing very well. There is a lot I am still learning from you. I love the way it is easy for you to make friends and keep acquaintances. You can talk to anybody, and go even further, by inviting them to your home for a barbeque. I love how you are comfortable with people. I love how you trust yourself. I love how you know who you are.

Chastity, I love how organized you are. You always make things flow easy. You always make things look pretty. You have a talent for style. It is natural to you. You do not realize how good you are at it. I love how many people follow you. You are a leader. People do not know why they do it, they just assume you are the leader, and take your word for truth. You can spread many messages to the world, with your leadership qualities. This is something I strive for in myself. I would like to learn your skill. I would like to learn how to do what you do, and do it as well as you. Thank you for showing me something that I strive to become. I apologize that I did not see it, like that, in the past. In the past, I was mad at you. Now, I understand it wasn't you, just a lack I wasn't seeing in myself. I wanted people to follow me, and now I know when my heart is in the correct spot; people will always follow me. As long as I am living truth, people will follow and learn from themselves. Thank you for being a good 'devil's advocate.'

This is where my energetic letters stop.

I feel better as I wrote them; though am hoping the feeling of forgiveness follows quickly. I have done all I can think of to let this go; I hope this was our last step.

Now, back to Sunday after church; at Sunday school, Aidan had issues. The teacher felt the need to tell us all the wrong Aidan had done. We get in the car, and I tell Aidan, we are either not going to church next Sunday, or he is not going to Sunday school. I told him that if he wants to believe that he is naughty, if he wants to believe the stories being taught to him, I was not going to sit back and watch it. Until a further answer came, I was not putting him in the situation to continue on with these ridiculous beliefs. He needs to take ownership and start turning these beliefs around; or he is not going back. From here on, I am affirming that he is seeing how awesome he is, and to expect to be loved, and adored in his class, or he is hanging out with us at church.

Sunday afternoon, I listened to predictions by the 'Twin Psychics' and Sylvia Browne on You Tube. This was my time to decompress and relax into the week. Brian spent the afternoon making Dreana's bunk bed. We had dinner and soon the kids were sleeping. Brian and I fell asleep. I slept through the entire night.

....

Monday morning I woke up early and had time to myself. I took Chevy on a walk around the neighborhood. Upon my return I realized, I still had an hour to myself before the kids and husband were to join me. I spent this time in beautiful visualization and being thankful for everything that I am!

I wake Brian up at 7 o'clock, and he informs me he is late; he needs to be at work at seven today. I left him in his frustration, and continued to affirm my beautiful day. The kiddos were then up, and breakfast was served. They made it to school, and I was home eager to write. I spent the majority of the day writing. I had a lot flowing out of me; I was irritated when Brian came home for lunch. As I came to terms with my frustration; he informs me he is exhausted, and he chooses to sleep for his hour and a half of lunch. I received much more time to write!

While he slept; I received my phone call. It was our confirmation call from our financial agreement/project that was beginning. We finished up thirty minutes later. I was relieved that all of this goodness finally started!

There is a small risk with the project. The risk doesn't bug me; it feels good, and I have a knowing that everything is going to work out for our benefit. I truly feel, this is what we affirmed, and everything will go smoothly.

I feel taken care of with this company; they are helping us move through our past debt. All the fear and worry that you would assume I should have, I do not. I know this was affirmed, and I know our answer was delivered. I know God is in charge. Really, I just had to hand over my numbers, and let someone else set up the payment schedule. Then, I just pay the bill for two and a half years, and let it go. It is easy; it is just weird how there is no fear.

I began looking at our budget. I opened the bank account, and saw only one other withdrawal had come out; it was for my car payment. I then began calculating all the auto drafts that should be coming out for the rest of the month. I did not add the credit card payments because these now did not need to be paid. The amount needed was still higher than we currently have coming in. I chose not to care! Until we received our money from our renters, we did not have the money to pay our mortgages; this had to be okay. Really what could I do, I currently could not manifest more money, so why was I stressing. I called Brian, and asked him to take all the auto payments off for our mortgages. I also noticed the bill for our movie account was coming out of our credit card. I did not want to use credit cards anymore; so I decided to open up a PayPal account to have this drafted. I asked Brian to set that up (he is the techy guy in our house.)

The PayPal account is significant all on its own. I have wanted to receive different therapy sessions over the phone, everyone I talk to asks me to pay via PayPal. I also considered some sort of business (Reiki or counseling) which requires me to be set up with a PayPal account. Ironically we needed an account set up, funny, how God always hooks you up with each of your intentions!

Now, concerning the mortgages, I do not care! Funny how all of the stress has gone away! I am figuring that God is hooking us up each step of the way, and I am positive He will help us know what to do with our mortgage companies until we start getting more money. I am positive He will help us with our two past debts: the money to Brian's mom and to my grandfather! I am also positive that He is going to guide me. He will create an easily managed budget, and will help fulfill our needs with Christmas, and all larger events when they come!

2:30 p.m. was here, and it was time to get the kiddos. We came home and finished homework and reading. Aidan wanted thirty dollars for an outing with his friend. He wanted it within thirty minutes; he was anxious with his request. I just 'knew' the answer. I am so proud of myself for not feeling guilty about my lack. I am so proud of my growth to be able to say, "No" when the supply is not currently funded. I told him, "No," because I currently did not have the money, and I did not find it important to hurry up, and figure how to get it.

He was persistent and found his ten dollars (from his allowance.) With his money, he was only short twenty dollars. I told him, I would not give him the remaining money. Instead, I suggested, he put the needed money on his goal board, and be prepared for another day. He was mad, but eventually calmed down. He then cleaned out his room! Oh, what a blessing to see his energy change so quickly! Maybe his energy change was due to me sticking to my decision, and not letting it alter, due to feelings of guilt of him not getting what he wanted. Who knows; but it felt good to see me so good.

Dreana was cranky. She wanted a peanut butter sandwich after she finished eating her left over school lunch. She can eat and eat, and stay perfectly fit; I think this is because she absolutely adores her food. What you love, loves you! Though, sometimes, it gets annoying that she constantly eats! So I told her, "No," she could wait till dinner. She was upset. Brian was also home; he was crabby. I needed to get out for a while; I took Chevy for a walk. We walked for an hour. It was a very good walk. I realized that I have been here before (in a past life;) I also had already succeeded in a past life. I realized (had a premonition) that I had lived a life beginning poor, and later becoming an author. This is the reason I have desired having the job of a writer since I was a little girl. I also realized this life time, my intention (that I made previous to coming here) was to succeed; this was my soul purpose. My whole intent was on succeeding and not living. One of my goals is to LIVE this time! It was neat to realize this. The rest of my walk I kept affirming that this time around I finally got it right, and was ready for the big shebang! I was going to succeed and learn to live a happy life. The walk was beautiful.

I was later home and dinner was already prepared. We ate as a family, a very happy time. After, I designated clean up and bed time to my husband. I went into my room with a book. I was asleep within an hour. I slept the whole night!

During the night I had a dream. I remember being in a room with my deceased uncle. He was showing me how much his family was hurting. He kept showing me movie slides, as if we were in a theatre, of his daughter and wife crying and missing him. It was a very calming dream. He told me it was okay that their grief was happening. He also was telling me that my recent awareness's were helping me clear, and I was on the right track. In the beginning of my dream, I felt sad, and by the end of the dream, I felt very connected, and relieved. Thank you for your visit; it was nice to see you and to see you so wise.

Tuesday morning, my son was my alarm clock. It was 5 A.M. and he wanted help with his birthday invitations. My husband was at work at 7. I cooked eggs for the kids, and they were off to school. I was later home folding laundry, then writing. I spent time visualizing being published by Hay House Publishing. I thought about literary agents, I had a name pop into my awareness; she was from a well-known agency. Here is a way it could all happen! Here is some make-believe! (This is my daydream, not currently happening; just a hope it could!)

....

My daydreams begin as a Thursday morning! I woke up at 4:14 A.M. with a lot of excitement; I just knew something incredible was going to happen today! I have coffee and soon am dressed, ready to walk out the door. I drive to the gym feeling excited! I get to the gym, at one minute to five, as I am allowed into the building with three others!

I get inside and head toward the bathroom. I slip off my shoes and step onto 'my' scale and see the numbers 138.5! Oh how exciting! How much better does today get! At the treadmill, the other two people who met me at the door were also jogging. We used each other as motivation. I ran the entire time, surprised by my speed! Nearing the end of my run, I slow to a jog and then as the 30 minutes come to a close, I find myself walking off my elevated pulse. Three minutes of a cool down left me calm and ready for a peaceful afternoon.

I drive home, still feeling the awesomeness of my run. I walk inside to see the clock says 6am! I still have an hour of 'me' time! Seven o'clock finds itself on the kitchen stove, and my kiddos and husband are awake. I begin to make lunches and eggs for breakfast. The kiddos eat, and Aidan begins his small journey on foot to his friend's house, then to school. Ten minutes later, Dreana and me jump in the jeep, and soon say our goodbye's as she enters into another day of kindergarten! Today is picture day! Oh did those two look adorable!

I am home now alone and at peace. I have this grand ole feeling that something even more amazing is going to be written today. I begin typing the events of the two days prior. Tuesday the 8th of October was my little man's birthday! There were lots of neat entries as we celebrated one more year; we are blessed with such an awesome Aidan!

I was soon caught up with writing and quickly saved the document; getting up for a break. I feel accomplished and on track! The house is clean; this is a good day! I fill the unexpected, extra time with some grocery shopping! I take the 25 dollars that was stored in the cupboard and my to-do-list hanging in the kitchen. There are only a few items on the list; this means I have plenty of money!

As I drive to the store, I am still feeling good.

I have a feeling that this day is going to get even better! I feel like I am flying down the road; knowing my directions without my GPS! I get to the store, turn off my car and step out into the almost vacant parking lot. It is 10:30 A.M. No one seems to be shopping today. I look down and of course I find myself 56 cents! I bounce into the store and grab the few items and move toward the register. Again, as I look down, there is a whole dollar calling my name! Today is good!

I pay the cashier and walk out with my three bags of groceries. I smile the entire way to my car, and start to pack my trunk. As I am getting in my seat I am stopped by a lady walking up to me. She asks me for directions, as she is new to the area. I laugh with her, and let her know I am usually the last one to ask for directions; though for some reason today I am the perfect one to ask. Where she wants to go is the same area I was at the day prior. She and I resonated very well; it was the mood and vibration I had found myself in that seemed to have all of these amazing things continue to happen!

We chit chatted for a moment; it seemed like 'the next logical thing to do.' It was as if we were 'old' friends. She soon tells me that she is going to meet a client in the area; this is why she needed directions. She was an agent that spent her time helping published authors. She worked with Hay House, and found herself in Colorado this week to work with her new client. My mouth dropped open, and I felt my heart begin to pump harder. I breathed slowly as the color of my skin began to lighten. She looked at me funny. I asked her if her name was Catherine. She looked at me surprised. I quickly said, "I do not mean to scare you, though I had a feeling you were coming."

(This next part is real, not make-believe; this really happened)

Quickly as I type that last sentence I am reminded of something I want to share with you. When I moved to Tennessee last year, I was excited to finally go to the Unity church. I felt okay with my decision, because I knew my mom was twelve hours away, and I would not be caught. I, at the time; Googled the closest Unity church and hoped for the best when I finally got to go.

Prior to attending my first Sunday service, I had a dream. This dream had me in an auditorium with a levitating man 'sitting' on stage. I was the only one in his audience. He did not talk to me; he only spoke his words telepathically. His message was one of teaching and guidance. I was his student, learning from him as a master. I had never met this man before. I had no clue of who he was.

And when I woke up from the dream, I knew he had taught me needed things; I felt blessed and peaceful.

I kid you not, two weeks later, I go to church. In the service they talk about a class that will be held after the service and that babysitting will be provided. I went to the class; there were only ten of us there. This man walks up to me to say, "Hi" and my mouth drops open! He is the man from my dreams! I introduce myself and attempt to act normal, as we all sit down to start our class. During the class I am sure I took quite a few glances at him (trying to be conspicuous of course) and for weeks after, I was curious of what all of that meant.

Continuing, the next few weeks when I would see him in church, I wanted to tell him of my dream. Though, I felt he would find me goofy, or think I was trying to 'hit' on him. I was nervous about how and if I would tell him. And because I was nervous, I did not act normal around him. Finally I had gone to Wisconsin for the month, and was back at the Tennessee church for Sunday. Maybe because time had elapsed, or I was feeling quite open from my month long vacation; who knows, but I finally found my courage to tell him. We were all hanging around after church, drinking coffee and having snacks. He and I had said, "Hi" to each other in the past; we were on an acquaintance level. I pulled him aside this time, and said I had to tell him something. I told him about the dream; and his response was many people dream about him. He kind of laughed it off, and said, "That was cool." I did not think much of it, I was only glad I finally told him and he did not freak out!

So here we are building our friendship; and one Sunday after church, this man's daughter is practicing (in the church) for the church Easter play. His three daughters and my kids were friends, so Aidan wanted to stay after church and watch his daughter practice. There was this man and I sitting in the chairs, watching the play. It was really weird, this was the same setting of my dream; in my dream, I was sitting in the audience watching him. Because it was just the two of us, I brought the dream up again. And this time he got it. He told me, that maybe I dreamed my dream because he had been affirming for years to be a spiritual teacher; and maybe my dream was to tell him he should be teaching people about their spiritual path? We also talked about the energy that came from my hands. He was the first person (not in my family) that I shared my secret with.

Now back to our day dreamed Thursday! When I asked Catherine if Catherine was her name, I had the exact 'weird feeling, knowing' when I had finally met that man in Tennessee. It was like De-ja-vu. I was in such amazement that all of this was happening.

And back to, "I do not mean to scare you, but I knew you were coming," Catherine is looking at me with a bewildered look. I tell her my story which consisted of me writing this book. I let her know that I had to pick out an agent so my affirmations and daydreams could have some details. I told her I had talked to God, and wanted Him to hook me up with my agent's name quickly, because the process of picking out an agent seemed lengthy. I explained to her that I Googled the website of agents for Hay House and I started breezing through all the names and waited to hear, "That's her." Within moments, I found her name, and accepted that this is whom God chose and went on with my day.

Now that we were actually meeting face-to-face, I was as surprised as she was. I knew she was coming, though coming in this way, was such a treat. She is looking still amazed and not speaking. I continue, and ask her if she would read my book and consider her services on my behalf. Still amazed, she quickly says, "Yes." We then talk over some details of where I would meet her to give her a paper copy of what I had written. It was now one O'clock; I was meeting her at the coffee house down town, where she also was meeting with her client. She introduced me, and told a synapse to her guest of how we had met earlier. The three of us had a chuckle, and I handed her my book and said my goodbyes! The whole time I was beaming, this was not just a meet-n-greet; this was all orchestrated awesomeness!

I left the two of them and headed to the school. I decided to go early and wait the extra fifteen minutes. I sat in the car in amazement of how awesome all of this had happened. My heart was still pumping, and I had tears pouring down my cheeks. I was thankful, and full of gratitude. I was feeling all of my dreams coming true; and that God really does care that I have aspirations and goals in life! It was confirmation that God cared about me, and the things I cared about. It was good. Life was good. I did not tell the kids about my 'chance' meeting. I wanted to keep it to myself as I watched it all unfold. I listened patiently to their stories of the day. We soon found ourselves at the kitchen table studying homework and accepting plans of play dates in the neighborhood. Brian came home excited about his day. He talked of all of his 'lucky' events. I let him talk and talk, as I was beaming with gratitude!

We had a great afternoon and prepared dinner as we had kids running in and out with joy and excitement as they played. We eventually told all the neighborhood kids to head home as we sat down to dinner. Brian was in charge of cleaning up the dishes after we ate and the kids were asked to go to bed early even though they had off of school the next day. I wanted them all rested and prepared for the arrival of grandma when she was flying in tomorrow!

I began my drive to the prosperity class at church. The entire class was filled with bliss and fun. Lots of neat testimonials were told; life is good! At the end of the class, we prayed together in our groups and again I found myself in lots of gratitude. I was beaming on the way home. I had tears of joy again and was thankful for my life!

I parked my car in the driveway and speed-walked to the house. Brian was excited to tell me about his evening and was happy I was home. We both grabbed a beer and I listened to all of his successful stories from the evening. He was in a great mood. My phone began to ring. With it being so late, I figured it was my mom calling with anticipation for her arrival the next day. It was not! It was Catherine!

She apologized for calling so late, though wanted to catch me before the evening was finished. She said she spent the majority of her time reading what I had given her. She said this was a best seller, actually she said the key words, "NY Best Seller." She wanted me to know she loved the book; she loved the story, and was excited to hear the rest! She said she wanted to be my agent and asked if I would like getting an advance. I did not know what to say except, "Yes" a hundred times! My voice began to shake as I was holding back my tears! As she ended our conversation, she told me she was emailing me a mini contract which said, "Until the Real contract was signed, this contract meant she was my agent!" I thanked her, and her reply was a very heart felt, "Congratulations."

She hung up the phone; I began to cry. All of this happened, and it had happened to me! I was in awe. Brian asked what was happening. All I could get out was we needed to get to his computer and print the pre-agreement, sign it and scan it back! He did not know what was going on, though he followed my instructions. Thirty minutes later, after I read the short document, signed and scanned it back; we went back to our beers as I let Brian in on the whole day! The evening ended with blissful sleep and a grateful mind!

The next morning I was informed I would be receiving an express check in the mail. The afternoon passed as we waited for grandma's plane to get here. We went to go pick her up and when we were home a large package awaited our arrival! Not only did the check arrive; also a dozen roses, cheese and sausage (we are vegetarians, ha, ha) and a hundred dollar gift card to a local restaurant. It also came with lots of info, and contract language stating Catherine was my agent! Of course my two kiddos and grandma wanted to know what all the excitement was; and then is when I let them all in on the events of the last few days! Oh what a beautiful Friday it was!

Day dreaming over; back to reality and our story. When that day dream comes true, I will totally let you know! Tuesday afternoon is here again.

I spent the remainder of the morning finishing up some writing. It is now time for the kiddos. The afternoon was filled with homework and then some playing. We ended up doing a quick, 'left over' dinner because it seemed the four of us were too preoccupied with life to create anything else!

Something neat that happened was my husband forwarded me a Facebook post of a buddy he went to war with. This buddy is now a public speaker, speaking with people and showing them how to follow their dreams, and their goals in life. I listened to what he had to say, and was utterly amazed at the truth that came through him! His name is George Montgomery. (You can find him on You Tube.)

The night was filled with kiddos that did not want to sleep, a husband Skyping his buddy, and me having happy thoughts filter through my head. Soon the night ended.

Wednesday morning I was up early. I decided not to work out. I was not feeling it; the quiet hours of sitting seemed a lot more enticing! I also figured that my field trip with my daughter would cover the exercise portion for the day. We were going to the pumpkin patch! I am excited about our field trip! These are things that I spent years with Aidan on, and now Dreana is having those same experiences! I am blessed to be their mother; I am blessed that the two of them chose me! I am a very lucky mommy!

I had an idea that came as I sat in my quiet. This may be scattered, but please go with it. You know how amazing this 'tithing thing' is, and how it showed up in my life. The reason I share this with you is because I want you to have the courage to do this yourself. As I have given this portion of my life to God; God is responding. He is guiding me, and directing me in each of my next thoughts.

Can you imagine if these principles made it to the 'poor' community? Can you imagine if these messages made it to the 'bad' community? Can you imagine if these principals made it to a group of people who 'really' need it? As this overextended community clears, then the rest of us 'normal' people only benefit!

Here is my idea. My idea is to be able to collect a group of people with 'special' skills. In the tithing class, it speaks of tithing of your talent, time, and money. Part of tithing of talent and time could be to spread these messages and help people learn to live better and bigger! Here is the start of the plan, the idea! In the prison, the prisoners are allowed to have a priest visit them.

My idea is that a member of the group will be an ordained minister, and another person in the group is a past-life regression therapist. If the prisoners are open to the idea to find out what has happened with them in past lives, there is a very good chance they could heal the wounds in this life. Can you imagine a 'bad' person finding out that all of this stuff they were doing, they also did in a past life. Can you imagine these guys and gals learning that this time around they can learn the trouble they are in, is past life triggers? It could be something they are picking up as a distant memory; that they currently couldn't figure out how to stop. Once they know they can release it, they can choose to release it! Can you imagine the tears as they learn that this stuff can go away? Can you imagine their different perspective on life? Can you imagine their recreation of the next, many years of their life! Can you imagine how you and I benefit from having these 'bad' people now expecting good! We all are so connected, as their hatred leaves them, our hatred leaves us! Our expectations as a society rise. Can you imagine a community that does not 'need' a jail? Can you imagine one prisoner after another 'releasing,' all of the feelings that no longer serve him or her?

The next check point on the to-do-list is to have a volunteer group praying for all of the prisoners. This idea correlates with a guy who already tested this. It was a study done, I am not sure of the name, where a guy took all the files of prisoners from one prison, and blessed each file each day. (He would put his hands over the closed file and send blessings.) He also blessed any characteristics the files portrayed that were also in him. He would say each day (paraphrased,) "I now love all of these things that are represented from the prisoners in me. I now forgive these qualities in me." As he would bless his feelings of hatred, there was no longer a need for murder to be in his awareness; hence the murderer would heal. Like magic, the prison was shut down; there was no need for it anymore. This is what I am talking about; life is an illusion! Let us all have the 'illusion' of the life of our dreams! Let us all choose to live in light and love and really enjoy this life time. We all deserve it; now let's do it.

My next idea is to also go to the really 'bad' neighborhoods and bring these prosperity principals to them. Teach them, via example that miracles can happen. Teach them miracles are possible. They are for me, for you, and for them. I really love the theme of my book. In a way, it is someone (me,) who is stuck, and has no other choice but God. Someone who led by example, who in the public eye, took a chance and learned to trust, as each day was presented. Because of that trust, was able to show the world what God really can do when you let go.

Continuing, we also address the people who are living on Government assistance.

Can you imagine them coming on board, and literally taking what they have and trusting by giving ten percent? Giving ten percent of their money, ten percent of their time and talent, ten percent of their trust and watching God redirect their present and their future! Can you imagine how their lives change? Can you imagine how our lives change by watching them? Can you see their new hope? Can you imagine a kid in a gang selling drugs, always fearful of his life; and out of nowhere, by applying these principals, turning into a spiritual person that now is a part of saving billions of lives! Can you imagine that individual becoming a role model to you and to me?

Can you imagine one person, in a community of many like him, all of them changing? Can you imagine a world without poverty, or violence? Can you imagine the beauty we would be seeing on a daily basis? Oh my goodness, this is a great idea; please show me my part and show me the directions and insight to make this happen! This is huge, this is large, larger than me, please continue to guide me!

There is our idea. Now back to Wednesday afternoon. I came home after our field trip, and had the house to myself. It was a mess, and I was having a 'mood.' When we have a 'mood,' it is because something has 'come up;' it has come up into our awareness so we can release an old, outdated belief. It is good when we have a 'mood,' though when we are having them, it doesn't feel good; instead we tend to judge them and ourselves for having them. Take my word for it, the next time this happens to you, learn from it, welcome it as the gift that it is. Ask it questions, such as, "Why are you here now? What are you wanting me to see?" 'It' will answer you; if you allow it. 'It' will teach you what you have wanted to know.

Knowing what these 'bad' moods in me represent, I allowed them. I found myself listening to an audio and allowed the answers to begin to flow. I saw my messy house and was okay with it. I knew as I cleared so would my exterior mess.

The audio was about the importance of breath. As we breathe deeper, we can hear God more. The suggestion was to lay on a hardwood floor (with a pillow) and for fifteen minutes a day continuously breathe in and out. All we had to do was do it continuously. We did not have to count or have the inhale or exhale be a certain timed breath. All we had to do was breathe in and out for fifteen minutes. What she said was when we usually breathe; we are only taking in a small percentage per day of what we could be. So by training fifteen minutes a day, many aspects of our life would improve, as we would be able to hear guidance a lot more clearly! I did my fifteen minutes and then started to want a cigarette.

Though, with this new beautiful breath in me, I did not want to ruin it with carbon dioxide. So in that moment I quit smoking. I decided I could not ruin my breath any more. I decided to quit; weird how things just happen.

That was Wednesday at noon. My withdrawal was intense and I basically slept from three P.M. until the next day.

....

I awoke on Thursday morning, very crabby and depressed, though excited that I did not 'forget' about my non-smoking when I awoke. I was very much aware of my decision, though still depressed. My husband got the kids off to school and I took my dog on a walk. The pain was intense. I soon encouraged myself to listen to the audio from the prosperity class and attempt to fill out my workbook. As you can imagine, the day was filled with pain and depression as I attempted to still function. I knew where I was, though kept reminding myself that this would be over soon. I would learn to be prosperous with my decision very soon.

Lunch time came and I found my husband's electronic cigarette; I took a drag! Oh did the pain quickly alter. I became okay with this decision and decided that the electronic cigarette was the way. I was okay having that guy around for a long while. I started to function a little better. I took another walk with my dog. I finished up my prosperity work book and was coming out of my depression.

I soon walked to go pick up my kiddos and we made it home. I looked on the counter and my open pack of cigarettes started chanting my name. I gave in and sat and had that one cigarette. Oh, I do believe that was the best cigarette I have ever had in my entire life! I was on an instant 'high' and was at peace with the world. After, I felt guilty, and resorted back to my room to Google, "How to quit."

Soon my husband came home and I had another one. Here I was feeding myself lots of guilt and not receiving guidance on how I could ever truly give up this habit. Though this is where I was at the moment. I understood this and continued to know, "This too shall pass." I was no longer as crabby as I had been. My husband warmed up lunch and cuddled with me.

Later it was 5:30 P.M., we watched a movie. The kids were home and I prepared for my prosperity class; wrote my tithing check and slowly slugged to the car. I really did not want to go, though I knew I should. Kind of like when the last thing you want to do is exercise, but you know exercising is the only thing that is going to get you moving again. I am positive the husband and kiddos were going to have a good evening. I was sure mine was going to get better.

I get to class, still feeling guilty of my 'failure' of smoking a cigarette. I am in the hallway searching the board for my name tag when I hear, "How are you? Feeling prosperous?" This came from a couple that in the last few weeks, appeared shy and unsure of being participants in the class. It was exciting to hear their excitement and chipper moods! I was still feeling down and said, "Actually I am feeling guilty because of my failure at quitting smoking." I apologized for my negative attitude.

We soon are sitting, preparing for class, and of course everyone around me is chipper. I know my mood is down and kept chanting to raise it. I was honest with all these guys and spoke of my smoking 'failure' and tried my hardest to raise my vibration. I soon remembered all the cool things that happened over the week and laughed with them saying, "You know when you really want to focus on the 'bad,' it kind of is hard when all the good is pouring out!" I then let the good pour out and watched it overflow into my evening.

Our leader began the class with a reading from the "Daily word." She declared (through the reading) that Prosperity was a state of mind. I agree with this statement; you first begin to feel 'taken care of' and then prosperity is a 'no brainer.' It is given to us, we already have it. Within moments of this class you feel the truth!

Our first testimony came from a lady who told us the prior week she 'lost' 200 dollars, she laughs saying she still had not found it. I tell you this is that 'feeling;' who laughs with a loss of 200 dollars? We all do, because we know there is something to it! She then tells us that her checkbook is always exact. What comes in is always accounted for. Though this week there is an extra 250 dollars that appeared with no documentation of its source! It magically appeared, and she is taking it as 'hers.' She added the new balance to her check book. Good for her! Another lady told us about a different group she attends weekly. In this group they go out to eat once a month. Well this specific month, one member of the group decided to pay for everyone's lunch; so our member received free lunch! Who says, "There is never a free lunch?" (Economics class 'saying'.)

Our next story is pretty awesome! Remember our quiet couple I talked about when I was finding my name tag. The next testimony explains why they were so cheery! Apparently his 'job' is to help sell businesses; he is a consultant in that field. He recently received a business and the sale is expected to close at the end of the month! Who hoo! And of course, he receives a commission on the sale! Good for him! His wife works in another company; she just happened to know someone who works with construction and project management.

She thought her husband would do well with project manager, and set up a meeting for the two guys to meet. The two gentlemen had lunch, and our guy has himself another source of income. Oh yea, prosperity all around!

Our next story is from the lady from last week. Remember she, 'out of the blue' received a call about her being eligible for a marketing manager? She went to that interview and told them, "No!" This job was not a good fit for her. Awesome, here is a woman who is offered a really good job and recognizes that there is something better; and is willing to find it! They wanted her to work on Saturdays, and she was good with her current weekend plans! Good for her. She knew something bigger and better was on the way.

Our same lady was also looking for different child care for her 3 year old. The perfect opportunity fell in her lap this week, as her daughter (starting today, Friday) starts three year old school/babysitting! This is the perfect fit for the two ladies, and our group member could not be happier with the unfolding of these events! Also the preschool program opens up at 5:45 in the morning. This was an extra blessing to this family.

Another story comes from two ladies in our group who are also sisters. One of the sisters celebrated her birthday this week and was offered free lunch by sister number two! Next the group leaders asked us what our thoughts were on prosperity, and if they had changed throughout the course. I piped in with saying that the ideas coming to me are so much more real. They feel like they are destined and orchestrated by God. They feel like they are God's plans, and I am blessed with letting them come to me. It feels like He is backing me and my goals up! They feel amazing and so 'Real!' They feel like they are finally coming together. I now feel like what I do is for a purpose! This is an amazing feeling!

This next comment is really awesome. One of the ladies said she was having trouble receiving prosperity when the source was her mom. Our leader piped in with a solution. She told us that when she was younger, she was a real estate agent. One particular year she was low on money. She received money from her mom. She did not like this either. Soon the realization came to her that God was the source of her money, and if He wanted the money to come through her mom, she needed to realize that the money was still from God. This helped a lot. And then our sweet gentleman piped in, with his view on the subject! He said, years earlier when he was working, he had an overabundance of money. He used to also give to his kids. His kids also did not like to receive from him. Though coming from him as a dad, he was letting us know it is the neatest feeling to give to your kids.

He asked us to think of it this way the next time we received money from our parents. Sometimes if we do stuff for someone else, it is easier. Next time you feel guilty about receiving, try to see it from the givers eyes!

Continuing on, we did our half hour of our CD, and then took break. Next came our next half hour, and then our prayer groups. We continued to pray for our members as they prayed for us. I told our group, the last prayer meeting left me in tears. I was not used to having someone else pray on my dreams. When it happened, I was full of gratitude. They are a blessing in my life and I am positive I am a blessing in theirs. Here is my prayer for these two! Our first member, I pray that only good comes into your awareness, and you are encouraged and able to receive all the good that you are! Our second member, I pray that God within you, helps you received your signed contract for teaching this semester and the contract outlines your teaching job for the next. Blessings and prosperity to you both. The prayer prayed for me was, "God within, shows me how to receive my advance for my book." We also prayed for Hay House as my publisher.

As I was leaving class, I was guided to talk to our prosperity teacher about my idea about bringing tithing to the communities I talked about earlier. She was excited, and told me to set up a meeting with the minister, and to continue to let it unfold! The ride home was amazing as I visualized all the amazing things that were to come. Even now I get tears in my eyes as I know our world is changing! I am very thankful!

Later I was home, I saw my kids peacefully sleeping. I quietly walk in their rooms and sent a prayer. My prayer was all of their past life gunk would release as they sombered. I affirmed they enjoy their current life, and remember how awesome they are. I also enjoyed my beautiful kitchen. My husband is awesome for cleaning! He and I then finished our movie in the quiet house. We later discussed our days and soon were asleep. I slept through the entire night! □

Chapter 5
So many happenings!

Friday morning I woke up late. I wanted to continue to sleep and sleep. Brian was nice, and made breakfast for the kiddos, and their lunch. I was up, seeing all of these duties complete, and decided to take a shower! No work out for me today, but I was okay with it! For some reason, I knew my 138.5 'weigh in' would be here on Thursday, with or without a work-out. Also, I did not want a cigarette like I usually do. I may not have wanted one, though I had one anyway. Maybe my intention of quitting smoking is working; as I start to not want a cigarette, I am sure sooner than later I will not want one forever!

Brian then offered to take the kiddos to school! Oh, how much better does today get! The kids and husband were off; and I cleaned up after breakfast. I now had a clean house, and some extra time. I made my calls that I ignored from the day prior. I made an appointment to go to the soup kitchen for next week. I also called the finance guy back, and received a to-do-list to continue as the program had already started! After all the chores I did some writing.

The afternoon was spent writing, a little research on our prison project, and then more bill collecting for the finance guy. I did some laundry, and I caught up with another Video Vlog. Brian was home for lunch. He only had to work half the day. His hands were full of groceries, as he told me about his plans for spaghetti and wine for dinner! What a great evening this was going to be!

He was quiet as he cut the vegetables for dinner. He likes to cook; it is his quiet time, his meditation. He was digesting his day, his week; he was happy, and I was pre-occupied with reading. Later, he was downstairs on the computer watching the news. I am not sure what he was going through, though I do not think I was supposed to know. I was only supposed to witness he had clearing to do, and he was fine.

Before we knew it, it was 45 minutes before the kiddos were finished with school. We took that time to go through the folder of bills; our first step was to pay all the Colorado bills. We've decided to take care of us first, have us be safe, and then go from there. I realized if we section off our bills via category, the bills are easier to go through, instead of only looking at a large pile all at once. One category was the bills for our Colorado living expenses; i.e. electricity, water, food. The second category was mortgages for our rentals. Another category was bills not paid by the renters; another category was bills accrued via the rental company and so on. We paid the electric and water, and the bills were finally in the mail.

I grabbed our donation bag (that I had been collecting throughout the week) as we headed to the truck to get the kids. We waited for a minute as the bell was ready to ring, and both kiddos were excited to see Dad; it is always a treat when dad gets to pick them up from school! After, we drove to the donation store; the donation guy was very sweet and grateful. The kids were talking the whole way about their excitement for the next day. They were going to be in their first school parade. We soon get home, and the kids gear up to go play.

Aidan headed to his friend's house, and Dreana played on her Kindle. I was in a great mood from all the editing and paying the bills. I decided to text Aidan's friend's mom, and ask if Aidan's friend could spend the night! I got a big ole resounding, "Yes!" I picked up the house and enjoyed my clean, flowing energy! The evening was very good! Later I remembered a credit card I forgot to add to the financial guy's portfolio. I made those calls, and had Brian upload the documents to the computer. It was now time for my awaiting wine! I poured myself a glass, and put the spaghetti on the stove. I was in a great mood. We then had dinner and lots of conversation. We soon found out that Aidan's friend's mom sews, and offered to sew Dreana's ripped back pack. After dinner, Brian took Aidan and the backpack over there and on the way home brought the friend! It was a win-win for all parties. The kids got to hang out with each other, I received a fixed back pack, and Aidan's friend's mom had the evening to herself!

The evening was filled with bliss! The house was nice and clean. Brian was occupied with movies, and all three kids got along, being quiet and respectful! I spent many of the hours talking with my girlfriend, and of course the wine tasted very good! Around eight o'clock, we received an unexpected knock at the door; it was the UPS guy dropping off our package with Aidan's Cub Scout uniform! The day just keep giving and giving; again we were all feeling very blessed.

We all were asleep and Friday came to a close!

Saturday morning brought a huge head-ache! I had enjoyed my wine a little too much, and had to figure out how to function for the remaining day. The three kiddos were up early. I made eggs and received a compliment from our friend. He told me, "For being vegetarians, you make the best food!"

I encouraged them all to get ready and we soon were out the door. We entered into a huge parking lot full of kids, floats, and lots of fun. We walked two miles to the high school; this was our parade. We had lots of fun.

Dreana, at times, walked with us, then her teacher, and then her girlfriends! Aidan walked ahead of us with his friend and his class. Both kids collected lots of candy!

We arrive at the high school, and we get in for free for the football game. We also received a free lunch, provided by our generous grade school! They served soda and chips and hotdogs. Not a very vegetarian meal; three of us ate the buns. My boy, being my boy, ate the hot dog! We had a lot of fun. Later we were home and the kids went to play. I took a nap.

I woke up and headed to the library. I found three good books, and came home to treats cooked by Brian. The treats were for this evening and Aidan's class so they could celebrate his birthday. The first book I read was a numerology book. It was very interesting. One of the techniques I immediately put into practice. I put a '6' on my door. The reason for this was that my address broke down to a 2, and a two represented nourishing and love. Nourishing and love is good, though I wanted more money to come into the house. I added a '6' to my address, and awaited my new blessings.

As I read; the kids, Brian and Richard (on skype) hung out by the bonfire. Throughout the night we all munched on the treats that Brian made. Before I knew it I was asleep. My body was thanking me; I finally was recovering from the dehydrated grapes consumed the day prior!

....

Sunday morning, I woke up with a much happier head! I was up early and spent time with me. I soon made breakfast and cleaned the kitchen. After my shower I put on the skirt I had been waiting to wear! It fit! I looked incredibly 'hot' and prepared for my day!

We later were packed in the truck. On the way to church we reminded Aidan that he was amazing. We encouraged him to remember he was wanted and adored by his Sunday school. We get to Sunday school and of course there was a rude comment directed to my boy. I squashed the comment, and reminded them that my boy was excited to be taught by such loving leaders. The face of our leader dropped in embarrassment, and here began the beginning of Aidan's great day at Sunday school!

Our sermon at church was amazing. The talk was about service. She said that, "We are God," and when we are asking how to understand and embody this as truth; the best technique is to serve more. When we are serving, we are giving; we are full of gratitude. We are in bliss, and we are in the flow. When we are giving, it is because we know we have enough; we have so much that it is easy to give.

And when we are feeling lack; we should give. By giving, we will feel our abundance. The way she spoke of this, it brought me right into the flow. It is true. Do you remember the last time you gave? What did you feel like? Wasn't it the coolest feeling ever? You feel like you are contributing. You feel your moment of happiness. You feel fun, energetic, and alive! The smiles and thank-you's you get remind you of how awesome life is! How fun it is supposed to be. You are reminded of joy.

The service came to an end as we went to go get our kiddos; they were having as great of a day as us! On the way to the car I stopped a woman who usually prayed with people. I asked about the prayer box they always talk about in church. I asked how it works. She told me that in each service the prayers are prayed for, and then the minister spends all week praying with the prayers. Later the prayers go to more churches, and our prayed on for an entire month. What this means is that a lot of people are joining you in your prayer!

I asked our friend if anyone ever read what was in the box, or if the box was only held, keeping the secrets only with God. She looked at me goofy and said, "Of course the minister looks through the box so she knows what and who she is praying for." I became reluctant, and our friend started to understand. She told me that as we grow within ourselves, we stop being ashamed at what it is we are asking for help with. She encouraged me to gain the courage to share my fears with those who would pray with me. I was blessed by our conversation; she encouraged me to begin to open up, and start to heal my deep, dark, secrets and fears. My faith became stronger.

We headed home, and Brian watched the remaining of the Winning Packer Game! The kids went to play. I found an ad on Craigslist. The ad was asking for people to volunteer, and become foster parents for dogs. There was a need for families to take in dogs for a time while permanent homes were being found. I emailed, and must have been in the flow, because I received an instant reply! I then found myself cleaning the house because in the next 45 minutes the dog agency lady was coming over! After the house was clean I let Brian know what was going on; I did not tell him earlier. I was nervous he would not agree. He was irritated, but quickly became intrigued and excited with the possibilities of our guest.

Our lady came over with an application and some stories and pictures of dogs that needed a temporary home. Our job was to love them, and take them to dog fairs twice a month to help them get adopted! The idea of this is so fun.

As the day came to a close Aidan fell asleep on the couch; his weekend was long, he was done!

Dreana ate peanut butter and jelly for dinner and was preparing for bed herself. I read one of the books from the library. Aidan was then up for a minute, and also filled up on peanut butter and jelly. He later talked with my father about what gift he wanted for his birthday. Soon, both kiddos were asleep, and I was on the phone with my girlfriend. It was funny because her vibration was low, and she did not even know it. She kept waiting for something to work itself out. All I kept getting told was for her to let it go, and trust that the best would come. Our conversation continued as she would not let go; instead kept bringing up point after point that kept her stuck. As she kept talking my thoughts went to Dreana's back pack; I realized we had not gotten that back yet. I took my own advice, and let the thought go; I decided to find a different bag for her to bring to school in the morning. Moments Later, nine o'clock at night, the doorbell rang. Aidan's friend had Dreana's back pack in his hand as he was apologizing for the late delivery. My girlfriend heard the whole exchange as she was still on the phone. She finally was able to let go as she saw my abundance and example!

If you let go; it does find its way to you. She left our conversation in a much happier vibration then when she started.
We were a sleep. It was a very good day.
....
Before I knew it, Monday morning was here. I was awake at 7:02 A.M. We had all slept in! There was a mad rush to our morning, though everyone made it to their destinations on time.

I noticed the house was messy and cluttered. I made an intention that this week was going to be filled with lots of deep cleaning and another collection of the donation bag. I cleaned up the kitchen and started the laundry. I soon found myself with zero motivation to do anymore! I instead choose to clean me out; I did some writing. My morning hours were spent with you. I also signed up for another foster class. This class taught techniques of how to love more. I later googled Sylvia Browne's website, and added our names to her prayer chain. This is really cool. These names are prayed on by a lot of people. When I add names to her list, I always feel a lift. A good suggestion is to add your name and loved ones to her list! (Browne)

The morning was calm and fulfilled, and the afternoon came with abundance! We received our first foster dog. Her name is Sammy, and she has really brightened up the week. She is happy; and she is potty trained! How much better does this get.

Later it was our Girl Scout meeting. Dreana's new Girl Scout vest came in the mail, and today she looked crisp and prepared for her fun!

The rest of the family was invited to her meeting, and we all had to dress in red, white and blue. We were going to the MWR! Our patriotic evening was fun. I love to see life through the excitement in her eyes.

One of the mom's at Girl Scouts was a woman I respect and adore. I love this woman, she is exactly like me. She is a very trendy dresser, and she is also a very driven woman. She is an amazing listener. Everyone assumes she is an open, beautiful person. Everyone assumes this of me also. Here is the secret though. She is a great listener, and a lot of people want to open up with her. Though, when you get too close to her, and ask her questions about herself; our lady gets scared. She is there for everyone else, though has difficulty letting herself open up to them. I know this because I am the same way. People figure I am the coolest person around, though these people usually just stay as acquaintances (with me) instead of friends. The reason is because it is hard for me to open up to them, and let them in. Even though letting more great people into my life is a huge desire of mine; I do not allow it to happen very often.

As I notice our lady, I see more and more of me. Here is the goofy part, I really like this woman; I want to be her friend! She is awesome. For me to get to be friends with her, I have to give a little and open up to her first. As I grow and uncover my fears, she has to (via universal law) do the same. As I clear, she also has to clear. Because I desire her as a friend, I have to make the first steps. I have to get vulnerable, to allow her to get vulnerable. I choose her as a friend; therefore I choose the uncomfortable growth ahead for me

Monday evening brought us home-made pizzas, and kiddos tucked into bed. Soon we all were dreaming.

....

Tuesday morning was Aidan's birthday! Lots of Happy Birthdays to my nine year old! We had breakfast, and began his morning with a very high vibration! We took lots of pictures, and of course sent them to Facebook receiving billions of 'likes' for our awesome dude! It is cute as my boy was telling me of his visualizations from the night before. They consisted of him (this morning) going down to the office for his, "Happy birthday" announcement to receive his special birthday pencil! He had planned today, all of his blessings, from the night before! I tell you our kids can tell us more about the power of visualization, way more than we might know! Listen to the little ones; they have lots of wisdom.

The morning was a success, and off to school we went. Dreana headed to her class as I snuck around the corner to the third grade with a bucket full of home-made granola bars! I see Aidan, and he is excited for his treats.

As he empties out my arms, I unexpectedly grab him and give him a big old kiss in front of everyone! Then with a very loud voice I sing, "Happy Birthday" as he runs away in embarrassment! I tell you these are the things us moms get to do! Happy Birthday Aidan!

The afternoon was filled with lots of cool stuff. I did not get a lot of writing finished, though lots of amazing things happened. I spent the majority of the day in bliss as my daydreams had a mind of their own! It was hard to focus, though as they say in the Bible (paraphrased,) 'it is better to do the things that make you feel good, instead of the things you feel you should be doing.' Remember when Mary or Martha, (whichever one) was mad because the other was not doing the preparing for the meal; and Jesus said that the one doing the 'wrong,' was actually doing the best thing she could be doing. She was happy, and this is more important than any task that needs to be done! (International Bible Society, 1984)

I had been listening to my CD from the prosperity class, when I received a call from a publisher! This was cool. The publisher was a self-publishing company; they received my information from my Google search the prior day. He was calling to see if I would hire him to help me market my book! At the time, this was not what I was interested in. Though I kept his information for the future if I later became interested! This may not have been what I was looking for, though it did brighten my day! This is what I had been waiting for; a publisher on the phone!

I then turned my CD back on, and was again interrupted by a call from my girlfriend. We talked for a while and enjoyed my excitement. I then received a call from the Foster Dog agency. They had puppies, and wanted to know if I would take them in. Of course! I then, again received another call. It was my friend asking if I would babysit on Monday. My day was awesome! See what happens when you spend your day in visualization; good stuff comes to you!

After school I had the whole neighborhood over; lots of kids. While the kids played, I cleaned and listen to my CD. I spent more time researching agents and enjoying my good day.

The rest of the day was in bliss and soon was over.
....
Wednesday morning I woke up at four A.M. to my computer playing every one of my video blog's simultaneously. I did not have them on the computer to be played. I was trying to figure out what was happening when one of the girls, in an online Law of Attraction group (Under Facebook the group Attracting Abundance created by Shanae Tomlin,) had (at that moment) commented on my videos. She was telling me how she enjoyed my messages.

I assumed she and I were to connect that morning; and this was the reason for my weird wake-up. I sent her a message explaining my morning. Later I found out that another girl from the group had been thinking about me and considered texting me at 4 A.M.; but didn't! The connection trying to be made was from this girl and me.

Brian woke up sick. On a physical level we can figure his flu was due to his flu shot. On a spiritual level, I think, he is preparing for his E8 board. He has had to go through a lot of layers during the last few weeks, and this was the week his E8 board was due.

That morning I also received a call from my friend. She called to tell me I would not be watching her daughter all day on Monday, only half of the day. She had gotten fired! I was surprised and inquired why? She laughed and said, "It is good." She is a nurse, and works for different clients in their homes. The current client had not submitted their insurance paperwork on time, and their family could not have a nurse. She laughed and said it was perfect timing because her family was coming to Colorado for a weekend visit. Of all the weekends to be fired, this was the perfect one! Talk about God always finding ways to bring our desires. I laughed, and told her she seemed very happy lately; I was not surprised she was getting what she wanted!

I researched more on Literary Agents. I almost had the courage to edit the first fifty pages of this book; though I chickened out! I also received an unexpected call from an old friend. I met him years ago when I bought my first house; he was our lender. At that time I looked up to him. He was a success, he made a lot of money, had a really nice office; he had a cool job. He was what I was hoping to be more like. Over the years he helped us get many of our rentals. Over these years I grew into more of the qualities he possessed. I eventually became a realtor, and was able to work with him and our clients. When he called I noticed how much I had grown. I no longer saw myself as lower than him; instead I saw him as a colleague, as an equal.

He called to tell me that he received a reminder on his computer stating that I did not pay my mortgage. I told him that was not possible because the payment was automatic. He looked into it and told me the mortgage was paid, though the five year balloon payment was now due. We needed to refinance our loan. In my head I knew we did not currently have the money to refinance. I also knew the appraisal rate needed for a 20% investment loan was not currently what our house would appraise for. I also knew our credit score was not eligible for the refinance. Knowing all of this, I knew I currently did not have the answer.

Therefore this one was easy to breathe through. I had no clue of the answer; I figured there was no need to stress. God more than likely orchestrated it all, and He had the answer. As I was thinking all of this, my lender friend interrupted the conversation and said he has never dealt with a situation like mine, having an investment property that did not already have 20 percent equity. He told me he had to go ask more questions, and get back with me. Crazy how quickly your desires manifest when you let them go!

Still all day, I was daydreaming! I googled more information about publishers. I guess I was getting scared as I thought of actually being published. Then something amazing happened! I checked my Facebook and I noticed we had a new member to our online group! (On Facebook, Attracting Abundance created by Shanae Tomlin) The question posted was, "What is a cool thing that has happened to you today?" One of the responses came from our new member saying they just received notification that their book was the number one seller on Amazon!

I immediately introduced myself, and asked him questions about his book. I asked if he had an agent, or if he self-published. He is sweet and told me all the details. He self-published and told me the entire process from writing to being number was all orchestrated by God! His book was about how he won the lottery via the Law of Attraction. Now you know what they say in, "The Secret," "When the opportunity is here, don't second guess; just move." (Paraphrasing) This is what I did! I asked him if he would consider being my publisher. I told him of my affirmation to have an agent by Thursday, and he is who had showed up. I told him I wanted an agent for the marketing; but if he already accomplished this, I could use his expertise! I also suggested maybe I was supposed to introduce him to the publishing world. I do not know where all of this courage came from, though I asked! He responded, by telling me he would be happy to help me be a number one seller; though, he did not want to publish my book! This sored my vibration throughout the rest of the day!

That evening I talked with a girlfriend. I told her how thankful I was that she had started the online group. (Attracting Abundance) The people she has attracted are amazing. We have published authors, producers, and many, more awesome people practicing, "The Secret." Everyone practices daily. The posts coming from these people are awesome. The courage of these people, how they put their dreams in front of us all is awesome! These guys and gals are amazing pioneers; they are helping make beautiful contributions to our world, to public consciousness. I am thankful for what we have been able to manifest as a group! I am blessed each day as I see where my life has come.

I later received a call from the lady with the dog agency; she was coming over to pick up Sammy. I was sad, though also excited; Sammy had a new mom to go home to. Sammy also received a job; she became our newest service dog. Blessings to her.

....

Thursday was very exciting. I slept well from the good fortune of the day prior. I helped the kids get ready for school, and sent them off for school pictures! I was home, and posted a new Video blog. My Video blog was full of thank-yous. I was feeling grateful, and wanted to let the ones I love know how special they are. I named them, one-by-one, letting them know of their significance in my life. They are. You all are special to me. I also received (via Facebook) Richard's new song, "Forgotten Freedom." This song is awesome. It is very inspirational. It reminds us of when we were kids, all we do is play; and as an adult we stop. In his song he reminds us we forgot how easy life is. He reminds us to remember. Between my Vlog, and Richard's song, the vibration of my day was consistently high! The whole day was exciting!

The afternoon quickly led us to three P.M. I drove to get the kids and had to run through windy rain. The kids and I then drove with the music blaring, we were going to go pick up the puppies! We were excited with anticipation of puppy breath and kisses! When we were there, there was an entire crate of five puppies. We were able to take them all home! Oh were we excited! I kept hoping that the rain would continue, and my prosperity class would be cancelled. It wasn't. I had to leave my family, and the puppies to go to class.

On the way to class I found myself in a large traffic jam. As I sat and waited I wondered what this was all about. I realized I still wanted to know how to forgive past friends. I was clogged, and did not know how to let go. I asked for guidance. I began affirming, "I am letting this go, I am now forgiving." Within a few minutes, the traffic started to move, and the sign on the highway said, "You are cleared." I thought that was hilarious; I finished my drive to class.

I get there a bit late. As I sit down everyone is telling testimonies. Our one girl from last week, who turned down the job, has now decided she wants to interview for bigger and better jobs! Her prosperity opened her eyes to more. Another lady received an interview for the teaching job she wanted. Another lady got to go to a workshop! Another received a free tank of gas from her son-in-law! And another received a new lap top, and her kids offered to teach her how to use it! How much better does that get! And yet another received 75 extra dollars for the photo shoot she worked. She also received free lunch!

I told the class about the success with my book.

I was trembling when I gave my story. It was neat to hear myself tell it. I also told them about all the puppies. Life is awesome! This reminds me of the post I saw this week. It said, "Speak your truth, even if your voice cracks."

During our class, it was hard for me to concentrate. I was vibrating very high; I was full of gratitude! I kept giving myself permission to relax and enjoy the current moment. By break time I was doing much better. During break I received another surprise. The leader informed me she told my idea about the prisons to our minister. The minister loved it, and said she had been praying for me. She had been praying for someone like me who would do prison ministry. This was cool. Last Sunday I put my idea on the back burner, and now my idea was being confirmed and honored. God is great.

We also had prosperity at our church this week. They had a book sale, and 1100 dollars was sold; this money went to the church. Yea prosperity all around!

The class was good, and it was then time for our prayer circles. We gained two extra members, and everyone was in an awesome mood. Our affirmations for the group were: gratitude for Divine source helping create a new client for our first member. Next, we prayed for Divine source helping create a teaching contract for the following semester for member number two. Our third member asked for Source to continue to create energy and resources in completing his remodeling project. We asked for Divine source to continue to create a perfect, healthy body for our next member. And for me, all prayed that Divine source continue to create even bigger and better miracles in my life. Blessings to us all!

Class was over, and I drove away happy once again! When I was home, I smelled spaghetti; and my house was clean. I played with the puppies and spent my time with my family. Aidan was at his friends for the night, and Dreana and I had special Dreana time! The night was very happy and prosperous. Thank you for my prosperity!

....

☐

Chapter 6
Time for Me (and Some for Others)

The next day was Friday; Grandma was arriving at 3 P.M.! Dreana hung out with 'her puppy' and her kindle all morning. I cleaned and did laundry. I was very anxious for my mom's arrival. A week prior to this, I had affirmed Grandma would be here early; some way, somehow, at noon. I did not know how this was going to happen; though I still held the intention! I soon received a call from her, it was now nine in the morning and she was in Denver with an unexpected lay-over until two P.M. I laughed, and figured I could pick her up, (her lay-over was an hour away) and this is how I could get her here by noon. Though the drive to and from Denver is not my favorite road trip. I then affirmed that God knew all things, and He would figure out the best, efficient, and easy way for Grandma to get here by noon! This was a hard one to believe. Though, each time the thought came that this was impossible, I shooed it away and said, "I trust."

I kid you not of what happened next! She called, and said she went to the terminal desk and asked for an earlier flight. They had one and switched everything over for her! Though they forgot to switch her luggage. They made her wait in limbo until it was figured out. It was eventually figured out, but because of the mix up, (on their part) they gave her free luggage (because now they make you pay a luggage fee if you have luggage that goes on the plane.) Within one hour from that phone call she was in Colorado Springs with extra, unexpected money in her pocket! Oh how exciting that was!

Brian picked her up from the airport. I did not tell the kids, hard as it was, I wanted to surprise them. To top all of this off, I affirmed all morning that Aidan would come home (he was at his friend's from the sleep over) at the exact moment that Grandma was in the driveway! This also happened. How much better does this get!

Friday night was spent with lots of gifts and conversation. Later, Grandma and I drove around town to see if she remembered anything from when we were here, when I was a kid. She also googled an old friend and found her address; her friend's house was only 10 minutes away from mine. We drove by the house, and saw the grass long and seemingly uncared for; we figured the house was vacant. But at least we tried!

The evening was filled with lots of talk, and happy moments, as we all celebrated having Grandma here! It was a good night!

Saturday morning we woke up with excitement for Aidan's birthday party! We also had his friend over; he had slept over as an early celebration for Aidan's birthday. We had eggs, and then sent Aidan's friend, Aidan and Brian out to pick up the birthday cake. Grandma, Dreana and I cleaned up the house, and prepared for our morning guest. A mom with a baby was coming over to meet us; she was interviewing us to see if we were a good fit for babysitting. We anxiously waited, and soon received a call of a 'no show.' The mom did not realize how far our house was from hers; she decided not to come. That was a bummer. I was also very anxious and nervous; I was feeling Aidan's party would likewise be a 'no show.' I worked all morning in releasing my fears, and affirmed for an amazing day.

Soon Grandma, Aidan and me went to the store, and Aidan found his Army uniform Grandma was gifting him. We had a good time at the store, though I still was trying to shake my nervous feeling. Brian and Dreana stayed at the house and set up the Army course. Aidan's theme for his birthday was Army Basic Training. When we arrived at home and saw the course, my spirits began to rise. I kept affirming that my vibration would continue to rise higher, and I was continuingly trusting for a great party!

One P.M. came and went. There were no kids. I was sad and upset, but knew I had to clear me and my vibration. I turned on the movie, "The Secret" and went to lie down for a minute, trying to center. I then took my dog on a walk; I tried to push through the doubt. As I headed back (after our walk) I saw Aidan's friend on his way to our house! Then, I saw the neighbor kids on their way to our house! Aidan was excited! I was excited. As the kids were finally here, Grandma and I went to the store for some chips and soda.

When we were home, the house was full of camouflaged uniforms, painted faces, and lots of rambunctious kids. The evening was filled with target practice, cake, an Army Basic training course, and a big ole campfire. The kids played, and Grandma and me sat by the fire. She then received a phone call. She had recently put her house on the market, and was getting her first showing. As I clear, so does she. The evening was a success. Aidan's friend spent the night again, and he and Aidan were soon asleep. Dreana, the puppy and Grandma all fell asleep in Dreana's bed. Brian and I had another piece of cake as we re-played the amazing night!

....

Sunday morning came as I realized I woke up late. We ran out of time for the nine o'clock church service. We instead had a no-church Sunday. We soon prepared for the puppy fair.

Aidan's friend shed some tears as he had a feeling Fluffy (the Foster German Shepard pup) was going to be adopted. He and the little guy became quite attached. The boys then went to the friend's house and were tasked with five hours' of dishes. (Well it should have only taken them twenty minutes, but you know how kids are!)

Brian did not want to wake up this morning, so we graciously let him sleep in. Grandma, Dreana and I took the puppies to the puppy fair. This event was a success! I enjoyed talking to people in the store, and introducing them to my puppy friends! It was very energetic and fun. I felt like I was in my zone. At the event, we were visited by Dreana's girlfriend from school. They were there shopping, but found themselves being loved by puppies! Dad had come thirty minutes prior, he was there to pick up Grandma and Dreana. Dreana missed seeing her girlfriend, though I have proof of our interaction because I have a picture! Dreana was reluctant to leave because she did not want 'her puppy' getting adopted; she wanted to keep him. I made a deal with her that I would guarantee the puppies return if she went with dad. They left, and I put him (Dreana's puppy) in my shirt, and made sure I made zero eye contact with any puppy prospects from then on.

The result of our puppy fair was six out of ten dogs were adopted. In that mix, two of my puppies found new homes, and Fluffy was going to be adopted on Thursday. I came home with Fluffy, the puppy, Slim, and Daisy. Daisy was a new one; her foster mom was getting a dog the next day. She could not have the new dog and Daisy in the same house. Aidan was still at his friends; Dreana was playing, and very excited that we still had her puppy. Brian and Grandma had watched the winning Packer game, and Grandma was napping on the couch.

Grandma later woke up and she and Brian began researching for her friend (the same friend we drove by the house the day before.) They did some incognito spying through Facebook, and narrowed their search down to an address. Address in hand, at seven O'clock at night, my mom and I drove the few miles to my mom's friend's daughter's house. We knocked on the door. After a few strange looks and an introduction; the daughter remembered us, and drove us a mile down the road to her mom's house. We stayed there for a few hours and the ladies talked and talked and talked about the last ten years.

Soon we were home explaining the reminiscing to Brian and the kids. Funny story, the original house we found on Friday, was the same house we were at this evening. We were confused by the vacant looking property, and all the tall grass. My mom's girlfriend lived behind that house.

She had one of those houses that are like a country setting in a neighborhood. This is why we could not drive through on Friday to find it. It was covered in trees, and way back in the neighborhood. Lesson learned, the answer is always there, it always exists. We just have to open our eyes. It was a very good day.

....

Monday morning was here starting at 5 A.M. I was up early. My little friend was to arrive at 6:30. Her mom called the day before, and told us she was no longer fired; her client turned in the appropriate paperwork, and received their insurance benefits. She needed a babysitter so she could go to work. I was very excited! We had balloons still lying around from Aidan's party; she loved this! She also played with the puppy, and was having a blast! Around 7:30 she walked into Aidan's room and woke him up. And because she is so cute, there was no crankiness from my boy! Soon Dreana and Grandma were up and became play mates with our little friend.

We had lots of fun, and some waffles too! I cleaned the house, and before we knew it my mom's phone was ringing. My mom's girlfriend wanted to take her granddaughter, my mom, and my two to Santa Clause land! (Santa Clause Land is a theme park here in Colorado.) They all packed up for some double-Grandma time.

Soon the house was only filled with dogs, Brian, my toddler and me. Soon our friend and the dogs were in dream land, leaving only Brian and I to a quiet house. It was nice; we had been nonstop all weekend. During our time we received a call from an insurance lady. She was recommended as a friend from one of the members of the prosperity class. We had been looking for insurance for a while; our coverage in Wisconsin did not cover Colorado. Each insurance company we called was going to charge us an extra one-hundred dollars. We had been waiting and affirming to get the same, or less of a price, then what we had. We have been patient, and are positive it will work itself out. So when I received the recommendation, I figured this may be who we were looking for. She gave us a quote, and she also came in a hundred dollars more than what we wanted to pay. We are still waiting, and knowing that we will find who we are looking for. I am affirming that by next Thursday, this will be settled (24 October 2013!)

We also spent time on the computer looking at Brian's DA photo. This is the photo that he sends in with his packet for his next rank. This was such a neat conversation. Brian loves his job so much, and can talk hours and hours about it! He was telling me that his 'rack' on his uniform looked large on the picture.

Apparently each award you receive, you also receive a pin, and these pins get decorated on the uniform and become the 'rack.' The pins get stacked together, showing the different accomplishments. This is good because someone can look at the uniform and know the story of the soldier. Brian has excelled in his job very quickly, and his 'rack' has thirteen pins on it. The average for his rank usually has eight. We talked about the board and his career. We had a really good time. It is meditative as I listen to him. Have you ever noticed how you can listen for hours of someone else's passion? The excitement and pride comes blasting through the story. He is happy in his career, and I love listening to him.

Later, grandma and the kids were home, and our little friend left with her mom. We cooked spaghetti, and grandma made cupcakes with cookies in them! Dreana wore her toy apron, and enjoyed her baking session with the pro. They were both so excited!

Soon the night was ending and the kiddos were in bed, each with their own puppy. Dreana was asleep with the little one; and Aidan with the German shepherd. Grandma was reluctant to go to bed; she was getting sad knowing this was her last night. Soon all were asleep.

Tuesday morning was here. Grandma had thought her flight was to leave at six in the morning. All weekend I kept affirming that she was going to see the kids off to school. I had wished and wished that they went to school on Monday (so this could happen,) but Monday was a holiday. She checked her flight schedule the night prior and realized her flight did not leave until eleven in the afternoon! My affirmation came true!

At seven 0'clock we woke the kiddos up, and the five of us had a big breakfast. We prepared the kids lunch and encouraged them to hurry and get ready. Grandma, this whole time, was fighting the tears. I was not sad, I received a 'knowing' that she is going to be back next month. For some reason her job is going to need her to travel, and she will be in Colorado.

We get the kids to school and it is cold. Grandma went to walk Aidan to his class, and started to cry. She then came over to walk Dreana to class as Dreana excitedly introduced her to her teacher. School was in session and I was left with a sad grandma. She and I then drove to the gas station as she graciously bought me a full tank of gas. We soon were home and then cleaned my house top to bottom, as we waited for ten O'clock to arrive. I think I was afraid of the goodbye; my emotions were occupied, as cleaning the house was a good outlet.

Grandma departed with her plane, sad, but enjoyed every moment she was here. I later was home, and finished the laundry.

I also (that morning) received a voicemail from the lender wanting me to refinance one of my houses. I checked my message, and all he said was to call him back. With no preemptive information, I could not prepare myself for the conversation. As I am about to call him back, I see I received an email from him! On his email he was a little more explanative. It said to sign this document, which would give us a few more months to figure out the refinance. God had given me a few extra months to figure what to do. I then returned his call. We had a nice talk. We caught up on old times, and explained the events of the last year. I told him all about Tennessee, and my book, and the foster puppies. He told me about his four year old son having heart surgery (this year,) and how his son is doing much better. It is always good energy when we talk.

He then told me the paper we should sign (the reason for his call,) would tell the computer that the bank was over-writing our balloon loan for a few months. He informed me I would stop getting delinquent reminders when the form was submitted. I was not getting delinquent reminders. I found that funny. All of this is God's doing, for our benefit. The delinquent reminders were only in his world, not ours, because it really was not our problem. God is funny at times! I also think it is funny that the letter we signed is good till February. I had been reading a "Secret story" on "The Secret" website describing how one girl made her 'magic check' for her birthday. That was her goal date, and I thought that was a really good idea; what a birthday present! I made a magic check because of her story, and my magic check was dated for my birthday (February.) Here he is telling me that my note is good till my birthday! What shows up in our awareness is there for a reason.

I also made a new goal list. I noticed that I am really good with the small stuff. It is easy for me to believe the small stuff will come. Examples are subway and car washes. Though the bigger stuff is what I have been wanting for a while. I watched, "The Secret" movie many times this week, and kept hearing, "Go Big." My affirmations have been pretty large lately! I made a goal list and had big stuff on it!

I affirmed I would receive my book advance soon. I also made an affirmation that the dogs we have, Daisy and Slim would be adopted by the end of the day on Tuesday. About two hours later I received a call from the agency lady telling me she was coming to pick up Daisy; she was getting her new mom. I tell you, affirmations work!

When I picked up the kiddos that afternoon, Aidan told me that at 10:50 A.M. he looked at the clock. This was the time Grandma left to get on her plane. At that moment, the two of them (Grandma and him) were saying some goodbye's!

Aidan also went to the store to buy toys with his birthday money. Obviously, that was a blast! In the evening we took Fluffy over to Aidan's friend's house for them to say good bye to one another. Fluffy was getting adopted the next day.

The evening came and went. It was good.

....

Wednesday morning my dreams ended at 4 A.M. I was up early and let all the puppies out. I made coffee. I checked my phone, and had received a text message from a friend wanting me to watch the movie, "I Am" on Netflix. I watched the movie as it occupied my morning hours. It was really good. It was a documentary about how what it is we really want is connection, not all the outer things we keep saying we want. We want to know we are loved. We want to know we matter. I could not watch the last half hour of the movie because my computer over heated, and requested me to shut her down.

So here I was with no computer, and still having the morning hours to myself. I looked for something to do; I decided to make a Video blog. As I was going through my phone to delete some videos to make room for another video, I was interrupted by a phone call. Now remember this is very early in the morning, and we are on Mountain Time!

The caller calls me by my name, Michelle, and tells me she is calling to let me know she is cutting her tree down today. She did not want me to be surprised with all the noise. I did not know who this woman was; I racked my brain trying to place her voice with any distant memory. I then asked if she was a neighbor from Wisconsin or Colorado; I was not remembering her. She tells me her address is on Home drive, which is right next to one of my rentals in Wisconsin. We both do some talking trying to figure out how she knows me. She repeats my phone number, the one she had stored in her cupboard. She called the right number, and asked for the right person, Michelle. Though we still do not know each other! Weird huh!

The conversation ended with us still not knowing each other, and a realization that it was very weird how she knew my name and number. She apologized for calling so early, and the both of us were back to our mornings. I do not logically know what that was about, but I am sure soon I will. My inner self totally felt a connection! We are all connected on some level. Our souls know what is going on; though our mind's get confused!

Soon I was back to my video blog with the memory of the phone call still in my head. My video was about all of this stuff. How we are all connected.

How it was ironic I was awake (so early in the morning) to receive her phone call. Why I received the call in the first place. Why my friend sent me the name of the movie now, instead of a week ago. You know it is all a puzzle, we may not know now, but our souls sure do!

My quiet morning was over; the kiddos were up and soon off to school. The day came and went. Nothing significant happened next. Nothing but routine was our day. Soon it was night, and the next day was preparing itself as we slept.

....

Thursday morning we all were up early. The kids and husband needed to get to school and work, and I had an appointment with the puppies. I met over at the location to drop off my three so they could hitch a ride to the vet. I have become attached to the little guy; we call him 'puppy.' He rode on my lap all the way to the store. I was sad giving these guys up. I felt for them; as I knew they were going to be poked and prodded, and that they had a long ride to the vet with a stranger. I was also sad knowing Fluffy was leaving us, as he was going to his forever home after they returned from the vet.

When I was home I cleaned the house. I then caught up with some writing, I dialoged the past week. We had been non-stop all week and finally it was time for writing. I also found myself daydreaming throughout the day. I was appreciating all the good in my life. I am living the life of my dreams. I get to do the work I choose. I love my 'job!' I get to lead my family, my volunteer activities, my writings, and my life! I know I am a creator. I know how important and awesome my gift of visualization is; this gift brings my accomplished dreams. I love what I do. I also spent the afternoon talking with my girlfriend; we also hadn't talked all week. We had a lot of catching up to do.

Soon Brian came home for lunch. He was only here for thirty minutes, but in that small amount of time he prepared chili (to cook all day) and let me in on a secret. Apparently late, last night we received a knock on the door. A tow truck guy was about to tow away my truck, and then realized it had Wisconsin license plates. He stopped and knocked to talk with Brian. He asked him if we knew where the people who used to live at this address were living now (because their car was who he was supposed to tow.) He did not know; the tow truck guy left.

That story surprised me. I wondered what all of that meant. How ironic is it that a tow truck guy tries to tow your truck! He also told Brian the 'story' of this woman. Why did we get the 'story?' Why did I not wake up to someone pounding on our door late at night? It all relates, and I am sure soon it will unfold. I will keep you updated.

One thing my girlfriend said was that it was my husband clearing; it was something he was doing for me. That, whatever it was, Brian took care of it. That comment resonated with me. There have been many daydreams going through my head, and it was sweet to know that Brian is taking care of some of my bigger desires.

P.S. A year later as I am editing this book; I get it. I was not towed away because I am grounded in Wisconsin. I have roots. As I venture out, I am safe. I am safe because I am grounded in my origins.

The afternoon came and I picked up the kiddos. They did not have homework, but wanted to hang out with their friends. That was good; I still had to finish up my work for the prosperity class for the evening. They did their stuff, and I listened to my CD's and finished my workbook.

It was 4:30 P.M. and Brian was home. I left to get my puppies; they were back from the vet! I was excited to get them back in my arms! I tell you they are easy to love. I get there and Fluffy's new owners come running to get their dog. Oh did that sink in! I was sad. I said my goodbye's, and reminded them to please be careful with him because he was feeling sore after his surgery.

A little sad to see him go, I was happy to take my two home. These two were sleepy and cute. They were sick from their doctor visit, and all I wanted to do was cuddle with them; though I had a class to go to. I dropped them off at home, gave instructions to the kids to be careful with them, kissed everyone good bye and headed out the door.

Driving to class was liberating. I was feeling very free, still realizing this amazing life I have. It was also mixed with a little sadness and a whole lot of changeable energy. I thought of my girlfriend as I drove; but talked myself out of calling her. As I headed around the corner, I realized I was going to be fifteen minutes early for class. I could talk with her and have her help me though my feelings. I was conflicted; I wanted her help and also wanted to work through these emotions by myself. As I pulled in the church parking lot my trash bag hanging from my gear gets wrapped around my steering wheel. I could have caused an accident if I was going any faster. I decided, at that moment, I did need to talk with her. I was feeling tangled and about to cause accidents with my thinking.

I called her, and of course she was thinking about me at that very second! I told her I was sad, and I wanted a friend. She listened, and we talked about my car overheating, and my computer overheating; I explained I thought I was overheating. I think the puppies were the breaking point. All I want is love; I want to be loved and to know that I am loveable. I want to connect.

I get into class and our teacher is ready to read us the, "Daily word." The topic was, "Let Go, and Let God." She quoted a verse from the Bible stating, "I am a channel through which God's power flows." (International Bible Society, 1984) This is exactly what I was experiencing all week. I received a lot of awesome stuff. I am receiving, though receiving is hard for me. It is hard to keep the faith, to remember how worthy I am to receive good things. When I was asking for my mom to arrive at noon; I had to go through a lot of work as I let my request go so I could receive. I wanted it, but it was hard to hold the belief that I would get it. Also I received lots of freebies from my mom; free gas, free food, free Pizza Hut, free everything. It was nice to get them, but I had a lot of guilty feelings about taking from my mom. I kept feeling if I am getting, she is losing. Also Aidan's birthday, I am glad it all worked out, though there was a lot of stress as I waited for it to work out. This is how the whole week went; I received a lot, though also simultaneously felt stressful.

When she read the verse; it was perfect. "We may not know; but God does." He wants to give 'this' (whatever it is we want) to us all. We are His channel. When we feel guilty for receiving, we should not; this is Him gaining as well. His part is to give, ours is to receive. We should not feel guilty because He is getting when we have the resources to do our part. (International Bible Society, 1984)

Our testimonies were next. Our first lady told us a story of her breaking her tooth. This appears bad, though it was good. She called for an appointment and was told no; they could not get her in for the week. She then called back and asked if she could see the assistant just for a few minutes. She got a yes and went in. The assistant fixed her tooth! Her tooth was fixed and she was able to afford the fee! She was happy.

Another lady spoke of her experience at a conference. She said the speaker was a handicapped lady in a wheel chair, who was also blind. The speaker talked of this lady's job each day was to help other handicapped people. She also talked about a neat tool she gets to use. It is a pen that when it touches lids of paint jugs, it can 'tell' what color it is! Isn't that a cool piece of technology? This woman is a painter and even though she has many disabilities, she was able to prosper with her dreams. She gets to uplift everyone who hears her story! She was described as a really happy, inspirational person. She is full of life. The woman telling this woman's story, said meeting this woman uplifted her whole week. She was an example of why small things in life really are a reason to feel joy! What a beautiful picture I have in my head of how awesome this woman is to all of us! This lady's story is amazing to experience. I am thankful her story was a part of our testimonies.

We also heard a second testimony. This one was for a daughter of one of our friends. Her girl is currently going through a fourth Chemo treatment. Each day our friend gets to be happy in each moment. Each moment she is happy as she gets to spend it with her daughter. She cannot be positive of how many more tomorrows she will have; though currently, in the now, she and her daughter are together. Each day was a lesson reminding her to be thankful. This is a gift each day.

Here is a special prayer for the two of you. May God within both of you, love all the parts of you, and now gather the healing that is inevitable.

Another member received an email from a friend requesting her to judge a teenage writing contest. All she kept saying was, "Wow, people want me!" How exciting is that! How exciting is it to be wanted, to know we are wanted. That's all we really want, to know we are loved, to know we are taken care of physically, mentally and emotionally. Our next 'lucky' friend told us he received a follow up with a pre-employment test! What this means is that his new employment is on its way! Here is another step. Good for him. And to see his excitement, his knowing that 'it' is on its way! Good for you, blessings to you!

Another testimony tells of a story spent at a metaphysical fair. This guy has a talent reading auras; though he is new at presenting his skills. On Saturday he went to the fair and was instructed he could only practice his skills; he was not to take any money. He followed suit. Though, Sunday morning, he decided he was done with this, he was good at what he did, and his skills were of value. He was now ready to receive all good life had to offer! He went to the fair with his new confident self, and was paid! I love, love, love this story! Blessings to him! When we decide we are worth it; God rewards!

Here is another story. As we began we had immediate results, lots of prosperity. And now that we are more in depth with our course, deeper stuff is coming up. This is the stuff that has wanted to be cleared for ages! It makes since that goofy feelings begin to surface. This story is how a woman went to the laundry mat and someone stole her laundry bag. Who does that? Though, she feels she handled it well. She decided that the thief probably needed a laundry bag and she could afford to give! Then as she was enjoying her new perspective, she received a call from her sister. Her sister was calling to ask her to buy her a loaf of bread and apples. This appeared goofy, though she went with it and purchased a new laundry bag, some bread and a bag of apples. She later gets to her sister's house and does not receive a refund for the bread and apples. She continued and said she must be excessively prosperous, and she can afford to give to those in need!

I am so curious to see how her next week comes together! Her story reminded me of my first week, here I am tithing, and what I receive are more opportunities to collect for other people. I went with it, and the next weeks were incredibly prosperous. I am positive this girl has a very prosperous week ahead for her!

Another point to bring up is we are at the half way point; it makes since for things to start shaking up. It is like cooking food. At first the food is frozen. As it begins to boil, it starts to unfreeze and change. It is changing form, it is becoming something different. Soon the food is cooked and ready to eat. As we are in the middle of our class, we are in the cooking stage. We are no longer frozen and stagnate. We are changing. We may not be ready to eat, though we get closer each day. As we change, things have to mess up. They have to go through stages of change and sit in boiling water. This part is uncomfortable, but at least we know it is normal; it is the process of change. We are changing; this is a necessary step in growth. This is when we get to chant, "This too shall pass."

Continuing on with our testimonials, another story came from a woman. She had an 'Aha' moment. This week she realized when she was little, she used to hear, "You should get an education, just in case." Just in case she was to fail, she had a backup plan. This gave her permission (according to her beliefs) to fail. This is why she subconsciously did not want to make money, and have her own business. She was supposed to fail, and her subconscious was ensuring it! This reminds me of the movie, "The Secret." In the movie it was quoted, "You expect a bill, so a bill has to show up; do yourself a favor, and expect a check!"

What is good is that she recognized her belief. Her realization has not miraculously created a billion in her bank account, though it has created the first step. It has created the path for her to have a spot to put her billion in! The path got mowed, and walking on it can now be scheduled! Her old pattern has stopped, and now the new pattern has begun. She now can work through her new belief. Her new belief is, "Making her own money used to be bad, though now it is good, and is expected." Here is another quote from, "The Secret," "Now that you know this knowledge, play with it!"

The leaders of the group were next. They asked us if we were having 'bad' things come our way. Some of us commented. He said this was normal. As we are changing, stuff gets mixed up and it soon evens out. Again, when we are changing, old stuff has to be stirred out so the new stuff can form.

We then listened to the first half of the CD. I was able to listen this time.

I needed to hear what was said, instead of being preoccupied with my thoughts. In the previous classes I had been excited, and found it hard to settle down and focus. This time I immediately found my center, and was very attentive to our teacher. This reminded me of when we come in for winter from a very playful summer and fall. In winter, we settle in our houses. For months we cuddle our thoughts, and wrap ourselves in blankets. The evenings become dark, it seems we hibernate. This is how I felt as I was attentive with the CD. It was easy to hibernate into the lesson and focus on learning, instead of reminiscing about playing.

The CD led us into break. The teacher, at this point, asked me my progress on our prison project. She informed me that her and our minister suggested I take the prayer class in March. I am going to need this credential to start ministering in a prison. Things move forward especially when the world is involved. The things we desire are not only for us, they are for us all. It was my idea to have this idea, though do you see how many people are now involved and encouraging the project. This is how much you matter. This is how much your ideas matter. They involve us all, and are necessary. You matter. When you see your value, the world also sees it. It is necessary for you to have desires; this is how the world continues, this is how we prosper.

After break we finished our CD. One of our members did not make it to class. She was in the hospital. Here is a prayer. The lady with her daughter's Chemo, and our lady in the hospital, may God within show you how you can now believe you are healthy. May the two of you see your beauty and your contribution to our world. May you now begin loving the parts of you that you have forgotten.

After our CD we went into our groups. Our prayers this time were, "God within continues to bring perfect teaching opportunities and continual guidance with our life purposes. He continues to give us reasons to live, continues to eliminate our debt, and allows more prosperity. He shows us how to expect bigger and better than what we already are receiving." Life gets even better when others continue to pray for us.

When class was finished, I asked a member to listen to me as I read my personal inventory. This is a practice found in our workbooks. Here we are asked to write a list of what we know we are good at and what we want to release. It is a very good, cleansing exercise. Our leader asked us to read it to another member. Reading it was like confessing. I chose to participate. It felt goofy telling another person my bad, my fears. As I was embarrassed, I continued to read. When I was finished, my person said, "It is all normal." That comment stuck with me. I have been holding on to this stuff for a very long time.

All he said was, it was all normal, nothing to feel embarrassed of, and nothing to feel the need to hide. It felt really good when we were finished. I released a lot, and am forever grateful. It is done, it is finished.

I was back in my car and on my way to pick up the new puppies. They were going to be at the location at 8:30 P.M. My class finished at 8:30, so I was on a time schedule to pick up the little guys. I get to the store and no one is there. I check my phone and learn that the pick-up was pushed back until 10:30 P.M. I drive home tired and disappointed. I ask Brian to go instead when the time comes; he agrees. 11:00 P.M. rolls around and I am asleep on the couch. I wake up to a lot of ruckus, as Brian and the dogs are home. Brian brought home two extra dogs. The lady that was supposed to foster the two, five month old Great Danes, realized (at the pick-up point) how big they were! She went home with no dogs, and we volunteered for a full house! We had our three, and a puppy from the last litter. We also still had Slim. Now we had four, three-month old puppies, and two large Great Dane puppies! We were full, though happy!

....

Chapter 7
A Dark Dream, a Light Realization

Friday morning was here. My first task consisted of shifts as I let one litter
out, and then the next. I enjoyed my morning, energetic as it was. I also
noticed the disaster the house was. I saw the amount of work needed to
keep an eye on all eleven dogs. The kids were soon up; they also were
loud and energetic. I had a war going on at seven in the morning; the war
included every toy gun my son owned!

I soon got them off to school and was preparing for my time away
from the house. Today was the day for the soup kitchen. (The soup
kitchen is an organization that feeds those who have no food.) A few
moments later I received a call from our soup kitchen lady, saying she was
going in early. She would not be able to meet me in the parking lot.
Instead I was to call her when I arrived, and she would come out to get me.
I now had extra time in the house because I had no one waiting for me.

I was feeling very grateful; I was noticing how great my life was. I
was happy. I may have a messy house and a lot of work to do with the
puppies; though this was work I enjoyed doing! My work was fun. I love
what I do. I am thankful that the life I envisioned; I am living. Also this
day brought us our first snow of the season. It was beautiful and peaceful.
I was in awe at how awesome I was feeling. I created a video blog to share
my vibration. I spoke about how cool it was that five different couples
came so late in the evening last night to pick up different dogs. Here were
all of these people coming together, for a cause they believe in. They came
together even though it was the middle of the night. Seeing all of this,
seeing my opportunity to volunteer, was incredibly neat!

Knowing that I do not have to go to work; I do not have to do stuff
all day that I do not want to do; this makes me feel incredibly blessed. I
get to do what makes me happy; I enjoy my work. My work is very
productive. Knowing all of this brought tears to my eyes. I do have a
really awesome life; I am blessed and am very thankful!

Still in my high vibration, an hour later, I drove to the soup
kitchen. I drove up and down streets trying to find where I was supposed
to be. I am in the wrong place. I have the wrong address. No one is
answering their phone. I wasn't going to be working the soup kitchen this
morning. Though my day was still good.

Here is the funny part, amidst the chaos of the morning, I had been
thinking the soup kitchen might be too much for the day. The dogs were
only on day one, and a tad bit of work. They were actually a lot of work,
though my thoughts were committed to my previous commitment.

This is why I decided to go, even though thoughts of cancelling the Soup kitchen crossed my mind. Funny, God cancelled for me. As I am leaving my 'wrong' destination, I started to laugh. This intention came true also! I came home and cleaned my house, and took many shifts to feed and let out all the dogs. Before I knew it, it was time to get the kids. The afternoon brought lots of kids in and out, and dinner. Soon it was time to sleep. Our day came to an end.

....

Saturday morning was here, and I was up early to enjoy it. I let all the dogs out. It was warmer than it had been in the last few days; so the dogs got to stay outside. I had my coffee and spent many hours re-watching all my video blogs. I noticed the large amount of growth the months had brought me. This was cool. When I first started my video blog's I imagined other people using them for a weekend marathon, and here I was doing that very thing. It showed me a lot of growth I have been going through. It helped answer questions I had from the past. The answers had come as time went on. It was a very reflective morning.

I have had an on-going dream all my life. The dream is me going to this vacation house once a year. I hate going to this house, because I know the house is haunted; though I still go because this is the tradition. We have to spend the night in this haunted house, though the ghosts are 'just there,' they really don't scare us; they only make us feel uncomfortable. During the day, there is always some kind of fair or carnival going on, like a Fourth of July event. The house is surrounded by a river, and according to tradition we are supposed to ride water rides through the river. This sounds cool except there are snakes that ride with you. I never found it exciting to go on the rides because I am afraid of snakes.

This is the setting of my on-going dream. I had this dream again a few months back, and talked about it in one of my earlier video blog's. This time in the dream I bought the haunted house. Also my kids were in my dream at the age they are now, 5 and 8. And when you look into the big river, I see 4 humongous snakes; they are as big as dinosaurs. The two outer ones look like real, (still large like dinosaurs) snakes, and the two middle ones look like cartoon snakes. The end of the dream has me sleeping, when I notice my daughter is giving a tour of my house to my aunt. I wake up (in my dream) and am scared, and hoping my aunt is going to approve of my house.

Here is my evaluation of the reoccurring dream. The house is a house I visit once a year, like a vacation house. It is not a house I enjoy, because it is haunted. A house represents you, your body. My house happens to be haunted.

Almost like a lot of old stuff still lingers in my awareness. I like to enjoy life 364 days a year, but once a year I have to deal with my demons. This time I bought the house. This time around I owned up to all of those demons! I was ready to finally let them go. Though first I had to look at them, accept them, and purchase them.

Also in the dream there is a down stairs and an upstairs. In the downstairs my husband decided to put a partial wall up to separate the downstairs. Part of the down stairs was now a bedroom, and part was a living room. I remember feeling comfortable in the living room part; though scared in the bedroom part. Why this is significant is because where we dream is also where a lot of clearing happens. I was scared of this. I am scared if I actually clear, I will not know how to live. Being cleared is an area I have not been; it is unfamiliar territory. I may want to clear because I am not happy where I am; therefore I want change. Though changing is not staying. Changing is going somewhere different than you already know. A decision has to be made, to stay in what you know even though you currently do not like it; or do we change. When we change, we become uncomfortable, this alone is scary. This makes us vulnerable. We get to be uncomfortable, but also we get to feel good. We feel good because we know we are on the right path, moving in the right direction. Though being on the right path is scary because you are unsure of how this new path is to be walked. You do not know the directions without a GPS, you do not know how long the grocery store stays open, you do not know what to wear to be cool in your new school. You know you are doing the right thing, but you are unsure of how to be in this right thing. These are things we learn as we go, though learning is being vulnerable. Being vulnerable is scary; even though it has an amazing outcome.

The other section was the 'living' room. This is where we partied and felt full of life. There was nothing to be scared of in the 'living' area. The living room was also down stairs. Down stairs is a symbol for where we have our past, our dusty files. In the living room part, I am good with my memories that make me feel full of life. I am okay with that part of my past. In a way, half of my past I enjoy, and the other half I fear.

In the dream my husband brought a muddy couch into the down stairs living room. For the first 3 days, (My dream was a 4 day period) I was okay with the muddy chair. I went with the flow for a while. By the 4th day, I was irritated that we had a mud soaked chair in our living room. I wanted it out!

This represents me being too comfortable with my problems. It is okay that I am not happy. I am not, not-happy enough.

A couch represents your comfort; it is where you sit and relax. It is where you digest your day. I am comfortable with my current outdated beliefs. My current beliefs are not serving me; though they are not bad enough, not yet. The couch was muddy; it is telling me my beliefs are covering up my goals. It shows that I cannot drive the road of my dreams because there is mud on my windshield. I cannot see; I cannot move forward. I have to get rid of the mud so I can move. The muddy chair needs be in the dumpster; I no longer need this. I need to let it go and get a chair that I can sit in. I need a chair that I can feel clean in. I need a chair that belongs in my life.

The muddy chair is in my living room; my happy room. It hinders happiness, happening in this room. It is messing with the comfort of my happiness. Why my husband brought in the couch was because he represents what I will not see in myself. He is bringing in the old beliefs because I am not telling him not to. If I would stand up for my dreams and my desires, than he would know that the couch does not belong. Instead he thinks I want the muddy beliefs, and brings in the chair thinking it makes me happy. He is a representation of my physical world. I say I want this great thing, but emotionally I feel I am not good enough for it. The universe hears our emotions, not our words. Therefore my husband hears I want the muddy couch, the outdated beliefs. 3 days into my dream; 3 means the angels are here to help, is when I decide I will not put up with the muddy chair anymore. I remove the chair, with help and guidance, from my living area. I can now continue to live and be happy when the outdated belief is removed. I am able to make this decision on the 3rd day because I have asked for help and guidance. As I asked, assistance was given. Just as Jesus rose from the dead on the 3rd day, I rose and continued life. 3 tells us it is time to make something happen. A new creation is formed. Chaos appears after, and it moves us from the dead to the alive.

Next to evaluate was our snakes. Snakes represent growth; old beliefs coiling out of us. They represent new life, new growth; a new us. This time around my kids were in my dream. They wanted to jump in the water with the snakes; and I was trying to get them to stop. Growth is scary; snakes are scary. They found the growth fun, not scary. The excitement of the ride was more important than the potential danger of snakes, of growth. My kids, (in my dream) represent the creative, courageous, innocent versions of myself. They see the blessings in growth. I, in my dream, represent the parent, the authority figure, the law enforcer, the warner of danger.

To grow we need to gather every aspect of ourselves; the hurt, the wounded, the courage, the adventurer, the innocent, and the wise.

We have to talk to all parts of ourselves and hear their opinion; hear their fears, their excitement. As each part of us brings a positive and negative list to the meeting, all the concerns can be discussed and then healed. When all parts of us are heard and then healed, all of us are ready for the new growth. We are ready to move. In my dream, all the parts of me were not yet in agreement. My dream was telling me that a group meeting was needed.

Then we have our 4 green snakes. Remember we had 4 days, and now 4 snakes. The number 4 means balance and stability. It is the four legs that create the stability in the chair. 4 appears when something negative in your life is being removed. 4 becomes 4, when 3 legs, no longer stabilize the chair. 4 legs eradicate confusion and unpredictability. In my dream I see 4 snakes. I see the balance in growth.

The two outer snakes were real, and the two inner snakes were cartoons. The snakes were large like dinosaurs. My growth currently is huge. On the outside growth seems scary. On the inside it is just one big cartoon, an illusion. We are here to play and be a cartoon; nothing to fear. All we have to do is push the reset button like they do on cartoons if anything 'bad' happens. We are safe, and supposed to move through our changes, and have fun with them.

The snakes were also green. Green is the color of healing. I am being balanced as I heal. I heal as I trust it is okay to rid the old; the old that is no longer serving me. I am a cartoon, a child on the inner which is growing. On the outside I am a wise mentor, grounded in this world. My color is green; I heal as I swim through the water. Water is consciousness. Water is power; water is thought. Water is growth. The 4 green snakes for me show I am becoming balanced. I am becoming balanced in my original values that I hid away as life progressed. Now I am back to the basics, I am back to my beginnings. I am back in the water; I am balanced.

Lastly we have my daughter giving a tour of our house to my aunt. When I woke up I was happy to realize that we live in Colorado, so my aunt, in reality, could not be here. What this represents is judgment and self-worth. My aunt has always been a mentor for me, someone I looked up to. As I change; I always hope she will approve. I am going through these changes and hoping they are approved by my family.

My family represents my tribe. My tribe is who accepts me. I was nervous of not being accepted as I grow back into myself. I in the past chose my tribe over myself. There needed to be a balance. I am now finding that balance. Parts of the old beliefs that are going away are that I have to have myself or my family. This chair does not belong anymore. Now I can have both; I can be me and have my family. This is the balance that is growing as the snake sheds its old skin.

When I woke up from this dream (this time around) I noticed all the changes in my reoccurring dream over the years. And then I realized I have this dream always when something large is about to happen in my life. This dream always forewarns me of large changes, life changes. It explains why things seemed to be (currently) so confusing around me. It made since that my life was changing in a big way. When I realized this; I found comfort. I still did not know all the changes coming, though I do know it was all a change for the better.

What has happened since that dream (a few months earlier) is I have moved to Colorado. We had all the rental problems; our budget was not in order. I was enjoying my writing and our new area; though felt like I should be getting a job to fix some of the money stuff. I inquired about real estate. I prepared for the license when my brother decided against borrowing me the needed money. My kids decided to go to school instead of home school. My role of 'teaching' my children seemed to have ended, and now I was looking for the next.

I now find value in my writings. My kids are happy and doing well in school. I am able to maintain a clean, organized house. I feel less stressed. We have progressed with our goals with foster children. We have fostered dogs. I started tithing. This is huge on its own. I have attracted a debt consolidation company for my larger bills, and my budget is getting on track. I am writing my book. I have learned of publishing. I have new goals. I have hope. I would say my dream is accurate in its timing. It is showing me the dramatic changes happing in my life.

Continuing back to our Saturday morning; I spent my time reminiscing and reevaluating. The kids were soon up, and the house became a mess. I had to get our dogs to the puppy fair. I became irritated thinking that all the hard work from yesterday, (my clean house) was now obsolete as the disaster was coming back. I looked at my husband and my two kiddos, and told them I expected a clean house when I got back! I reminded them I was not their maid. It is not my job to clear for everyone; it is my chosen job to show others how to clear. I can assist, but will not do it for them!

Out of the house, my irritation subsided. The puppy fair was fun. There were four different agencies (there is that number four again) at the store. We had to bring our clan outside. The weather was chilly but not too cold, so we made it through! One of our big puppies found an adoptive home. (He goes to his new home after the vet on Thursday.) Slim did not get adopted; he instead went to another foster home. The foster dad wanted him to help with the puppy at his house. I thought this was funny because all week I affirmed Slim would find a new home. He did not get adopted, but he found a new home!

Affirmations always come true!

I brought home the four puppies, and the two big Great Danes. I also came home to a clean house, and scrubbed floors! The bed sheets were hanging outside. The house had a brand new beginning, perfumed in clean! The evening was filled with Pizza Hut, quiet kids, and sleepy dogs.

Brian and I watched a movie. It was about four magicians wanting to join a certain prestigious club. They had to do some pretty big stunts to gain the achievement. One thing they did was rob a bank on national television. Of course they got arrested, but this is what they wanted. They had to go through the 'bad' times to get their prize at the end. Their prize was their admittance into their chosen club.

What I loved about the movie was their ease with the 'bad.' They must have had to repeat over and over, "This too shall pass." These things were necessary for them to grow into their goal. They had to play the game and get arrested, to reach their outcome. They were not moping around saying, "Why me," instead they went with the flow. It is easy to go with the flow when you know it is all just a game. It is easy when we do not get wrapped up in the circumstances, and instead know this as the process. When we do this, we know we are on the right track. This is the goal all along, to stay on the right track.

The evening came to an end.

Sunday morning was here bright and early. No working out again. I think I have taken an extended vacation from the treadmill! Later the kids were up. We prepared for church. The service was nice. Our minister was finishing up on the topic of service. It was one of those services that hit the heart. Church was very good, and much needed as I have been feeling shaky lately. I know I am growing, though this certain spot keeps swaying me. I know I am grounded and will not fall over; though I am being pushed around a lot. Her service was comforting and reassuring.

The church talked about needing a new building because the congregation is growing. I think this is funny, because the first day I went to this church I affirmed soon they would buy a bigger building. I wanted to be a part of this church family, and see it through a really large growth! And here we are months later, seeing its reality. Even the small intentions find a way to surface.

During the service I was also thinking, if everyone was tithing correctly, they could easily afford a new church. They could afford the new building and the existing one.

They could have a minister preaching at this church as another one teaches at the new one. One of my intentions, that only God, you and I know, is that the minister begins to teach and expand these principals. She could be in charge of opening up a few churches. Instead of preaching, she could train ministers to preach! This message could then be spoken on a huge scale. This intention would be neat to see come true.

After the service I talked with the minister. I told her of my intention coming true of her needing a larger church. She smiled like she knew. She was affirming the same thing. When two or more come together, miracles happen. The bigger our church; the bigger the message! I also talked with her about the prison ministry. She told me to email her. We left church and headed to the store. We were getting our Halloween costumes. After, Brian dropped us off at home, and went to the bar with a friend to watch the Packer Game.

The kids and I spent the afternoon reading and googling. The kids were soon asleep after some peanut butter and jelly sandwiches. It was eight O'clock at night and Brian was still not home. I called him and he was drunk. I was worried about him spending lots of money. He ended up only spending thirteen dollars, I was relieved; though still irritated that he drank too much. He eventually was home and was passed out. I was mad, but soon was over it. I was happy and grateful he at least drank on someone else's tab and he was home safe. Soon I also was asleep.

....

Monday morning was again a no-gym day. Though I had a workout getting all the dogs outside for the morning! I prepared lunches and cooked eggs. Soon it was time for school. I had warmed up the car for twenty minutes, and my car was still frozen. We sat in the car for five minutes trying to get the windshield defrosted. The kids were late and experienced their first tardy.

They and I laughed at it though, how cool is it to only get one tardy instead of Aidan's first year of school when we were tardy every day! We entered through the office and both kids headed to class. I picked up my name tag and prepared for my fieldtrip with Aidan's class. We went to the bus safety organization and learned all about how to be safe. I was impressed with the order his teacher had for her class. She had twenty-three third graders, and every one of them was well-behaved. I enjoyed spending the morning with Aidan. He was also happy as he gave me some public kisses and hugs! Funny how that works, at first I am ordered not to hug him in public, I follow the rules and before I know it he is hugging me!

After the fieldtrip I said my goodbyes and was home.

I had my initial rounds of letting the dogs out, and then found myself dialoging with you about the last few days. Life is a blessing and I am excited to see what's next. I have a feeling it is even more amazing then what has currently shown up!

Later the evening came and my happy feelings began to change; they became darker. I was feeling confused. I was feeling like I was in the middle of a clearing. I knew it would soon pass, though I was currently in it. I was talking with my girlfriend and telling her about it. I told her the events of the last few days, to give her an idea of my confusing times. I told her it was warm outside, but it was October, so it was supposed to be cold. This was my in-between feelings, and an exact replica of what the weather was like. I told her about Saturday, about watching all of my video blogs. How I recognized what I was feeling was a pass through phase. The pass through phase was a reflection and memory of what the last few months brought. As I was finishing up my story my friend began to tell another one. She said to me that 'now was the time' for her to tell me something that she noticed a few months ago. She did not tell me prior because now was the right time. She said when she was watching one of my Video blog's, there was a glitch in one of the videos; a male voice had come through and said, "Die."

This scared me. This has been (in the past) one of my deeper, darker fears. Ghosts, demons and the unknown scare me. This is all ironic because I am the one choosing to be on my spiritual journey, and choosing to learn all about this world.

As I got off the phone with her I attempted to work with this new info. I kept reminding myself that this will pass, and that this belief (of being scared all of the time) has to finally go away. I needed to look at it, and finally say my goodbyes. Ironically that evening, I was not as scared as I have been in the past. It was not sticking as it had in the past. I was very thankful for this. I then went and found the Vlog she was talking about. I made myself watch it. Half way through the Vlog, my phone (during the recording) had said, "Droid." I watched that video a few times, trying to catch what she heard. I took in the new information; maybe the big ole scary thing was just a normal, "Droid" from my phone.

The evening came and soon it was bedtime. Usually when I have another layer of fear come up, I go through a phase of not sleeping. This night I did wake up in the middle of the night, though was able to fall asleep twenty minutes later. Usually when I am awake in the middle of the night, I am too scared to go back to sleep. Last night I did wake up; though was asleep again quickly. I am making progress.

....

Tuesday morning I woke up still bothered by last night's phone call.

Though noticed how well my body and conscious were accepting it. I was nervous about being alone in the house while the kids were at school; though I was willing to be okay with it.

Soon the kids were off and I was again entering my house. What I noticed was how peaceful my house was. It really did not seem scary. I was alone in my bathroom putting on make-up, and I was fine. Feeling this, I became inspired, understanding I might actually be letting this huge scary belief go. I began to feel 'ready.' I prepared to make a video blog, and tell the world my big dark secret (of being so scared.) I decided to give it energy, to look at it and finally let it go. I told my story of the conversation with my girlfriend the night before (on the video.) I then told a story of how the Ouija board worked for me when I was a teenager. The moment of when I saw the Ouija board work was very scary, and seems a good starting point of where my fears began. I could not believe I was allowing my fears to be spoken about. I was bringing them into the open. I was looking at them. I was not keeping them hid away to haunt me for the rest of my life. I was done. I was going to admit them with some energy.

And now, I am here, telling you about this. I do not know the outcome of giving these fears of mine energy. Though I do know what I have done in the past. I hid these stories, these fears. I currently know what it feels like to be scared and all alone in the middle of the night. I may not know what it yet feels like to talk about these fears, but I know what it feels like to not. I decide to take this different route and talk. I am now feeling the different energy and decision flow through me. I think I may be clearing these beliefs.

This has been one of my biggest fears all along. These, and the fear of not 'making it,' are fears that I would love to look at and finally let them go. I have wanted to write about my fears for a while, though I did not know how to do it. I thought that if I wrote about it, they would become true. I thought if I gave them energy they would come true. Though, I think, I was giving them energy (in the past) by trying to hide them. But now I just gave them some air. I opened up the window, and yes they could have easily gotten out, though they got out to the outside. And in the outside is a whole big outside that sucked them up. Air circled in their dark, dreary basement quarters. Air cleaned them out.

Amidst my realization with my fears and their outlet, I also was dealing with foster puppies puking non-stop all morning. It is now noon. It is warm enough outside to let them stay out there. As I was letting them out, I thought about the clean outdoors cleansing their sickness.

All we have to do is open up a window when we don't feel good. Confining ourselves in a closed room makes us sicker as the same 'sick' air continues to re-infect us. Sickness permeates when there is no air to 'air' out the disease. Fears permeate when we do not open windows.

I feel really good right now. Thank you for listening. Tuesday evening came and I spent a lot of time cuddling with the puppies; that were still sick. Brian went to Girl Scouts with Dreana as I was starting to feel sick as well. Aidan stayed with me and showed me all of his creations he made on his video game. This is a game where he builds different cities and structures. It is a great game to create many different realities. I also spent a lot of the evening editing. Soon we all were asleep.
....

Wednesday morning I woke up and began my day. As I walked through the house I noticed pools of blood everywhere. I walked in the kitchen, and saw all the puppies separated in different bins. On each of the bins was a dialoged synopsis of what they encountered the evening prior. There was one bin empty.

I looked around for the fourth puppy; I eventually woke Brian up asking him what was going on. He told me the puppies were sick all night. He stayed up with them the majority of the night. He cleaned them up time, and time again as the night turned into day. We eventually found the lost puppy underneath Aidan's bed.

Brian told me he tried to wake me up to help with the sick puppies. He couldn't get me to wake up. He said he emailed the foster agency telling them the pups needed to get to the vet immediately. I grabbed the phone and tried to tell the person in charge of the puppy organization, what was going on. She did not answer. I was crying on the voice mail. I then texted her. I needed to get my entire message out, one that was not interfered with tears. Through all of this I also got the kiddos ready for school. Ten minutes prior to when I had to leave; the agency lady called. She told me she was trying to get someone to drive the dogs to the vet. She asked me to give the puppies sugar water; this was to hydrate them.

I took the kids to school. On the way my boy asked why I woke him up in the middle of the night. I told him the only time I woke him up was when I was looking for the puppy, and that was early in the morning. He kept saying, "No, it was in the night. You kept waking me up." He said I was on his chest, petting him. And I got it! The puppies were so sick; they were in and out of consciousness. When they were out of consciousness, they could travel and be healthy. One of our puppies came to play with Aidan in the night.

I came back home and the agency lady called asking me if I would take the dogs to the vet. She could not find anyone else who could do it. I called Brian and asked him to come home to help me load the puppies. I was emotional and was having trouble doing the simplest of things. The vet was also far away. I needed his help on planning my trip. Brian came home and started putting the puppies in a bin (they were all so sick, we did not want them in a crate.) At this time, one of the puppies died. Here is where I broke down. Brian called the agency lady and she instructed us to bring this puppy to the vet with the other puppies. What was wrong with this guy was what was probably wrong with the other three. The vet will be able to diagnose the other puppies by seeing what went wrong with the puppy that died.

I soon was on my way to the vet. I was going through a mixture of feelings. I was sad and crying, though also realizing that some intentions of mine were coming true. My road trip was something I had been craving for. No kids, just the open road. I was also thankful that this was my life. I was spending my Wednesday morning volunteering by driving puppies to the vet. I was thankful to have this opportunity. I was thankful to be the foster mom of the pup that died. I really loved the little guy; I got to be here for him in his last moments.

I get to the vet and soon the doctor takes over. I had to leave my puppies there. This was hard. As I was leaving, one of them (my favorite one) looked at me with his sick eyes, almost saying, "Don't leave me." I responded to him (telepathically) saying I had to go, and the doctor would take good care of him. I told him I loved him, and he was going to be fine. When I was later home I called my girlfriend. She was a really good friend as she comforted me and my loss. I described how comfortable, I noticed I was with death. I missed the puppy, though I knew his current transition was a very happy, pain free, place.

Later as the day came and went; evening was here. As I was lying in bed I was sad again. I think this is the process; as we do get to accept death, we still may be sad. It is okay to be sad, but it is also good to know we are moving through it. This correlates with all of our goals. As we move through them, we may be sad and not believe in what it is we want. These feelings are all A-Okay. When we understand these feelings as what they are, just feelings, we can know that we will move through them. We will rise above and learn from our moments. When we get wrapped up and think that they are 'our forever;' this is when we get lost. As we accept our grief, knowing it is okay to feel it, we accept it as our now and also know it is passing. As it is passing it is healing, and new beginnings are being created. Death is a normal passage of life. It is a part of life, just as each of our moments are parts of life.

We learn to love every moment, even the sad ones. They all are creations of who we are. All our moments are us. Every part of us brings peace.

....

Thursday morning came. I was feeling a lot brighter. I had my morning to myself; my kiddos had the day off of school and were still sleeping. I recorded a video blog. My Vlog was about the process of life. Each project that we do, we go through different layers of life. My example was our book. I explained that when I was a child, I wanted to be an author. I told how I loved writing class in my years as I was growing up. I wrote many novels when I was a kid. I talked about the time I quit real estate; I started writing again. And then the years since, my writings have become personal; my writings have become consistent.

It is all a process. Each thing we go through. We have an up, then a down, then the next up. When we accomplish one layer; the next layer starts. We continue to go through the process of life, over and over. I then was inspired to do another video blog. This Vlog referenced yesterday morning. As we were in the middle of our puppy crisis, we heard the garbage truck and remembered we did not take out the trash. I rushed outside hoping we were not too late, when I see our garbage man finding our trash can and emptying it in his truck. I was thankful that he took such good care of us. Later that evening I was cleaning my house and remembered to call their company and tell them how these men were so awesome. When we called, it was after hours, and our complement could not be conveyed.

I thought about the irony of this. When we do something for someone else, we expect a thank you; though sometimes we do not get one. It is not because we do not deserve a thank you, it just means it was 'after hours,' and the thank you could not be delivered. This also goes for "Sorry's." For a long time we may have been waiting for a sorry; though the sorry might not have been shown in physical form. Maybe there was embarrassment to say the, "I'm sorry." Maybe they lost your phone number and there is no way to tell you sorry. Maybe they thought they said sorry and they no longer feel they need to say it.

An example of this was when I was a teenager, I had a boyfriend. He and I broke up on bad terms. Years later I was at a bar, and he was there too. He came over to me and apologized for how he treated me (from the past.) This was an apology I had been waiting for, for a very long time. I never received that apology (then) but he was giving it now. Understand that you do receive what you are hoping for; it sometimes shows up in a way you may not recognize. It may come later; though it always comes.

People say sorry on many different levels.

Sometimes it is not the level you were hoping for. My message to everyone that I have hurt, "I am really sorry. Please accept my apology and move on into the bigger and greater you that you are." "Anyone who has not received my thank you, please know that you have all contributed in my life. You are miraculous. Because of you my life has only gotten better. You matter. You mattered then, and you matter now. Thank you for how you show up in our world."

Here is a thank you that I have not thanked. When I was younger, I had a girlfriend that told me I would do well at public speaking and uplifting others. At the time this was not my career path. Though that comment stuck with me and has brought me to where I am today. To this person, thank you for letting me know. Even though we do not talk now; I am still thankful for your kind words. You have helped design my life as of now. You contributed to me; you were and still are important.

As I was uploading all of these messages (my video blog's onto YouTube) I received a message of my own. Another puppy had died. Here again is our process. Here we were high on life, enjoying the beautiful thank yous and sorrys; we were receiving, and we are hit with grief. Life is full of ups and downs; this is our natural process. Good comes in, and so does sorrow. Sorrow is a natural part of life. Our second puppy has to experience death to make it back into the spirit world. Our puppy is not sad, just wanting us to enjoy each part of our existence. He wants us to know that life is good, and when it appears bad it is just life. We are to not engulf the grief, just feel it. We are to know the heart ache will also move on. We are to create more growth in our heart as the next steps are here.

I want to thank my puppies for finding me and asking me to be their mom for a little while. You really contributed to me and showed me many more reasons to be thankful in my life. I am happy that you chose me, you wanted to be with me. Thank you for choosing me to spend your last moments with. Thank you for loving me and letting me love you. Thank you for coming into my world. I am blessed by you.

Our afternoon continued. I was later at teacher conferences. The conferences were good. Both teachers said my children were above average academically. The skills they were learning were social. Dreana is incredibly smart. Her current growth is motivation. She is learning she has to do the things the teacher asks her to do, even if she does not want to. The teacher has been motivating her with a game. She connives Dreana into doing the things she does not want to do, as a joke. As Dreana does what is needed, the teacher says, "I knew you could do this; you were just pretending that you did not know how." In the end, both are happy.

Aidan's teacher adores him. She said he reminds her of herself. He is a very good leader, and he helps her teach the class. Though, at times, she has to remind him that she is the teacher.
She is capable of teaching the class.

Each of these qualities I notice in my children as well. It is amazing that each of their teachers benefit from what my children are learning. It is exciting when a lesson to be learned wants to be learned. The lesson shows itself in how my kids and their teachers found each other. I also noticed that both teachers kept complimenting me. They kept saying my two are so smart, and so good because we have a good family. This was a desire of mine to be noticed as this kind of family. We are getting noticed for our values. It was neat to see the validation.

Soon I was home from school. I relieved Brian so he could go back to work. I was able to hang with my kiddos and enjoy with them their day off. The afternoon came and went and soon it was time for our seventh class of our prosperity course. I drove to church feeling sad. I was processing all my feelings. The puppies brought a lot of stuff up from my past. These feelings were never dealt with. I was feeling all of those memories again. This time I forgave all of the 'bad' memories. I think I finally let them go.

The class began with our "Daily Word" for the week. This message was about Guidance. We have guidance all the time; all we have to do is let it in. As we are moving through something sad, we can receive guidance; we can receive help. All we have to do is ask for it. I can guarantee you that you have this guidance. You and I both have it; we all have it. If we would just listen. It is here; just ask and know you are worthy to know this love.

Testimonies were next. Our first testimony came from the woman whose daughter is experiencing cancer. Remember last week we prayer for the both of them. We prayed that they would remember how awesome they are, and that they can heal their fears. Our outcome from that prayer came from another woman who did not attend last week's class. She gave blood in honor of our patient. This story brought tears, tears for the kindness and act of love. It was also neat how the message of the patient came to her through our prayers, instead of her hearing about it in last week's class. Thank you to you all, for your continual awareness of all of our healing powers.

Continuing, our leader purchased a bottle of, "Prosperity spray" from the book store! He said it was four dollars instead of twelve (this week.) Funny what a play on words we can create! And you know how goofy the conversation was about this spray, that the spray can actually cause prosperity; the class was laughing away.

Though it is true; we have tools to help bring about our powers. When we can hold something, or believe in something, a lot of the time this is what helps us use our powers!

I was privileged to be sprayed with our, "Prosperity Spray!"

Another member, this week, did some tapping (EFT.) She was tapping away at fears she had about prosperity. As she finished up, in that exact moment, she received a phone call. Her phone call was telling her of a new real estate job! Blessings to her and her current growth!

Another lady during the week, was preparing to get money out of the ATM. This lady keeps money in a spot in her house, and when the money is out, she goes and gets more. This specific morning she really did not want to go to the ATM. She knew she was out of money, but decided to check anyway. She had forty dollars! Yeah, blessings to you!

Another woman in our class told us about a bone disease she had been experiencing for years. Because of this disease, it is not good for her to take certain medicines. This is an issue because there are other parts of her body which want the medicine. This has been a challenge with her. She has been trying to balance different medicines she can take. This week she went to her doctor, and he introduced her to a new holistic choice for medicine. This medicine actually cures her current ailment. She is finally being healed from years of pain. She said this is what her biggest goal of our prosperity class could offer. Blessings to her!

Our last testimony came from a woman. She confessed that she had been nervous about tithing. She recently retired and was on a limited budget; though she decided to trust and watch prosperity unfold. She said currently she was receiving new flooring for her house, and this next week, she was going to Costa Rica! Look what happens when we trust, not only are all of her bills covered; we also receive many gifts from life! Have fun, and enjoy the sun; be beautiful!

We then began the first half of our CD. Soon it was break, and again our leader came to ask my progress on the prison project. It is sweet to see this manifest. She also told me 'sorry' for telling of my project to the minister. She thought she was being non-confidential. I laughed and said that it was okay. She had held on to this all week. I was not bothered by it at all. When we hold onto grudges or grief's, a lot of the time the other party is not even affected by it. As we let go, we finally move forward!

Before we knew it break was over, and our CD began again. After the CD we had discussion. We talked about how important it was to forgive God. When we forgive, we can move forward. Some people were confused by this. Though here is our explanation. We are all God, and when we do not forgive ourselves for perceived mishaps; we do not move forward. If we do not move forward, we cannot inject the world in beautiful ways. When we do forgive ourselves, the world benefits.

The world is better when we know we are better. When we forgive, we know how great we are.

We soon were in our prayer circles. Our prayers were: that God would bring offers for a woman to speak at fertility clinics; speaking of miracles. We asked to live in the here and now, and complete mindfulness. We asked for financial abundance, and to live through our heart. Each of our goals were spoken by one member at a time. We decided to pray for each person's request and then to add those same requests to all of us.

The example is each of us asks to speak our truth. Each of us asks to live in the here and now; each of us asks for financial abundance. As we clear and accept these blessings in us, there is no need for them to show up as a lack in another member. I now receive for every one of us, our biggest and best intentions. I now draw them forward. Thank you God!

Thursday evening came and went.

Chapter 8
Letting the past go

Friday morning I woke up and had my morning. The kids and the two big pups were loaded in the car, and I drove to the location for the dogs' vet appointment. The agency lady was there, and asked how I was doing with the loss of the puppies. I told her I was sad; but moving through. She said that not only was Zeus going with his new mom after the appointment, Cisco also was being adopted Saturday morning. When I came back for 'pick-up,' I was only taking Cisco home. She also updated me with the sick puppies. They were doing fine, though they would be there for a few more days.

Later we were at the kids' school. The school was having a big Halloween carnival for the evening, and we were there to purchase the tickets. They also were having a book fair. Here we saw Dreana's Girl Scout leader. She had the, "Lady Bug girl book." We laughed and told her the story we experienced with the book.

The story of the, "Lady Bug Girl Book" consists of my dedications as I make intentions. I make large and small goals every day; the numerous small goals I make, and see come true, build my belief for the larger goals. One day when my daughter was little, I made an attention to see a girl with lady bugs pass my house. This was such a small goal, that it did not matter if it came true or not. Though the importance of these small goals is to watch them manifest. When they do, it teaches us what great manifestos we are! The reason for the small goals is that it is easy not to get attached to them. The more we are unattached, the faster they show up. By practicing daily little goals, our larger goals become easier to believe.

I made this attention in the morning, in the afternoon I was in the garage, and my daughter was in the house. She came running outside crying, saying a book had fallen 'out of nowhere' on her. I found out the book that 'fell' on her was the "Lady Bug Girl Book!"

I tell our Girl Scout leader this story, and she is looking at me in amazement. I am surprised by this. I then continue on and tell her I make these small intentions all the time. I receive free gas, clothes, food all the time! She then asks how I do this. I explained I first learned it from, "The Secret." In the beginning it was all about stuff. As I have grown, it has taught me how to love myself, and know my worth in the things I desire. This woman is almost in tears as I am telling her my stories. She then asks me if I can speak to the Girl Scout girls about this. I said I would.

This conversation has stuck with me all day. I was surprised she did not know the principals I was talking about.

When I speak this truth, I usually do not receive such a bewildered look. Most people say, "That positive thinking stuff." This gets annoying because I want people to really understand their power. When they brush it off, they cannot experience this love, this magic. When this woman reacted the way she did, it threw me off. She received it so well.

I also thought about how ironic it all was. Here I am intending to speak to millions about this awesome power, and my first gig comes from a normal, day-to-day conversation. We really are connected. How amazing it is that all of life comes to us. This happens when we know what are goals are; when they are easy to identify. I may have by-passed this opportunity if I did not recognize it as my goal. I feel blessed.

Later in the evening we headed to school, all dressed up in our costumes. There were lots of games and fun. An hour into the carnival I left to go pick up the big dogs from the vet, and the kids and Brian continued their fun. As I was loading up Cisco and Zeus, the agency lady told me one of the puppies (from last week,) had died of dehydration. This was the long awaited diagnosis. This really hit. Here I am, the one in charge of them, and the puppies die from something basic. I thought about this a lot over the weekend. In our lives we move on with our bigger and better; at times we forget about the basics.

There also was a lot of guilt. I had thoughts of how bad I am, and what I should have done better. I had to keep reminding myself to watch my feelings, and not get wrapped up in them. This is how depression begins; it happens when we take our current thoughts as forever truth. I am allowed to feel sad or guilty, though these feelings should not consume the rest of my life. As I was consciously in charge, I allowed some old stuff to come up, and was able to let it go. A lot of my hate and sadness from the past got to come up. I forgave it. This is the benefit in watching; we can use our emotions as tools, to relieve old heart-aches.

Another thing I evaluated was the puppies may have been healed from the disease they came with. What if the puppies, from being around me and my family, were healed, and this is why they could only be diagnosed with dehydration. The vet assumed because of all of their drastic symptoms, that it had to be the puppy disease Parvo; though when they were tested, the test came back negative. The doctors were in shock. They looked at me and said, "I do not know then; this has to be wrong, we are going to test them again later in the day." What if they had this disease and the disease was healed; and the only diagnosis the vet could come up with was dehydration? I do not know.

What I do know is that as hard as this situation was, it was also good. There is good in each bad. I experienced death, and learned to be okay with it.

I experienced the blessing in being with those puppies as they transitioned. I experienced release. I get to know they are no longer in their sick bodies. I get to feel peace. Ups and downs, yes, though also peace.

Our evening was over.

....

Saturday morning was here and I enjoyed my morning to myself. I spent my last hours with the big pups before they were to be adopted. Soon I was off to the location; I was fifteen minutes late. The agency lady called to tell me their new owners were waiting, and my 'lateness' was noticed! Good for them, they were wanted.

After I unloaded the big guys, I noticed my puppies were back! They were picked up from Denver that morning, and looked healthy and happy. The week that I had had them, they were very skittish. This morning they were playing with all the dogs and looked eager to be adopted!

We had a good time at the puppy fair. My little ones did not get adopted, but lots of other pups found new homes. There also was another agency there that had a lot of older dogs. An older German lady comes by us, and she and I got to talking. All we had were puppies, so I helped her pick out an older dog from the other agency. This experience was really cool. Helping her made me feel really good. I was of service to an agency that wasn't even mine. As we help others we get that awesome feeling; and that awesome feeling continues into our days!

On my way home I evaluated my week and how cranky I had been. I had a lot of dense emotions with the puppies, and a lot of old stuff that had cleared. Again, this was the half way mark with our class. Logically, it made since that my feelings were downers. When I was home with my two healthy pups, everyone could see my mood had shifted! I was happy to see them. I was happy to see them live. They brought hope as they were an example of someone 'making it.'

In the evening we played with the pups and my dogs. We also watched a kid's movie that showed the power of following your dreams. It showed the power of listening to your higher self, as here is where all your answers are. I love kid's movies; they bring truth and knowledge to a population that understands it. When I was a kid I watched these movies and wished life was like this. I was told over and over that it was just a movie. Now as I revert my life back to magic, I see those movies were true all along. I tell my kids to believe, as the movies do.

Life is magic, magic is real; you are supposed to accomplish your dreams, and the answers are always within you. You are love.

....

Sunday morning I woke up and enjoyed my morning. My mornings have been great lately. Though I was very frustrated when everyone else started getting up. I was frustrated with the bills. We had to start doing these and I did not know where to start. I was frustrated that my husband slept-in all morning. I was frustrated that it appeared I was supposed to be frustrated all by myself.

We soon were ready for church. I was trying to shake my vibration, but it was sticking. We get to Sunday school. The instructor stares at my daughter as she is welcomed into class. I snapped, and told him she is uncomfortable around him because he stares at her a lot. I knew there was some truth to my comment, though I seemed to spit it out at him. He quickly told her she could go with a different teacher.

Church was really good. The minister said, "Receiving is just as important as giving." She told a story of a woman who currently was training to be a minister. She had gone far in her training, and felt like she could not go any further. She was out of money and wanted to drop out. She called the minister and explained her situation. Our minister asked her to hold off for 24 hours, she was going to see if a miracle could be created. What ended up happening was our minister sent a mass-email asking for donations. Within 24 hours, fifteen hundred dollars was collected. This allowed the woman to continue her education!

Our minister also told another story. This weekend she received a knock on her door, as a man was excited to give a donation. He donated a hundred dollar bill; he also told his story. Years earlier he felt guided to quit his job; there was something more for him, though he did not know what the 'something' was. This decision was hard because it was during Christmas, and at the time he had young children. Though he knew it was the right decision. What happened next was our guy received a phone call from someone in his community. The lady asked him to come over with his kids, so his kids can share their awesome energy with her dying mother. Our guy agreed. When the visit was over, our guy received a hundred dollar bill from this lady. She wanted to donate money to him to ensure he was able to have a nice Christmas with his children. She knew of his financial struggles, and wanted to help. Since this day his life prospered and a new job, which he loves, was brought into his life. Every year since he gives a hundred dollar bill to someone he knows will benefit. He has continued this practice for years. When we are in need, and when we see our need taken care of, it becomes easy to be a part of the givers. Such an amazing story! This vibration was our entire subject of Sunday morning. Now you get to feel it too.

Sunday morning was great. After the service my mood dropped again.

What a roller coaster we are in! On the way home I again was trying to raise my vibration. I kept asking over and over for guidance in rising what it was I was feeling.

I began to try to involve the family. I asked them all to tell a story; hoping the story would bounce me a little. Each person in the car refused. They were starting to feel my grumpiness. At that exact moment my girlfriend called, and the first thing out of her mouth was, "Tell me a story." She was feeling down, and was hoping I could lift her with some conversation. I thought it was funny that we were feeling the same vibration, and we used the exact, same words! I talked with her for a minute. I realized I was not alone in my vibration. This helped lift me. I then had the idea to go out to eat with the kids. Eventually we all agreed on Subway. We would have a picnic at the dog park with all the dogs! As this plan began to unfold, I found myself much happier!

We had a lot of fun at the dog park. I talked with a lady that was also there with her dogs. It was amazing because she knew and wanted to talk about how beautiful life was. She wanted to talk about how we create our realities! It is such a blessing to talk with someone who 'gets it!' She told me her whole life was guided, and she lived each moment by what felt right. Years earlier she lived in one state, and her son and his family lived in another. One day she had received a call from them, asking her to move states to be their new nanny. Our lady took the steps to sell her house, and moved near her son. All of this cost her twenty thousand dollars. At the time she was irritated. Six months later her son unexpectedly died. She said the whole ironic move was because her and her son knew, on some level, the future events were to happen. She said if someone would have told her it would cost twenty thousand dollars to spend the last six months of her son's life with him; she would have done it in a heartbeat. In hindsight, the money spent was the best money she has ever spent. In hindsight, it always makes since. In the moment if it feels right, go with it. Later the pieces unravel themselves.

Sunday night came and went; a very happy vibration filled our dreams. We are blessed; we just have to remind ourselves at times.

....

Monday morning was here. I had my morning, and then helped the kiddos get off to school. Soon it was 9:30 A.M. and I went to pick up the new puppies. As I was gathering all the new love, I talked with the agency lady. She was stressed, and feeling overwhelmed. She no longer wanted to be the only person in charge of the puppies in Colorado Springs. She needed help. She was running around town all week, meeting new foster parents, and also taking in phone calls.

She also was the one responsible for getting the dogs to the veterinarian each week. She said it was all too much for one person.

I talked with her about, "The Secret." I explained she was attracting all of this; we all were attracting this. She said over and over, in our conversation, that there was not enough time; lots of people are not committing like they said they would. I asked her to watch the movie, "The Secret." I told her my current intention was to bring in more help, because this agency excites me so much. I am doing my best to not get overwhelmed. I trust all the pieces are coming together. I have been intending to bring this organization into something really large; where we can save a lot of dogs. I knew I did not have these answers of how to grow this organization; though I did know how to intend it, and to trust it. I was able to leave her with peace and hope.

When I was later home I noticed she texted me. She was telling me thank you for my kind words. She also said, since then, she received a whole bunch of new applications from people wanting to help! All we have to do is relax, and trust, and miraculously it all starts happening. I also received a call from one of the new adoptive moms (for the puppies.) She wanted to help with fundraisers, to help money for the pups! Later that evening the agency lady called to tell us about all the new foster homes we were attracting. We also talked about a lot of ideas to fundraise money for the organization. It is cool to see the ideas coming together! I then emailed our minister, and asked them to help with any donations. The second part of my email addressed our idea about prison ministry; I asked to set up an appointment with her to gather her input. The evening felt like a success. Soon we were off to bed

....

Tuesday morning was here, and I felt goofy from the evening prior. I was in such a high when I sent my emails, and when I was listening to the agency lady with her ideas of fundraising. And today I felt like I do when I drink too much, and say goofy things and later regret. I was evaluating these feelings. I am not sure if they are good or bad. Should I have not discussed ideas when I was in such a high vibration; or was it my ego that currently was telling me our ideas were bad? I am not sure, though I am intending to find our answer.

The day went good. Soon it was time for everyone to come home from school and work. Brian told me that one of our renters was not moving out. We had to pay a five hundred dollar eviction fee to get them out. Now I was mad. I felt taken advantage of and hurt. I called my girlfriend and yelled and screamed. She just listened. I was thankful for that. After my fit I was telling her about my bills.

Here is a synopsis of the last few months, again.

This is what I reminded her of, as if she didn't already know. Years ago I used to do the bills, and I knew what was coming in and out. We always had enough, but never much extra. Eventually I got so mad, not wanting to live this average life anymore. I decided to go for my dreams, and hope the finances worked out. I gave the bills to Brian and told him it was his turn! I went to Tennessee, and while I was there, all the bills got paid, as well as monthly gas trips back and forth to Tennessee. Christmas got paid, as well as all the mess-ups with the rentals. (This is when all of that started.) They all got paid. I have no clue how, the same amount of money was coming in and more was going out; it all got paid for.

Now, here in Colorado the rentals are really bad; though we are still managing. The money is getting less and less, and we have some large bills to pay back because of all our borrowing to make this work. Seven weeks ago, amongst the mess, I decided to tithe. So amongst the financial mess, I am tithing one thousand and more a month. Where is all of this money coming from? I do not know; though it is all working out. This is God stretching our budget.

Last month I took over the bills from Brian. Where I found this courage, I do not know? I am sure God has been helping me. I had not looked at those bills in years, and now I am ready to clear all of my fears and find some solutions. I gathered all of the bills and collected the new ones. It was a large mess. We spent most of our time gathering and going through the mail to find what was what. I then was very confused not knowing what was auto-pay, what was paid, and what needed to be paid. The first month was a big ole mess. We also spent this time taking any bills off auto pay we could find. And of course, our debt consolidation company took all of our credit card bills; this lessoned the load a little. We made a little progress last month, though we still had a long road ahead of us.

I was still very overwhelmed by it, so I only paid a few, the few I could figure out. I just kept asking for help from God, as we go through this and to help me see. I let the money collect in the bank account knowing that some stuff was not being paid, I had no clue what bills those were. I did feel comfortable knowing that there was money in the bank account though; there was some safety to that. Even know there was money, because I was not paying the bills, there still was the safety of the collected money. There was money to pay my tithing check each week. This felt amazing.

Each day of this month that passed, I had thoughts of our bills; I was scared and nervous. Soon the 28th was here, and I knew the month was almost over. I was getting really scared.

Brian came home for lunch as we had a date to finally do the bills. This time around the mail was not a mess. It actually was a stack of really pretty envelopes. There was organization to it all. The growth from last month to this month is something to be proud of. It is more peaceful, as we now are feeling comfortable looking at the mail.

All I could do was go one step at a time. I kept asking for guidance as we sat down. I checked the bank balance first. Second, I made sure all the checks (written in the past) were cleared. This was a decision I had been feeling for a while. As everything got messed up, we were taking care of everyone else. We stopped taking care of us; this time our Colorado bills were high on the priority list. I then separated all the mail into categories. Here was my checklist of importance. One: God got His money. Two: all Colorado bills got paid. The rest of the money was split up from all bills from Wisconsin.

All the checks for Church cleared. I wrote out the checks for our Colorado bills. And two of the mortgages were auto pay which already came out. Next was a credit card bill. This bill was not included with the debt consolidation company because it was a credit card from a credit union. The debt consolidation company said that if this one was included, the bank could mess with my car payments. I was happy with that. At the level I am at, only one credit card bill helps!

I paid that credit card bill. From the beginning of each month we also transfer fifteen hundred dollars from our Wisconsin bank to our Colorado bank. This covered our rent and our food. So again, this is taking care of us before we take care of our renters. After all of those bills were paid, I checked the amount left over, and I started deciding which bills to pay next. Side note: we did this on the 28th, for some reason all of the due dates were after that date. We lucked out. God had our back.

The bills left were a few water bills that renters never paid. We had two mortgages we had to pay. We still had to pay our mortgage to our grandfather (this months and some back payments) and we have a five hundred dollar tax bill to pay for 'my grandfather's' property. We also had an old electricity bill to pay for the month we stayed in Wisconsin this summer. We also have to pay Brian's mom back for the three thousand she borrowed us. And we have a handy man fee we have to pay from the past. Also we have the handy man fee we have to pay to the rental company. So as you can see, there was a lot to choose from.

Also we never took one of our credit cards off of auto pay. This money was taken out of our account instead of being consolidated with the other company. Lessoned learned, the next time we pay bills that amount will be added to our budget.

What we ended up paying was all of the old water bills from the renters. We paid one mortgage. We paid our old electricity bill also. We have two hundred and fifty left in this account. What was not paid was the fourth mortgage, my grandfather, the rental company bill, the money to Brian's mom and the tax bill. This may seem bad; but it feels better. I only have these bills left! We are making progress. Compared to last month, there is progress.

We also received a seven hundred dollar check in the mail. This money came from Brian's work from years ago! So far God is hooking us up. I do feel peaceful; we are making it! Even though we still have bills out there; I am learning to trust more and more, that God also knows and chooses to help. He is helping us; this feels good.

After this explanation to my girlfriend, I felt good and started to feel taken care of. I realized that we have not been receiving rent from these properties so far, and look at us stay taken care of. So if we did not receive money from them this month, we were going to be okay. I also realized that now, I only have a few bills to look at. I know the forth mortgage will get paid on Friday. I at least know this! It is not mixed in a pile of bills. I can see it now. Also the water bills, and old electricity bills, will not need to be paid next month (because we paid them this month.) The money for next month can go toward other stuff. Here is hope. I felt better as I talked with her. We were being taken care of. It is all manageable.

I felt a little less hate with the renters I had to evict. I still felt mad that they were getting a free ride; but not as mad. I felt what they were doing was wrong. They were a sucker punch in my belly. This sucks, though God is helping hug us, as we sit with our wound.

I later went to the gym. I needed to run. I ran a lot, and hard at the gym. When I was leaving I had an awesome thought. I realized (again) that I am taken care of. Extra money would only help us pay off our debts; the monthly payments are currently manageable. With more money our life style wouldn't really change. We would spend the same amount of money; we just would not have balances to pay back. We were fine. Then I realized it was great to not need money; but I wanted it! I asked God if He would let me have the money I wanted. I really did not need it, but I wanted it. It was my goal; I wanted to make money too. Then I asked myself what kind of money I wanted to make. I thought about when I worked at the YMCA, (years ago) there I made seven dollars an hour. Nope, I did not want that. Then I thought about Brian's pay; that was good, but I wanted more. Then I thought about my goal of forty thousand per month. Yes, this is what I wanted.

I thought about that for a while. Again forty thousand a month was not what I needed. What I have is plenty. Our life style would still be the same. We don't need more money. And all of our (desired) travels just make it into our budget anyway. A new car just makes it into the budget. Really what we have going on is plenty; anything more we always manage. More money would take the balance of the debt away. We do not need forty thousand per month; though I realized I wanted it. Just like when you go shoe shopping; you do not need a new pair of shoes, you just want them. I was so excited to have this realization. I do not know if this is closer to the right answer; but I do know that this is a different thought than I am used to. It was a break through, and now I get to see it unfold.

After the gym I went to the agency lady's house to pick up another puppy. A foster mom had taken the dog in, and then did not want him anymore. I told her I would go pick up the puppy, and take him home. This was another excuse to be by myself, instead of going home. This evening I needed to get away, and work through my emotions.

As I was driving to her house, I asked myself if I had forty thousand dollars a month, would I still be volunteering with the puppies. The answer was yes; I know what I am doing, I want to be doing. Then I realized something new. If I were making forty thousand per month now; I would still be irritated when I was taken advantage of. I am willing to do my part with the puppies, but I cannot be the only one. Again this goes to the agency lady. It is not our responsibility to be doing foster home checks, and picking up dogs when people change their minds. This stuff makes me feel taken advantage of. And now, and when I have forty thousand a month, I do not want to be dealing with this. I am willing to clear all situations where I feel taken advantage of.

I then see a car with a license plate of 771, and then another one of 117. 7's are lucky numbers. Seeing them, I realize, I want to help with this organization; and I am willing to change so I do not attract people who take advantage of me. I am willing to change this now, so I am prepared when I have forty thousand dollars a month in my bank account.

I then went through another layer. I want to take care of the puppies, but I also want to be making money. And then I realized, the work I do is needed. I always do a good job with the work I do. Because I am working, it is inevitable I will get a paycheck. God is my boss. As I work for God, He pays me. This answer felt pretty good. It made me feel like God was paying me. I asked God for a raise. My belief is getting stronger.

Then came another layer; I was lost. All I kept seeing was my gas tank getting smaller and smaller. I again was frustrated. I then realized this was my opportunity to not be taken advantage of.

I needed to tell the agency lady's husband that I wanted to be reimbursed for the gas I used, for the home visits and all of the running around I did for the dogs. They were getting paid, and I was doing some of their work; I should get reimbursed also.

I get our puppy, and I asked about the gas money. He agreed and told me he would have fifty dollars for me at the next puppy fair. I take home the new dog, Meatball. The reason he was given back was because he was naughty. I figured his naughtiness could have come from his goofy name. I changed his name to George. George is a sophisticated name.

Brian and I later talked. I told him about my realizations throughout the evening. He reminded me that when I am clear, I always attract people who want to help. I do not attract people who want to take advantage of people. When my vibrations, my moods, are high, I attract the 'right' people. He encouraged me to continue to think forward, and to keep clearing my thoughts.

Soon we were all asleep.

Wednesday morning was here. I had decided that I needed to start working out again. I gained five pounds from the month prior. Beyond the weight gain, I also know a work out helps me center. It gives me routine each day to take on the new.

Still, I did not work out. I will get to it eventually. The morning was peaceful. I think a lot of it was due to my run the night before. I saw an ad on craigslist. The ad was for a woman with three kiddos. They all went to my kids' school! One was in preschool, and needed me to take them to and from, two days a week. The rest of the time, three full days and two half days, were to be spent with me. She also had two older kids. She needed me to pick them up from school, and have them stay with me until five. This job was Monday through Friday.

This is goofy because I wanted babies; though her ad intrigued me. With her I get a little one three days a week. I get a break the other two days. This way I can still have time to myself. Also between three and five, we do homework. Why not add a few more study partners! It would be different if she wanted me to watch her kiddos from five P.M. to ten P.M. This works.

It is a win-win for all parties. I told her I would charge two hundred a week. This amount seemed less than I should, or more than I should; I couldn't tell. So really, it ended up being right in the middle. It seemed like a perfect price! This family seems like a great fit.

Brian offered to take the kids to school today. This was a nice break. I had extra energy to clean up the kitchen. Also, all the little puppies, all six of them; smelled.

I had extra time to scrub their little bodies. They all, then, took a nap and thirty minutes later, peed in their kennel! They all smell again!

I later spent time writing. Soon it was time to go to a home check for a new foster parent. The meeting with him was great. I laid everything out. I said we love foster parents, but he has to commit. I said if he was going to change his mind in a day; I would prefer he change his mind now! He looked hurt; I had to explain our run-around to him. I told him that we love foster parents, though our luck has not been great lately. He was a sweet-heart and completely understood. The original goal was for him to take in one or two older dogs that would be coming on Friday. As he talked, I understood his interest a lot more. He wanted a puppy to add to his family, and his family dog. George was a perfect fit. I called Brian, and had him drop off George. I called the agency lady and told her I would be taking the other two, if they did not have homes.

After, I received a call from the lady who was in charge of the agency lady. We will call her June. June is in charge of the whole agency. Our agency lady, we will call her Melinda, is a division of June. Because Melinda was going to be out of town, she designated me as the one in charge. This is why June was calling me. June was very chaotic on the phone. Her phone kept going in and out of reception, and she also had a strong English accent. She rambled on, without any real sequence to her story. Eventually, she told me about all the dogs coming in to Colorado Springs. Then she told me some dogs she was to pick up today, were not being dropped off. She decided to go to another pound and get other dogs. So the whole schedule changed. She was bringing the same amount of dogs back, but not the original ones she was supposed to. She then starts telling me all the dogs' names, as if I know them. Then she tells me all the foster families; as if I know them. I attempted to tell her, I had no clue what she was talking about, though she just kept talking! She then repeated the dogs were coming tomorrow. Tomorrow is Halloween. I tried to explain to her that they were not, they were coming on Friday. She was still confused. She eventually said she would figure everything out, and call me this evening.

After her phone call I talked with my friend. She had called earlier as I was walking out the door. I was telling her about earlier, when I was leaving for the home-check, there was a dog pound van outside my house. They were talking with a neighbor, who appeared to just be walking by. The neighbor was telling the pound lady about a barking dog he was concerned with. As I saw this, my heart started to pump. I thought I was in trouble with all my dogs. I walked over to the two of them and asked if they needed help with a lost dog.

I was hoping by me approaching them that they would tell me why they were here. No such luck, they just looked at me funny, and wondered why I involved myself in their conversation. The whole way to the home-check my heart was pumping incredibly fast. My thoughts were on the pound. As I told my friend this, she says, "Oh that's past life stuff." We did not go any further into it. Though I am still very curious why that happened.

We then talked about her synchronistic day. A few days ago, she was feeling down and called me to get her in a better mood. She told me she made an intention to receive a bouquet of flowers. She wanted to feel loved. She, at the time, did not see anyway of how this would manifest. Currently she is going through a divorce, and she doesn't have a boyfriend. She asked me if I thought it was possible for her to receive her intention. She asked if her request was too large. I told her it was on its way. We always receive one-hundred percent of our intentions, this or something much larger. Therefore her flowers had to be on the way. When we talked it was later in the day, all she could see was that the hours were dwindling away; and the chance of her flowers coming, seemed limited. I reminded her that the evening was not over yet. I could feel her intention, and knew it was on the way; though I had a feeling she was receiving it in the next few days. I secretly waited for that story to unfold, and hoped it would soon.

Now in her current phone call, excitement was pouring out as she told me how she received her flowers! The story goes like this, the evening she requested the flowers, they did not show up. The next day her sister called. My friend called her back, and the sister could not talk. One of those synchronistic weird things going on! They finally got to talk the next day; that next day is today. The reason they didn't talk the other day was because it was not important, there just needed to be a reason for them to connect today. The sister called and said she received flowers on her car windshield with a note. The note said, "Sorry for getting these to you a day late, the flowers are for you, and I hope I have found you. If this is the wrong person, please enjoy them anyway." The note was signed with an unreadable signature.

The sister was telling her story. As my girlfriend was listening she was not 'getting it.' The conversation continued with more details, the flowers received were only a single red rose and a single white rose. Now the light bulbs in my girlfriend's head went off! Yesterday, the day the roses were received, was the anniversary of my girlfriend's almost X-husband's mom's death. Every year my girlfriend would give one red, and one white rose to her husband in remembrance of his mom.

Of all the flowers to be ironically placed on a windshield, it was a single red, and a single white rose. And the flowers had to be late because they had to come on the day of the anniversary. The note was legible, though the signature was not! You can believe what you want; though my assumption is that those flowers manifested themselves out of the spirit world, and into our physical one. Miracles happen all the time!

The reason they showed up in Wisconsin, (where her sister lives) instead of Tennessee (Where my girlfriend lives) is because her sister had to witness the miracle as well. This helps her see how significant magic is. Also the week prior, my girlfriend's (almost X) husband visited Wisconsin. These flowers had to show up in the place that needed the most growth. This way all parties grow; we are all connected.

As the afternoon passed, it was time for the kiddos. They had an early release from school. I picked up Dreana. Aidan did not meet me after class. I couldn't find him; I hoped he would soon show up at home. I was alone with Dreana, and we did her homework. I started to get worried about Aidan. I texted his friend's mom asking if he was there. At that moment, Aidan comes walking in. He had desserts from his friend's mom. I sat him down and said, "I had been worried, and that was not really nice to make me go through." He promised to not do it again.

He later finished up his homework, and the kids and I agreed to carve our pumpkins later in the evening. Both of them wanted to go play with their friends. I spent the next little bit of time talking on the phone. My girlfriend and I only had a few minutes, all day, to talk each time we called each other. I was hoping to finally be able to have a whole conversation sooner than later.

I call and she tells me she only has twenty minutes! My goodness, here is our time limit again. I try to get her to tell me all of the stories of the day, and she doesn't want to tell me! She uses her limited time to tell me over and over, "It was just a very synchronistic day." She then asks me if I want to talk; then there was a lot of silence. Soon I look down and notice my phone is on mute. I had been holding this phone the entire time; how did that happen? I tell her what is going on, and she starts laughing. Earlier in the day she was talking with her girlfriend, and her friend's phone also went on mute.

As she is telling me all this, her other girlfriend beeps in. Usually we ignore when this happens, though instead she decides to answer it. Her girlfriend called to tell her she was in a make-up store. In this store she saw some boots. She was calling to see which ones (there were two sets) to buy. Question one: why are there boots for sale in a make-up store?

Question two: How is my girlfriend going to help her with a shoe purchase, if she is not even there? Goofy story, right, just wait it all connects!

Both these girls have been friends for a long time. My friend has always had this thing with boots. She eventually decided to donate all of her boots when she lived in Wisconsin. One day she moved to Tennessee, and now did not have any boots in the big ole cowboy city! Since then she has been intending some boots! The story continues that a while back, the two girls got into an argument and stopped talking for a while. This was the same time as my friend's birthday. For this (past) birthday, they discussed a good gift would be boots. The gift never came because of their argument.

Now years later, during this awesome day, the conversation between me and my friend was interrupted with talk of boots. There were two sets to choose from; her friend wanted my friend's opinion. My friend pipes up with, "What size are the two pairs." The girl lets her know the sizes are nine and ten. My friend says, "The 10's are mine, you are supposed to buy the tens for me!" (Later in the evening my friend told me she received the boots as a belated birthday gift!)

I was off the phone with her moments later. Now my phone beeps with a new text message. The text message said, "I think you have the wrong number. I'm just fostering Berlin." I had no clue who this text message was from, though I thought it was probably someone with the dog agency. I checked my phone history and this was the first text message I ever received from this person. I thought they were probably texting Melinda, though ironically replied to my number. But they could not reply to my number because they never had it. I knew this was not that important, just funny, how they had the ability to reply to me. I called my friend again, hoping to get a hold of her for a minute; knowing she was getting ready to take a shower.

She picks up my call! She was about to get in the shower, and realized she had no shampoo. She left the bathroom to go get shampoo from her son's bathroom. This is the only reason she was around the phone when I called. Funny and ironic huh! Then when I was telling her about the text, she thought I said the name Lynn, not Berlin. Apparently, Lynn is someone in her life that relates to this whole crazy day!

Continuing on with our evening, here is another story. In the, "Attracting Abundance" online group, there was a guy who did the 28 day challenge presented in, "The Magic" by Rhonda Byrnes. He documented each day and all his emotions as he went through the practice. His story was amazing.

In the beginning of his journey he walked away from a movie project he created; he handed it over to the director. This was hard for him, though he knew he no longer enjoyed where the film was going. At the end of the 28 days, he had attracted different people and began a new project; this time a project he enjoyed! It takes a lot of courage to quit; to leave everything behind and instead 'be empty' as 'the new' comes in. A lot of the time we hold on to 'the old' because at least we have something. Life is not meant to be lived with something; it is meant to be the best. We have to let go if we want to grow into the best.

Later, I realized a party I was invited to, was this evening. I had forgotten about it. I was not prepared for that party. I wanted to rush and go because it was a kids' Halloween party; instead I had to stop myself, and follow my heart. I only wanted to go to the party because the kids would enjoy it. If I would have gone, I would have felt drained. My heart told me to take a break. Decisions like these are hard; soon we see their benefit. We instead took the time to carve the belated pumpkins. We ate dinner, and soon the kids were off to bed.

Brian went to go get the mail. According to the kids, it was, "Devil's night." This meant the teenagers in the neighborhood play pranks on all the houses, the day before Halloween. Aidan made sure our freshly carved pumpkins stayed in the house for the evening; and Brian protected our mail. One of the letters from the mail came with a five dollar bill, as a payment for Brian doing a survey! This was a blessing; money in the mail, how much better does that get!

Here is something better, he told me he checked his LES (his pay stub) for the first of the month and noticed, the Army is still not paying us for the extra money we are to receive for living in Colorado verses Wisconsin. He had called the finance department and they said he would be receiving the extra by the fifteenth of next month. That extra is 350 dollars a month! He also told me that he is at 16 years of service now, and this also receives extra pay. This pay comes next month as well! More money to us, yea! Money is everywhere we just have to let it in!

Some more points from the evening. My dog Chevy has been sick all day. My eyes are wide open, as I experienced last week with the sick puppies. I am positive he will feel better in a day or two; though I felt for him today. I wondered why he was sick. Was this represented in me? He is frustrated with all the new dogs; I think his body is finally trying to accept that there is going to be new dogs for a while. At first he was mad and put up a fit; though I think now he is starting to accept it. And maybe his body is doing some releasing, to finally find its acceptance. This relates to me also. I have been frustrated lately; I have to do some releasing to finally accept the new.

Another point, today we all made plans to trick or treat with Aidan's friend's family; the mom suggested we go tailgating in their truck. This was cool because we always had Halloween as a tradition, with a group of friends from Wisconsin. We would always tailgate on the back of their tractor for extra fun! I was excited to be getting our tradition back. We could not trick or treat with our Wisconsin friends anymore, but we could with our new Colorado friends.

Yet, another reflection from the evening; Aidan is receiving an award on Friday. We do not know what it is for, though he is receiving a Renaissance award at school, during an assembly. The whole family was invited to watch his success. This is cool. This is something really exciting to look forward to. I am impressed with my kids and also their school. This school has offered many blessings for our family; if I wanted I could spend an entire day writing thank you after thank you to them!

Later in the evening my girlfriend called back. She went to a networking seminar, and was hoping to connect with people after. She actually was hoping for a 'night and shining armor' to find her, and confess his love. It did not happen; though she still had the entire evening to herself. Instead of going home, she went to a café and had dinner. After a while she was feeling lonely, and wanted to know if I could be with her via text message, while she sat. We talked for a little bit, and then my phone sent me a message saying I was sending too many text messages. I thought this was funny. I have an unlimited text messaging plan. God is funny. He wanted her to date herself for the evening. She was her date, not I.

Those stories end our Wednesday night. Good night to you all!

Thursday morning, Halloween 2013 is here. I had my morning to myself. I was a tad grumpy. I was not too grumpy, but I knew my vibration could be higher. I had coffee. I let the puppies out. I fed them. I cleaned up after them. I woke up the kids. I made lunches. It was just one of those days; I was feeling drained, but kept chugging along. When I am this way, it is easy to not care; I become numb. I was not caring that the kiddos were loud; I just heard them. I did not care if Brian had a problem with it; I just asked him to take the kids to school. I did not care that there was laundry to fold; it was just there.

After the kids were in the truck; Brian comes back in the house to tell me my car was spray painted. Now I am getting frustrated. I am not frustrated at the teenagers (from Devil's night.) They were just having fun. I am mad that I have to do more work, to clean off the spray paint. Seriously! I am really not mad at the kids, I am mad at God! Seriously, I am drained.

Why do I also get this extra project? Uggghhhh! Though I also understand that the vibration I am in, only attracts other things in this vibration. So I 'get it.' But I am still mad that this is how it works. As I am mad, I am doing my best to release being mad, so I can clean my car and do the laundry. I am releasing this mad, so I get my awesome creative energy back. I want to enjoy Halloween. Here is a great lesson. Being mad sucks. Though even at the toughest times, the only way to get out is to bring ourselves into joy or neutral. When you're mad, joy is so far away, it seems unfair. When you are down, you need someone to pick you up; but no one will. This is a law in life. You have to pull yourself out. Anyone who hangs out with you in this current vibration is not a savior; they are in the same vibration as you, because this is law. Do not trust the outside and think they are helping you. They are keeping you stuck. Know this and work with it; you are your own savior. This process will only take a little while, you can do this, and I can do this. This too shall pass.

A little love note your way. As we write all of this, my little puppies are getting bigger! Moments ago, they climbed the stairs all by themselves! Yesterday this was impossible. There is always joy and light in the darkest of days.

Here is another note of, "I am pushing through this, like it or not!" Yes I know pushing is not the correct vibration. I am intending, my pushing, to be motivational. I have edited 37 pages so far of our book; I am going to edit all the way to at least page fifty! Fifty is what we need to submit to an agent. I am doing this; I am going to use this frustrated, mad energy for the good! I am moving forward.

Here we are, a half hour later; I edited one whole page. I received a phone call from my husband. The rental company called and left a message saying we need to talk. We have not returned their call yet, though my husband has some pretty good guesses of what they want to talk about. They did some work for us, and we owe them money. We have a renter that is not moving out. We have one of our properties that is currently trashed, and they need to know what to do with it.

I do not know what to do. My belly is crying. I took a shower, begging God to help me. The only thing I came up with is to write all of this down.

I am hoping to release some frustration, and start trusting in the miracle I need. I am trusting God knows what I should do. I forgive me. I forgive me for having hateful thoughts towards my renters. I forgive me for getting so mad. I forgive me for not seeing how good I am, and understanding that God wants to take care of me. I forgive me for the decisions I have made that have brought me into failure. I forgive me for failing.

I forgive me for feeling like a failure. I forgive me for holding on so long, and focusing 'there' instead of asking and trusting for help. I forgive me for having fear of asking for help. I was so concerned I had to do this all myself, because I did not want anyone to fail along with me. I forgive letting myself fail, because I did not want someone else to fail. I let my renter take advantage of me for so long, because I believed in him; I believed he would pay me back. I wanted him to know the only thing he had to focus on was success. I took his burdens of paying me, off of him and onto me. And now I feel left out and overwhelmed. I forgive me for doing that. I forgive me for making the 'wrong' decision. I forgive me for being in this whole mess. I am sorry I got us here. I forgive me for not knowing what to do. I forgive me for not having the answers. I forgive me for being so vulnerable right now. I am supposed to be the smart one, the adult, the wise one; and I do not know what to do. I feel like giving up. I forgive me for this vulnerability. I forgive me for not letting go earlier. I forgive me for being weak.

As I was typing all of this, my friend called. I asked God to give me my decision, if I should sell my houses. I wanted the answer during her phone call. I was okay with either; I just wanted to know what the best decision was. During our phone call I was mad and frustrated. I explained everything to her that I could think of. As I calmed down I realized, it was my attachment to the properties I was afraid to give up. These properties were my memories; and now I was growing into something else. I was going through grief. As I learned this; I had direction. I knew it may be painful to let the properties go; though it was the right decision.

Soon it was time to get my kids. As I walked to the car I realized Brian cleaned off the graffiti. I was moving forward, a little sad, though moving forward.

We soon were getting ready for Halloween. Aidan was crabby and mouthy. I think he could feel the energy that went on during the day. We headed to his friend's house at 4:30. For an hour and a half there were very few houses that were giving out candy. The kids were also the only trick-o-treaters. I began to feel like we were in the twilight zone. I started to wonder if we had the wrong day! I also noticed the people giving out candy were rude. There was one guy who told me to be patient; or he threatened to shut his light off for the rest of the trick-o-treaters. I watched all of this, part of me wondered if this was Colorado people (maybe they were ruder than Wisconsin people) or if this was still my mood. I kept affirming all of this (bad vibration) was passing.

Soon there were more trick-o-treaters and lots more houses giving out candy!

My daughter became lazy and went in the car, while I took her bag and pretended I was five again. The boys and I were having a blast! We were having a lot of fun, though the boys began arguing. They both wanted to be the leader and kept racing to the door, and pushing each other out of the way. This perpetuated all evening. I again just watched this, affirming it all would soon get better.

The evening was ending, and we were at Aidan's friend's house to drop them off. The boys were in the back as they continued their aggression. Aidan's friend ended up falling out of the truck. This was the moment where we scream, "Enough is enough." We sat there for a minute making sure he was okay, and then we headed home and the kids went to bed. I was mad; Aidan's aggression could have really hurt his friend. I reminded him of his life purpose. It is to be a leader, and to also learn to accept and work with other leaders. His lessons are to learn to use his leadership skills with other leaders, and not be the only one. He has to trust others to lead, just as well as him. Each of our lessons may be hard to learn, they come up over and over, and eventually we will learn them. As we all calmed down, we reminded each other that we rocked and were of course, loved.

We had skipped our prosperity class this evening because of Halloween. Years ago I had learned this lesson; though it seems I am challenged with it each year. My two largest desires have always been and still are: my family and personal success. It is a dual battle. When I was in college, there was an exam that was scheduled on Halloween; my son was one. I decided to choose my exam, and asked a friend to go trick-o-treating with my boy. I did not like my decision. From then on, I made an intention that my kids will always come first for every holiday. I let our teacher know I would not be at class this week; she was disappointed. I said, "Sorry, my kids come first."

Our evening ended in dreams.

Chapter 9
Weeklong Journey with an Old Friend

Friday morning was here and it was hard to believe I decided to sell my properties the day before. I got the kids ready for school and was alone with my decision. I had decided to use my mom's realtor. This was a big decision. When I was a realtor it seemed my family did not support me. Then it seemed like they used me. They would have me prepare their listings, and drive them around town to find houses; and then they would call another realtor for the transaction. My heart was broken. And now, here I am deciding to let go of my properties. And I am using her realtor for the transaction. I knew this was the right thing to do. I also knew this would be painful to go through.

There I was at the kitchen table, and I called her, the realtor. I told her about two vacant properties, and asked her to run the numbers. She was very nice, and treated me respectfully. I needed this, it was hard to sell my properties, and it was hard to have another realtor do the selling. The rest of the afternoon came and went. Brian was coming home for lunch to help me with the bills. I decided to start them by myself. By the time he was home, they were done. As each layer of the bills had come to pass, they kept getting easier and easier.

We soon left for school because Aidan was receiving an award at the assembly! I really do love my kids' school. They are very involved as they inspire the young ones. They find value in rewarding them, and encouraging them to be the best they can be.

Soon we were home and the kids occupied themselves with friends. Brian and me talked for hours about how I was feeling. As I was selling the properties, a lot of old stuff was coming up. He listened to me as I screamed about everything. I was screaming about how unfair it was that I had to be the one to get my mom's realtor. How I had to be the one to sell my properties. How I paid all my bills and all my renters' bills, when they got off 'Scott free.' I was mad and hurt. I wanted it to all go away, all the hurt emotions and feelings. I wanted to finally let it go.

Before we knew it, it was eight o'clock at night. We packed up as a family and went to 'the location' to pick up more dogs. This was really cool to see. It was a chilly, dark night, though lots of people were there to help. As each person took their dogs, we were to pick up the rest. We ended up with two six-month old pups, and three tiny ones. The three little ones were coming to our house for the weekend until Melinda was back from a family funeral in Kansas. It was an adventurous night with all the new dogs. Soon everyone was asleep.

Saturday morning was here, it was very warm. I spent the morning getting all of the dogs outside. Brian was up and we continued to talk about the houses as well as all the dogs. We were going to be picking up another load (of dogs) that afternoon. I was expected to drive thirty minutes to get them; this made me irritated. What I wanted to do was ask for gas money, though was feeling afraid. I knew this was my stuff, and I knew asking for the money had to be done.

I get to the new location for the dog pick-up, and our transport is not there. I was getting really irritated now. If they were late, like they usually were, I could not just go home and come back. It was too far of a drive. Forty-five minutes later, someone else, not June, showed up. Now I am really irritated, because now I cannot ask June for the money. Three other couples take their dogs, and I am expecting to pick up my seven puppies. The lady tells me I am also picking up a six month old pit. I flip out. I tell her I am not taking the big dog, I have no more kennels. She told me to call June. I yell at June for a minute, and we decide she will come down and take one of my big dogs (from Friday's pick up) and I will keep the new one. I am feeling a little better that I got to get some of my frustration out. As I did, some solutions came my way.

I soon was home with eight extra dogs, 22 total. We had our three. Amongst the large number, 3 of the 22 were huge dogs, not cute little puppies. We had Lexi and Twiggy, and 4 pups from the previous litter. We brought 7 puppies home and 3 tiny pups from Friday. We had a house full, though it was fun.

The kids and Brian were picking up toys and raking the yard. I started picking up dog poop! We had a fire going to burn all the leaves when the cops showed up to tell us we could not have a fire without a fire pit cover. This was okay, we still had a blast as we all were hanging out in the yard and watching all the fun with the dogs!

The contract for my first property was emailed, and I was trying to make myself sign it; I wasn't ready yet. I also received a call from June. She told me she was bringing me money, dog medicine, and coming to pick up one of the big dogs as well as taking three of the puppies. She was going to a puppy fair in Denver on Sunday, and planned on selling the pups there. I then received a call from another foster mom. She said she wanted Lexi, and asked if she could come over. She spent three hours here as she cuddled with all the puppies to choose from. Her and her husband ended up taking, not Lexi, but two other puppies!

June then showed up. She had previously said she would be at my house after she did four home visits. She had ended up running out of time, and only went to one home visit. The reason she was late, was her transport was late coming to her.

She brought with her two 6-month old labs and a big ole fluffy large dog. Apparently she has been trading dogs! She picked these guys up from other homes, and planned to bring them to her dog fair on Sunday. Some of the dogs she had were aggressive. Her aggressive one did not seem to be as bad as the one I had. Brian told her we would keep her fluffy one, and she took Deja (one of the big dogs we had.) I also took her two labs. I know, crazy! She took three of my pups and Twiggy for the puppy fair the next day. Now we had less dogs, though a lot more big dogs. The evening was loud, and I had started to doubt my generosity.

Our contract was still not filled out for the realtor. We went to bed.

....

Sunday morning was here. I was cranky because of the noise all night with the dogs. I began affirming they would be adopted soon!

We went to church. Church was okay; they rearranged the chairs and gave it a make-over. That afternoon they were having a 'member vote' to decide what they were going to do for expansion. We had more people then room for. I was kind of irritated at church. I felt like an outsider. Our minister also seemed very arrogant this day; I didn't like it. This stuff was all mine; I just watched and affirmed I would see the bigger picture. I knew I was getting more irritated, only because I was already irritated. I was also mad that the minister had not responded to my emails. I felt like I was unimportant.

We soon drove home and I made plans to go to the store to buy more bowls (we were running out with all the dogs.) I also really wanted my baby gate, and was hoping to find one today. I let all the dogs out before I was off to the store. We then had a surprise visitor. Our landlord came by to drop off some woodchips. Here, he was witnessing all of these dogs. He laughed and thought they all were cute. I felt relieved. He also dropped off some wood for our lower level fire place. He is really a sweet landlord. He is a blessing and seems to understand the 'real' us! He also came with gifts; a bag of apples for Dreana (Dreana eats way to many of these) and some bananas for Aidan. He also gave us twenty dollars for when we fixed the toilet ourselves. I now had fifty from Saturday and twenty from today! I took my cash and headed to the store.

There were no baby gates or bowls (we were at the thrift store.) Though, their books were only 99 cents each! I picked up two and Dreana picked up a Tinker bell sandwich container! We then drove around looking for a rummage sale. Nothing, we soon were home. I spent the rest of the afternoon thinking about the properties, and reading. Soon it was Pizza hut and some wine; and then we were in bed.

....

Monday morning was here. I spent a lot of time getting all the dogs out. The kids were soon at school. I knew today was 'the day.' I finished reading the real estate contract, and I only had two questions. I forgot some terminology I knew as a realtor. I needed clarification and I did not like that she (the realtor) was recommending her title company because I wanted to use mine. I called her, and she did not answer. I then started thinking about the renters that were not moving out, and who had not paid. I called the rental company to let them know we did want one of the newly vacant properties rented out. I also asked about the status of the non-paying renters. There was no good news here.

I sat with all of this. It was going to cost me five hundred dollars to evict them. I was out of money and very frustrated. I googled the Appleton Police department and on the phone, asked them if they could do anything to help me. The officer was awesome, though had the same answer I started with. He told me it sucked, though for future reference, don't give so much lenience when the problems begin.

The reason it was five hundred dollars instead of one hundred to evict the renters, was because in this certain county, the only one who could go to court was us or a lawyer. The five hundred was for the lawyer's time. I then had an idea. The year prior, Brian had to go to court with another tenant. It was scheduled for when he was visiting in Tennessee. The court allowed him to do a phone appearance. I called the court house for this county, and asked if I could file an eviction on-line and then have a phone appearance for the hearing. This county did not allow this. I hung up the phone and was again feeling defeated. I started crying and begged God to help. We did nothing wrong; why was all of this happening? We paid all our bills and theirs, why won't they just go away! I then went to check the balance on the one credit card we had left. I really wanted to be done with credit, but was seeing this as an option. There was only three hundred dollars as an available balance. I started to cry again.

I then humbled myself and called my mom. I cried throughout the call, and asked if she had the five hundred she owed me? I could really use it. I explained everything and she said, "I know, they did it to us too." What she was referencing was her very first renters were the renters we chose as we managed her property. They ended up not paying and had to be evicted. They were a big financial strain on my mom. And all we said, as she was going through this, was to trust the renters, give them some time. We seemed to side with the renters instead of my mom. My mom ended up borrowing some money from us, and had not paid it back as she had a long list of people to pay back also. It seemed that during this time, she had hard times and slowly they were getting better. Our hard times just started.

I was mad at her comment, and I said she was just as 'bad' as them. She never supported my properties, and she never supported my dreams. I was the only one with enough courage to go after my dreams while being discouraged by her and her family. I told her she sucked, and now it is unfair that all of this is happening. I cried and cried. She soon told me she had a work-call and was going to call me back. She wanted to help. She took all of my screaming; she took it all. I felt good to get all of that off my chest. I also felt bad that it was on her now. Soon I was on the phone again; I was on the phone all day, with call backs from the police department, court house, realtor, Rental Company and Melinda.

It was funny how I would get off one call from crying, and dial the next number and switch to a professional, centered voice. As I was on the phone with the next person, my brother was beeping in. After I did not answer, he sent a text asking where to put the money that my mom had asked him for. I was mad about this. My mom owed me the money; and now I was going to owe my brother. I was also mad because my brother had never been there for me before. And now that I was in dire need, here is where he comes through. I found his money as blood money.

Brian was home and I explained the events of the day. I then told him about my brother. Eventually I decided to call Cletus (my brother) back. I began the conversation with, "You are probably going to hang up on me, but this time $250 (my mom was going to give me 250 and Cletus was going to give me 250) was so small that I did not need to give up any more of myself. He was going to hear it all, because it was only 250 dollars!

I reminded him a few months ago, when I asked him for money for my real estate class, he said, "No." If he would have given that to me then, at least I would have been able to afford my renters living rent free. So really, that money would not have solved the big issue, which was to not have them as renters. Though, I said I am mad, because he would have given that money to anyone, anyone that was not me. I yelled and said I have always supported him, and he won't even encourage me. I said now the $250 he was willing to give me, I did not want. I would rather lose the house, than to take his petty change. He screamed at me a lot also; though he never hung up. We screamed back and forth a lot. We said a lot of things we both wanted to say for a long time. At the end, we talked about my issue and came together like people making a business decision. All in all, the conversation with my mom and my brother were worth the entire head-ache the renters had cost me. It felt great to have all of those years clear, and to accept help from my family.

Then Brian and I submitted our real estate contract. We told the realtor we wanted to use our own title company. That was done.

Brian left for work and I had another five minute phone conversation with my girlfriend. Throughout the day, I would call her, but only have a few minutes. Though, those few minutes would help me, as I entered into another phone conflict. Soon the doorbell rang and it was Melinda. She was there to pick up her three puppies, and her puppy gates (she gave them to me while she was gone in case I had a puppy fair.) We gave updates on all the things that went on, while she was gone. She was surprised by how two of my puppies had doubled in size since she saw them two weeks ago! I told her about my day and all the issues. She told me her next meeting was with a foster mom who refused to pay for a puppy she had adopted. It was funny how her story and my story correlated. We are all connected. The energy we are experiencing is the energy all around us. Of course it makes since that the problems I am having, she is also. Though we both got to talk about it for a minute, we got to diffuse; this helped both of us go on with our days.

Soon I picked up the kiddos and they finished up their homework. They went down stairs to watch a movie. I used this time to listen to my prosperity CD and do some of my work book for last week's class. Soon Brian was home, and we chit chatted about his day as he made dinner and prepared for Aidan's Cub scouts. There was a Packer game on during the same time as Cub Scouts. Aidan suggested he get dropped off and then picked up after. Brian told him, "No," Aidan was way more important than the game. Though he asked Aidan to be ready to leave the moment they were released from the meeting! Brian really wanted to see that game; he got to watch the second half!

I spent my evening with Dreana, my prosperity CD and catching up with my friend. Soon we were all asleep.

....

Tuesday morning was here. Brian woke me up nice and early, reminding me of my intention to work out. I spent my time with coffee, and then Bub (one of my dogs.) I walked around the neighborhood for an hour. It was chilly, though I was glad to be exercising. I was glad I was back on track with my routine. The sun came up earlier today, and I was wondering if it was already seven when we made it back home. Nope closer to six, I was very excited about my morning with the extra time I was given because of our sun! I walked inside and Aidan was up! Him and I let all the dogs outside and had some Aidan and me time. Soon the rest of the house was awake. I cleaned up the kitchen affirming more and more that some of these big dogs were going to be adopted today!

Brian took the kiddos to school. I spent the rest of my morning letting dogs in and out and catching up on all our writing.

The UPS truck came by, and dropped off Aidan's belated birthday gift from my father. Aidan is going to be so excited when he gets home.

I also have changed my visualizations since we began our book. Listening to my CD last night, I held on to a specific phrase. The speaker wanted us to daydream about things we wanted; though he said we were to get them without debt. He said we should be done with debt. I like that. I (currently) do not want any more loans! My credit card debt is taken care of by the debt company, my houses are being sold. I want to pay off our cars and keep pulling money for payments until there is enough to buy a car with cash. I also am renting and like this freedom. I want to live in 'this world' for a while, a debt free world.

I have been thinking about my Cleo (another one of my dogs) lately, she is getting older and I know she will be passing on soon. I always wanted to have her die at a house we stayed at forever. I want to bury her in 'our' yard. I have not had one of 'those' houses yet. My visualization came on this weekend, that maybe there will be a country house here, only five minutes from base that will be inherited to us. You never know! It will be a horse farm that is all updated. The farm is in great condition, and the house is large and modern. The house has all hardware floors. There are ten bedrooms and a finished lower level. When we move in we will put up a chain link fence for part of the back yard; this is good for all of the puppies we are fostering. My dogs will have full rein of the rest of the yard.

The property will also have extra houses on it. We could rent them out to farm-help and people wanting a country setting. The yard will be at least thirty acres with at least a four car garage. We will spend the first month moving our furniture out of here, as well as cleaning and painting. We will also use that time to put up our fence for the new house. What I really like is how our dreams change. As we grow we want other things, other goals. I am excited for where we have come, and excited to see how it all unfolds! My day came and went.

....

Wednesday morning is here. We called the guy who sold us one of our properties, and asked him if he wanted it back. He had called last year and asked if we would sell the house back to him. At the time it was a good idea; I wanted out, but only if there was a profit. Now it is different. We called him and told him we would sell the property at what the property cost us. He said he would consider it.

What I have most recently seen is that we can write all of these losses off during tax time. This is a bonus I did not previously realize.

The losses include: the loss of rent with all five properties, the unpaid water bills, and the two-thousand dollar bill we paid to the rental company for maintenance. All of these losses could be written off. I am also feeling a lot better about letting this part of my life go. I am ready. I now trust God, as He takes this part away and brings something better in.

....

Thursday morning:
Last night Richard flew into Colorado. We had a fun evening of catching up with him. Everyone wanted his attention, when he fell asleep, he slept hard!

I was up at 4 A.M. today. Brian had a P.T. test and I wanted to make sure he was prepared. As I walked through the house this morning, I learned Richard was also up. I never remembered him being a morning person; in Indiana our 4 A.M. was 6 A.M. to him. (Because of the time difference.) Though this still seemed too early for him. He told me he always is up this early. He helped me with the dogs. He even took our Grumpy on a walk. Grumpy had jumped the fence the night before, so he could not be left alone outside. We talked about my book, and how cold Richard was! The little time alone was nice. I then had to corral Brian out of bed. This is no fun, though it needed to be done. Richard ended up jumping in bed with him encouraging him to join our morning!

Brian was up, Richard was up, and then Aidan was up! The house was full of energy prior to the sun rising. Richard went with Brian to cheer him on his P.T. test. I fed the kids and helped them get ready for school. I dropped Dreana off, and asked her teacher if she needed any help in her class today; I was hoping Richard and me could go visit later in the day. She alluded to a no, though left it open to, "If I really wanted, I could come." I was sad as I drove home.

Brian did not have to be to work until ten (after his run.) He told me he thought he failed his P.T. test. He did not think he did enough sit-ups. I have been affirming since then, that he has passed, and it is going to be a great evening with the news when it comes! Richard ended up going to work with Brian. Now it is me and all of these dogs! I am frustrated.

The idea of this book was to let you know what really happens when you tithe. I wanted to give you a big ole result to help encourage you. Though I think my prize is not a large win, though small bouts of progress. This frustrates me. I feel I have to have a big win, to encourage you to tithe. I feel without a large gain, that my small gains may not be 'good enough.' This 'I'm not good enough' is what I have been dealing with for years. Though I think each day, each moment, there is an opportunity to let more and more go.

I was hoping that if I did the one thing, tithing, that all of my problems would disappear. Kind of like, if you win the big lotto, all your problems should go away. Though I don't think this is how life is; life is a process. I guess, we learn, we grow and we move to our next steps.

Here is what has happened since we began. I have redefined my goals. I no longer want to buy my rental that I am currently living in. I instead want a country house to be inherited to me. Now again, this intention of my house being inherited to me is like winning the lottery. Currently I am so done with debt. The mortgages that I am holding do not seem to be paying me what I thought they would. My credit card debt is costing me and reminding me of past 'mistakes.' I am done with car payments. It seems the way I have been living is a form of slavery, and I want out. The only thing I can currently think of is that all debt is 'bad.' An inherited house would make me feel better. I know this is not the only option; though it is the opposite extreme of where I was with everything on credit. There is a balance I will eventually achieve. Further growing is inevitable. I also do not want to buy all of my landlord's properties anymore. I am finished with single family homes. That was a past goal. I have been there, done that. I now am finding courage to go with another goal, going for what I want. What I want is a prosperous apartment building.

Other things I have done, I have looked at my finances and made many steps towards making them better. I began by being afraid to open bills; I now open them, and work at getting them paid. I have given up my credit cards and am only living with what I currently have. This is working. What I have is enough; I did not know this before. As I spend what I have, I have eliminated the need for further credit problems. I have learned how to put my expenses on a budget. I have learned to live 'within my means.' Each month I transfer fifteen hundred dollars from one bank account to the next. We have been using this amount consistently, for our food and rent. This is working. I have learned this small step, and I am sticking with it. It is no longer a struggle to decide if we should go to the grocery store. The answer is always, yes, because we know we can afford it. This is an amazing feeling!

I have decided that my nice car is not necessary. My car was a pride thing, and I am now willing to drive a car that I can afford. I am willing to take the mask off, to live a healthier life. The expense of switching out my car is not as easy as I wish it would be. I currently owe more than what the dealership will take my car for. I am moving in the right direction. I do not need to have all the answers now; each answer gets revealed in time.

What matters is that I have decided, I am ready and willing to let my car go and receive a better option. God will figure out the details. I have also decided that I can let go of my properties. This was another pride thing. These houses were a definition of my success; I was successful for accomplishing these. And now that they are costing more money than I have; I still was trying to hold onto them. I had to decide enough was enough. I had to let go and admit defeat, instead of holding on and hiding from the truth.

I had to learn it is me that is successful, not something I did. I had to learn I will accomplish again. I had to let go, to let something better in. I grew since I created these properties; I am now growing into something different. I was afraid to let go, because I thought this was all I had, all I would ever have. I had to trust more would come. Coming to terms in this subject created some tears, though because of it, I am becoming a better me.

Now that I am ready for the properties to go; God is not just taking them away. He has a different plan. I think he wants me to sell some, and keep some. When I finally made my decision; I wanted it all to go away. And they are not 'just going away;' there is a process that has to happen. I have to now strategically make them work, until I can get rid of them. I cannot let all five stay vacant with a 'for sale' sign on them. If I do this, the properties will go into foreclosure. If I want to finish this the right way; I have to let them go when I can afford it. And in the meantime, they probably will become successful rentals again. Funny how that works, huh? Then when they are successful, I am going to have to decide again, if I want them or not. I cried to get to my current decision; you would think this is good enough. The strength it took to get to my knees and give up should be enough; though it isn't. It was enough for now; tomorrow's now is decided tomorrow, not today. Though today's decisions create a path for a better tomorrow.

Here is the status of the properties; one property is listed. Another property is rented, because the realtor said it was worth less than I owe. Another is rented and this is the one needing to be refinanced. I do not currently have the equity or money for that. This is the one I called the investor for and asked if they wanted this property at a cheap price. If I sold to him, I would make no profit on this and all the money I stuck into the house, I would not get back. Though, I would not have to refinance. This of course is a hit, though moving forward also feels good. I am curious to see how this unfolds. Am I growing into forgiving my loss, or is this property going to turn around and create me a profit? I don't know. All I know is what to do today. And today I asked someone to buy and gain on my loss.

Another one is where the renters did not move out. They have not paid rent for a long time; this is a loss. I also had to give another five hundred to evict them. The realtor called today to tell us the selling price would be $85,000, and her fee is around 6,000 dollars. I think I bought it at 82,000; so selling it through her does not make (current) since. As of now, selling it does not make since, renting it to someone else does. It would be great to let this one go, because this one made me cry. Though I think God wants me to hold on to it, and make it successful. I do not want to make it successful; I just want to forget it ever happened. I think God wants more for me.

What I want is to move on and let my losses be in the past. Though I think what is happening is God is showing me how to learn from all of this. As I go through the entire process, I think I am gaining the skills of a successful business person. This is what I want more, to learn to be a bigger me. I want the problems gone yesterday, but if I can't have that because I am gaining something better (a better me) instead; I will take that. I will be patient and watch myself grow. I will probably get frustrated as this happens; though my destination is now a permanent tattoo to my awareness. Tithing has given me this. It has not (so far) given me a lottery win; it instead has given me a stronger foundation to make my own lottery.

I wrote this book for you and for me. I wanted to grow and learn how the 'rich' do it. I also wanted you to learn from me, and decide on your growth, as you learned it was possible (as you watched me.) I really hope my experience was 'good enough.' I hope as you read what we write, you find it large enough to tithe yourself.

What I feel is peace, and a knowing that things are being built with a solid foundation. I wish my foundation was built years ago, and I was not here; as I am. Though now is all we have. I am learning to forgive myself; this is also what is shifting. What's shifting is me letting me off the hook. I also wish I could have a billion dollars; though I feel I am learning how to get it. I feel tithing has benefited me, and I do not think I will ever stop. I hope you feel the same way. There is something special in going through a problem. You get to experience everything it offers. You get to feel the raw 'you' and you get to learn to trust something new. You get to grow into areas for the first time. It's like a 'first kiss,' it is nerve-racking, though also exhilarating, all at the same time.

Another point I want to bring up, is that as I am in the middle of each project, I wish it was already accomplished. I wish I could just have my book finished. The reason is, as I write, I have many thoughts of 'what's the point?' I am so scared to fail 'again.' It is a lot of work to continue to believe, as the rest of my life unfolds.

If my book were finished now, I would know the end result. Instead I have to hold faith that I am 'good enough.' I have to hold the faith that I am moving in the right direction; that I will be rewarded. I have to hold faith that you will want to learn from me. I have to hold faith that what I am learning, is worth learning, and then later worth reading about. I have to hold faith that what I want; wants me. This is another process, just like my rental mess clearing up. It is not enough to want it fixed; I have to be willing to grow within my desires. My desire is me, and I am becoming me.

    Earlier today I received a call from a mom for babysitting. I had emailed her the other day; she is the one with the three kids. I saw her ad again today, and emailed. She called and we connected. After I was off the phone with her, I found the irony. I want life to move forward with my book; I want my book done, fast. I am now babysitting, less time for my book. Though this is how life works, it all unfolds as we live it. I should not spend 24 hours a day on my book, because my book would be about nothing significant. Life is significant. My book is about my life, and my life needs to be lived to be written about. My book will get done when it is supposed to. I have to let go and trust as I live. Living is what makes it a NY best seller! I love you guys and gals; thank you for being on my journey!

    Thursday evening came with chili for dinner. It was time for my class. As I was preparing to leave, the kids, Brian and Richard looked excited for their evening as well. It felt good to get out of the house. I was me, without kids, dogs or any responsibilities related to the house.

    Our class began with the Daily word. Again the theme was 'Let go and let God.' It spoke of welcoming abundant good, and being grateful for our tenacity till the end. It spoke of the many races in life, and us not needing to be in every one. We need to trust God that our role will be revealed. God will take care of the rest. Some projects are better accomplished when we slow down and trust. We are to continue to pray for guidance in knowing what our roles are. When I let go, I make room for unlimited good to come through unexpected channels. This is referenced from Job 22:21 in the Bible. (International Bible Society, 1984) We make peace with God; this is how our good comes.

    On to our testimonies; remember the other week how we prayed for one of our members to have their financial situation cleared up. This week she received a refund check of $2,242.50. She said it felt amazing to pay the tithe on this amount! The money was spent on all of her debts and some left over for gas! Blessings to her! Another member was asked to dinner. The occasion was only to tell her how special she was. This is an amazing reason!

Another lady talked of the cool people she is attracting. She has a friend who was at a restaurant, witnessing a very tired waitress. He wrote our waitress a check for one hundred and fifty dollars (as a tip.) The waitress cried and said that her furnace had just gone out and she had no clue how it was to be paid. This man was an angel for her. A few days later, that same man received an unexpected IRS refund of 1,500 dollars. The IRS had 'forgotten' until now. The IRS mistake was from three years ago. God always finds a way. What he gave was exactly ten percent of what he received. God is good. What an exciting story.

Another lady had a very prosperous Saturday. She went to pick up her paycheck from a photography job she finished. As she was there, her client bought her a yogurt. She then drove to the other side of town for another client, and was hired by a neighbor for another job! The new neighbor also was a mechanic, and quoted her 'only parts' work on her vehicle. How cool for her! I love it!

Another girl spoke of her job hunt. This week she received a, "No" but she was okay with it. She knew what was meant, was coming. This is cool because when we receive these, 'No's,' when we are not in the flow; they hurt. Though when we are in the flow, we know it is because something better is almost here! I told my stories and noted how they correlated to this woman. I told everyone that I was selling my properties, and on the surface it seemed as though this was 'bad.' Though I knew it was the next step, into getting me where I now want to be. Even though I am receiving something 'bad,' it really is good!

Our last testimony came from a man who was excited to be 'hired' at a volunteer hospice center. This is where he enjoyed his volunteer work. Now he had the opportunity to share himself with the world!

As our class was ending, I asked a question. As I am moving through many big decisions in my life, I wanted to know how to know if God approved. I wanted to know my affirmations were also what God wanted for me. One of the members said that when I have excitement, this is exactly the thing I should be doing. She told me when I talk about the puppies, she sees the joy in me, and she says this is an example of God agreeing with my affirmation. The reason I ask this question is because I want to move forward with my affirmations. When I get stuck, I feel like God is not approving. I feel like I am pushing against the grain. I want confirmation that I am doing the right thing. My intent is to do well in the world. I feel the things I strive for benefit the world; I just get confused at times. This is what a group of friends does for you; they help lift you up when you are not feeling very high.

Next we had our groups. Our prayers were, "Divine spirit within all of us, provide healing and abundant health.

God within all of us approves of all our desires, and offers us guidance as we move forward. God within all of us provides speaking gigs to help spread messages of healing. And God within all of us moves us forward with our academic pursuits."

One more story was told by a prayer member that I want to share. He said years ago, he had wanted to go to a baseball game. All week he affirmed he would somehow get there. The day of the game, they (him and his buddies) decided to tailgate because they still did not have tickets. As they were in the parking lot, a man came to them and asked if they wanted tickets. Our member got his ticket, and it was half the price the ticket was originally selling for! There was only one ticket so he went to the game while the other two tailgated in the parking lot. The plan was to meet up after. After the game, our guy went looking for his friends and soon was lost. He walked the city for hours; there were no cell phones at this time. He finally found a pay phone, and left a message on one of the friend's home phone saying, "I am lost, but will be at the meet-up spot." By leaving this message, he hoped the guys would check the voicemail. These guys were in a different state then their home state; they were only here for the game. The only people they knew were the three of them.

Our guy was getting discouraged. Soon hours later, a random person offered to drive him around the neighboring streets, to find the car and the meet-up spot. Finally, he found the spot where the car was supposed to be, but no car was there. Our guy decided to sit and hope his buddies would show up. His plan was, he was to sit for thirty minutes, and then he was going to call a cab to take him to a hotel and figure things out from there. Fifteen minutes later, his buddies showed up. They said this was the last time they were coming to this spot to check for our friend.

This is a perfect example of how we get frustrated, but God always knows where everyone is. We can only see what we can see. God can see everyone and everything! He always knows how to connect us all. We just have to let go, and trust that He knows what He is doing. Our class was over; soon I was home to sleeping children, Richard and Brian.

Chapter 10
Replacing: Who Knew?

Friday morning I was up early. I was getting the kids ready as Richard played the guitar. It was very soothing as I listened to him. The morning was great until it was almost eight o'clock. I had to have the dogs and the kids to school by then. The plan was for me to take the dogs, and Brian to take the kids; Brian was still sleeping. I eventually started to yell, and Brian was finally up! We lifted kennels, and very heavy dogs; and they were ready for the road trip. Richard and Brian headed to school with rambunctious kiddos. After they dropped the kids off, the boys were going shopping. They were going to have the day to themselves!

I dropped my dogs off at 'the location,' and learned I could (in the future) drop the dogs off at 8:15 instead of eight. This helps for next time; I will be able to drop both the kids and dogs off myself. All week long I had been affirming that the four big ones would get adopted. They had been a bit much for me. They did not get adopted, but they were the only ones who went to the vet on Friday. So my intention came true, I just had to wait until Friday. I stopped at the gas station on the way back to buy a pack of cigarettes. They were seven dollars; this surprised me, they are supposed to be four. I made a quick decision and said, "No thank you." I walk outside and find a penny on the ground! Awesome, I am on the right track. (Every time I find money I know I am making the right decisions.) I go to the next gas station, and get two packs for seven dollars! When we listen, we save money!

I soon was home and had the house to myself. I had a whole to-do list waiting for me; instead I sat, and enjoyed the sun. This week was long with all of the dogs. In my relaxed moment, I decided to make a video blog. I had a lot to catch up on. My Vlog was a lot of updates and explanation of how I was feeling. The overall was that I was feeling frustrated, and sad that I had to give up my properties. Though I knew it was the right move. I was moving forward, but owning my feelings. Soon the boys were home, and we spent the afternoon listening to Richard and Brian on the guitar. It was nice. It was like we were all on vacation. I kept checking the time, assuming it was time for the kiddos, though it stayed early. This day light savings thing can be pretty cool at times! After a while I went to go get the kiddos. They were having a candy bar sale at school. This school is so good with fundraisers! I thought it was also neat that the candy bars were only 50 cents. If we were at the store, we would have spent $1.50. It was a win-win.

We were later home, and Dreana wanted to go meet the new neighbors. Three girls moved in! We took a puppy over to say, "Hi."

We learned our new neighbors wanted a new puppy; win, win! They came to our house and began choosing which one (puppy) they wanted. We had some conversation, and then offered to keep the girls for an hour, to give mom and dad a moment alone in their new house. I eventually skedaddled out, and went to go get my four big dogs from 'the location.' It is always fun to hang out with the dog agency people! We got some updates, and a little alone time without kids. I ended up taking an extra dog home to drop off to a foster family in my area.

The evening was filled with the four big dogs, the rest of the pups, and our dogs. We all sat by an awesome camp fire. Soon I retired to my room and read, while the boys and kids finished out their night.

Saturday morning brought the same amount of work as Friday. I was up for a while planning to get the dogs, kids, and all of us adults into Brian's truck for the puppy fair. We planned on having the boys stick around at the puppy fair while another clinic was going on. A local veterinarian was at the store that Saturday, giving discounted shots to all who stood in line. My dogs were due for their shots. After Brian, Richard, and Aidan were going to take our three dogs home, and then rummage around town for some Saturday fun! This did not happen, we ran out of time. Instead we got all the dogs into the car, and it was just me that was going. The boys were going to clean the house, and have some fun time with the kiddos.

I get to the event, and have help getting all of these dogs out of my car. It took three loads back and forth, soon everyone was out. I then took my three, and sat in line for an hour, as the pet clinic had quite a turn out. As I was standing there, I saw one of my foster puppies being carried through the store. I stopped the couple and said my goodbyes to the adopted puppy. That was cool to see, as I am doing something else, my little girl pup got adopted! Just like that, God is in charge; I don't always have to be!

As the line got smaller for the vet, I realized I did not have my wallet. I quickly called Brian and asked him to drive to the store. He did, he paid and took our three back with him. Funny how stuff works out. I really did not want to waste the gas, but God knew I had too many dogs. Brian was needed for help!

The event was good. Many dogs and puppies went to new homes. We were very busy, and it was three instead of two when Brian called to find out what we were doing. He wanted to know why we were not home yet. I left with my puppies, and an extra one. I also came home with only two of my four big dogs, and still we had big old Oliver.

When I was home, the house was clean. Everything was clean, even the weeds! It was a nice feeling.

The long week with all the dogs was cleared out, the kids were good, the house smelled of pine sole; it was awesome! I soon learned we were having a party for the evening. The boys had invited some Army friends over. We were going to have a big camp fire, and lots of music!

A while back, we had had an Army party and met Jackie. We decided her and Richard were going to fall in love. This would happen if only we could get them in the same state together. Today was the day they both were in the same state! The evening was nice. Richard and Jackie hit it off. My kids had friends over. The boys played Legos, and the girls played dress-up. It was a lot of fun. Soon Richard and Jackie decided to leave and hang out at the bar by themselves. This was their time to get to know each other. This was unexpected, but whatever! Maybe this story will be told to grandchildren when the question is asked, "How did you two meet?" The rest of the clan left, as our main attraction was no longer there. We soon were asleep.

....

Sunday morning was here. I was the only one awake. Richard had invited Jackie over for the night, and they both were still asleep. I noticed chili on the stove, and figured there must have been partying going on last night as I slept. I spent the next few hours letting dogs out, and enjoying my coffee. Soon Richard joined my morning.

I asked him how his date went the evening before; he said it was, "All right." I figured it was because she was more immature then I had remembered from last time. His reason was because she was 'rich.' I was baffled by that. I told him I do not know why he has such a problem with rich people. He is the richest person I know. He has this weird ability to give everything he has away, and receive it all back moments later. He never has a need. His needs always come to him. He said he did not have a problem with her being rich, but that she flaunted it. He has a problem with rich people, not wealthy people. The reason she was rich, is because her father was wealthy. She still had to learn how to be wealthy on her own. She was attracted to Richard because he is wealthy now. Richard was not as attracted to her, because he wanted wealthy, not rich women. Here was a different perspective then I had ever received from him. At that moment, I gained a lot of respect for him.

That comment continued for a little while. He said he seems to attract very wealthy women. Each interest of his happens to own a business, come from a wealthy family, or has inherited a large amount of money. We talked about how I also attract these people. I could name at least twenty people I know who have millions in their bank account. This makes me feel good; because my intention is to have multi-millions myself. I also recognize that I currently do not.

I have a lot of growth within me to receive that money. I attract knowing these people; however I usually only work with beginning entrepreneurs. The contractors I hire are motivated but 'new.' The people I work with are just beginning their businesses. I would like to get to the point where I work with people who have already succeeded. For this to happen, I have a limiting belief that I have to succeed first. This is a belief I am trying to figure out. My intention is that I start working with people who will help me succeed, because they already know how. I now choose to know how to make it, and work alongside others who have already made it.

The morning continued on with Richard being the sweet-heart he is. Even though this was not the woman of his dreams; he still bought her breakfast and let her know she was a princess. She soon left and continued on with her day. We skipped church. The weekend was long, we wanted a break. I still had frustrations with church. I was still mad that our minister had not emailed. I had a hard week with my entire life. I knew I was in the middle of a storm, and it soon would be over. Currently I just wanted a break.

The boys took advantage and went to go play pool. Soon they were back, I took a nap, Richard took a nap, and Brian rebooted my computer because it stopped working earlier. Soon it was time for Richard and Brian to head to Denver. Richard needed to be dropped off for a treatment he was in Colorado for. The kids watched a movie, and I received calls and texts from my neighbor who wanted a dog. This was the neighbor we just met, and now he was getting annoying. He called, and tried his hardest to talk down the price of a dog. He wanted this, and that, and it all his way. I was irritated, and recognized what was happening. I did my best to just watch, and try not to get my emotions wrapped up in what he was representing. I took the calls, answered his questions, and then dumped him out of my awareness.

Brian was soon home, and later we were asleep!

....

Monday morning was here, it was still the weekend with it being Veteran's Day. Bright and early, I was up because I was babysitting my toddler friend! I met her mom outside, trying to avert barking dogs, and to give her a helping hand as she had a lot on her mind. She had an annoying weekend as well; she needed a break. I told her I would not be shopping on Black Friday, so she had the option to go.

Within moments, my little one was waking my two up. My two were happy for the early morning as long as she was involved! The three played, and ate Halloween candy. We then had breakfast. Our friend ate a whole piece of cheese bread! She is getting so big.

As the morning continued, it was apparent we should have let Dreana sleep in. She was cranky. Aidan went to his friend's house and I filled out extra real estate papers (for the property listed.)

The next project was with the foster agency. The list that was remaining were things we needed to do. All other parties had done their part; it was now, only us, who had a to-do list. Some of the items were easy. We had to darken and rescan an, "Exit Diagram" for our house. The next was scanning our veterinarian documentation; both done. What is left is for the agency to go over our income, and for us to get new vehicle and renters insurance. This is the hard part. We still have not switched over our insurance because it is one hundred and fifty dollars more than what we were paying. And currently we have not been able to pay every bill per month, with the big ole mess. So adding expenses into our budget seemed like something I did not want to do.

We sat for a minute an evaluated the situation. We have been affirming for a while, though it has now been a few months. We considered just paying the extra 150. Then an idea came to call a company we had not yet called. The quote came back as a hundred extra. We were down fifty dollars, not the 150. We decided to continue to wait, and expect a better option.

Next was our income. We talked about this one. In my head I figure our income would work. I have always been able to buy houses with our income. There is always a jigsaw to work through; but it always works out. Though, this time around, I am done with the jigsaw puzzle. I want it to be easy. I do not want them to look at my income, until I know it looks 'picture perfect' on paper. I decided my dream of me becoming a foster mom could wait, until this area of my life became easier. As of now, we have a lot of paper work in, now it is just the waiting game as more stuff clears up. I am okay with being patient. Months ago I was not. I think this is what my tithing is teaching me, to be patient until all areas of my intentions feel good; not just part of them. It is not just about extra kids, it is also me, and my life, that are taking a cleansing bath. I am in the process of getting rid of a lot of old, and building a stronger foundation for the new.

The afternoon was here and our little one's mom came to pick her up. I had all of her bags packed because her mom tends to not want to stick around. Today was different; she did not want to leave. She told me her husband was expected to be back in December (he was at war.) He originally was not supposed to be back until May. How cool was this! She instead was nervous. She said she enjoyed her current routine, and when he came back, things were going to change.

I understood this, when Brian came back (from war) I was happy; all the same, my life became much more entwined as it again revolved with him. I listened to her as she vented. She also said she had a Christmas party (for work) coming up that she was considering going to. She wanted to know if I would be available to babysit; of course I said "Yes!" She still did not know if she wanted to go. She has been frustrated with work lately, and was afraid of drinking too much and saying stuff that had been repressing on her mind. She was frustrated with many aspects of her life; things were bubbling up for her.

The evening continued. Spaghetti dinner came and went. The kids went to bed, exhausted from their long weekend. It was now Brian and me. We cleaned and folded laundry. I (out of nowhere) became excited with moving. When Brian receives his next rank (in a year,) we might have to move. His new rank will need to be in a different battalion, or he will receive an E8 slot here in Colorado Springs. The E8 slots are limited. Obviously because it is a higher rank; and there are less people needed every time there is a promotion. There are fewer job openings, and basically where there is an opening is where we go. We knew this was coming. This summer, as we fell in love with Colorado, we began affirming that Brian would be picked up for an E8 slot here. This was a smaller chance, but this is what we wanted. However this day I was open to moving! This new desire of mine also opened up many more options for him to be E8. I really want to go to Texas. We talked about this, and thought how funny it was if we were only here in Colorado for a year. Colorado seemed to be where I was supposed to let go a lot of my past hurts, it was a place of clearing. If we were only here for a year, it was because I had to come back to clear the old stuff. And this only needed to be a year. When the clearing was done, we could move.

The idea of going to Texas was fun. We would go there on a clean slate. We no longer would have our rental properties. We would have our credit debt company almost finished with their settlement. We would know we like helping with a rescue agency. We know we are okay with renting. We have learned how to live within our budget. We know we do not want debt on cars. When they are paid off, we start collecting money until we have plenty to purchase a car in cash. My book would be written and published by then. We know we want a farm only minutes from town and Brian's work. We know we want Brian to be in the military for him to achieve his SGT Major. Brian would work within his new rank for a few years. We could take a year for him to get settled with that. Then we would begin the process of patenting our product that we will be bringing to the market. It is all perfect timing.

There will no longer be any old stuff lagging us as we begin new projects. It will be calm; a perfect place to begin a new creation. We can now begin to affirm our house that we will be attracting. We have a whole year, lots of time as this creation comes about. And when we get to Texas, maybe this will be the time for foster kids. Maybe all of this had to happen in Colorado for us to be prepared for the new as we enter Texas!

I was happy affirming, and hoping to have Brian join in. He instead was stressed from his failing P.T. test. We were downstairs by the fire. It was very peaceful. I googled many things about Texas. I was in a great mood. Brian watched football and tried his hardest to forget his worries. Before I knew it Brian was waking me up; I had fallen asleep on the couch. It was time for bed.

....

Tuesday morning was here. Aidan was up very early; we made breakfast and packed the lunches. Before I knew it he was out the door excited about his new week. Dreana was poking around, and felt her time was best spent with putting make-up on. She looked adorable, and felt very pretty. I brought her to school and she portrayed the look of a model, as she glided through the playground. She asked a teacher walking by, "How do you like my look?" This of course brought many smiles her way! She was a very happy little girl, as she walked into her class; I knew both my kids were going to have an amazing day!

I soon was home, tired of the dogs. It has been a long few weeks, and I was ready to quit as each day progressed. As each dog took their time to bark, I tried to ignore it. I felt I needed to write, though was not in the writing mood. Instead, I outlined all that had happened, so I would know what to write when I was more calm.

I gave Bentley (one of the big dogs) a bath. He smelled. As I washed him, I chanted over and over, "Today is your day, you are getting adopted today!" I figured a bath would clean his energy, as well as mine. I had to prepare him; hopefully this was 'the day.'

The morning was filled with weird occurrences. The realtor texted and asked me if I knew if the property listed could be converted to natural gas instead of LP. She wanted the answer in case a buyer was to ask. I found this a tedious request. I used to be a realtor, and found myself finding all of these questions and answers, before they were even asked. It is the buyer's responsibility to find out these answers. And only the really interested buyers, will actually research the answers. The rest (of the uninterested buyers) just create unnecessary work. Sometimes we have to realize this. When we find ourselves doing extra work for someone else, we have less time to do the work that is relevant for us. This is where we get sidetracked and overwhelmed.

I recognized all of this in her question. I made a designated decision and told her, "If a buyer asked, then to direct them to the electric company to find their answer." It felt good to say, "No." Fifteen minutes later she texted, and told me she called and the answer was, "Yes, the property could be converted." Her text was happy. I was happy. She got her answer, and I did not have to do work that I found irrelevant. If she found it relevant, cool; but I did not.

Then Brian calls 'to talk.' He never calls unless he has something to say. Today he just wanted to chit chat. I watched this, and was curious for my answer of what it all meant. Why was I attracting all of this irrelevance for the day? I did not get wrapped up in my question, I was just aware of it. He also told me he received a call from an old friend. I found it weird this friend was calling. We only talk to him here and there; so the timing of his call was goofy as my morning was already goofy. He told Brian that his daughter's friend lost her mother this week. The mom felt sick one day, and the next day she died. I wondered why this was in my awareness. What did it all mean? Also our friend asked for the foster agency's phone number. He wanted to call and finalize his part in our application. This is goofy because on our check list from the day before, our friend's name was not on it. We get updates of what still is needed to be done from the agency. For a while it was a letter from our friend and another girl (stating their opinion on us as foster parents) that we were waiting on. Our friend never wrote his letter. However the agency crossed him off the list as if he did. I thought this was weird. I also found it weird that he was finally motivated to write the letter. Why now, after all this time of us begging him to do it; why now? Brian gave him the phone number for the foster agency.

Next Brian told me the MSG board (Brian's promotion board) was pushed back six weeks. The reason was because of the Government shut down. Everything was pushed back. I thought this was funny. We were waiting for this board, and now we have to wait a few extra weeks. The whole morning was something to wonder about. I do not have the answers; all I can do is wait and watch them unfold.

There was still more! Next I received a call from my mom. She wanted to know the status of the properties. I was kind of frustrated with her question because I am still hurt from the past. I am trying my hardest to work through it all, though I am still hurt. I do not want her involved. Though, it seems that she needs to be involved, for all of this to clear. She told me her husband, ironically, called the rental company to find out why they had not cashed his check. Remember his check is what paid for the eviction on one of the properties. The rental company told him that they needed an extra 110 dollars to move forward.

Good thing he called; a synchronicity I am positive God was involved with. And number two: I was pissed that the rental company did not call to let us know. They had that check for a few days, and would have had it forever if he would not have called. You would think they would have called to let us know they needed more money; nope, story of all of this! The eviction was pushed back because the eviction needed to be paid for. My step father got them their money, and the eviction had been scheduled. Here is a good and bad. Good thing my mom and her husband were so involved. Bad they had to be involved because my rental company is incompetent!

Next I found myself looking at Craigslist. I checked the babysitting site, then the free sight; nothing for me. I decided to check the jobs. Right away I found an apartment management job. The ad was very long. They first were looking for someone to manage the rentals they had. They were a company that flipped homes, and kept some for rentals. They also were looking for someone to help manage the whole production. This person would look for discounted materials, look for good properties to purchase, and set up projects to flip. This was a very cool job. I wanted this. I want to be around people who are successful with flipping homes. I want to manage properties for someone else, and get a weekly paycheck. I want to still have my flexible schedule. This job is a dream job.

They wanted a resume', a cover letter, and my salary requirements. I was so excited. I called Brian and told him about it, and said I wanted all of this information out by the evening. I needed his help. I wanted his help to make sure I got an interview!

He came home and we argued about what I should ask for pay. We argued for a while. I was glad to argue with him instead of my subconscious. My goal was to have all my frustrations out before I typed my letter. I did not want to type one thing, and be thinking another. I wanted my energy to be clear, so I could receive this job!

Soon Brian took Dreana to Girl Scouts, and I typed my resume'. For recent work experience I put my time and experience in Tennessee. Here I was not paid, though I found it relevant to describe the relevance of all I do. I do the same stuff all day that my husband does; he gets paid, I do not. This was important to me. I have a lot of junk in me. I am mad that I am an unpaid stay at home mom, unpaid author, unpaid volunteer for school, and an unpaid volunteer for a rescue agency. All of this work I do, does not get paid; while everyone else does. And to top it off, most people doing what I do, make at least sixty thousand per year. Instead, I do not get paid. This is something I am working with as I know it is a very large trigger of mine.

I feel I love the things I do. This is what we are to do; love our work. We are supposed to get paid big money to follow our dreams, and excel at our passions. I still am not getting paid. I instead am paying for my renters to live rent free. Something is off, and I am trying hard to figure it out. I want to get paid! I want whatever this is, to clear!

It felt good to put that section in my resume'. That was me standing up for me. I wrote my cover letter, and stated that I googled, "What the average rental manager was paid in Colorado Springs." (The ad asked for salary requirements.) It was fifty-six thousand a year. I also stated that in Wisconsin, the going rate is 8-10% per rental. As I typed this, I figured they were looking for a thirty thousand dollar per year salary. The numbers I googled did not support that. I am glad that I went with my numbers. At the end of my letter, I stated I was willing to negotiate. I was happy with a happy medium of what they were looking for (in pay) as well as what I was looking for. I was eager to begin this job. I wanted to be paid. I wanted this job.

I went to submit the pages on the website that the ad provided. It was on a company website, and the only place to submit is where a customer would submit a question. This was frustrating. All this time to prepare my info, and there was no good spot to send it. I replied to the craigslist ad with my resume and cover letter. I also emailed a message saying there was no good spot other than where I was submitting, for my information to go. I was nervous. I kept thinking, she was not going to get my resume'.

Before the evening was finished I received a call from Brian's aunt. She works for another agency that helps dogs. There were some dogs that were going to die on Friday, if they did not find a foster family. She called asking me if I had any pull in my agency, so I could help these dogs. I was upset all night about this; I made some calls and hoped for the best. I even considered taking the extra seven in my house and also driving the ten hours to get them. I cried and realized I could not do any of that. I had to trust that God had it taken care of; I had to release my guilt.

Soon it was time for bed.

....

Wednesday morning came. I spent a lot of the day typing and catching up on writing. I had been worried about the seven dogs, and knowing how soon Friday would be here. I was still bugged that I was saying, "No," and not being able to take them in. I finally accepted the fact that I could not help, and let it go. I took a shower, and when I was out I received a text message saying the dogs found homes! Oh this was a big lesson in letting go and letting God!

Another puppy was showing signs of being sick.

The entire day I held him, and asked him to get better. I just went through this a few weeks ago. I did not want to see it again. I wanted him to know he was loved. He hung out in my shirt all afternoon. I kept remembering story after story of animals and children healing from just being held. This was my therapy for the little guy. He was under my watchful eye all day. I asked God to make him better; I also sent out a prayer for him on Sylvia Browne's prayer chain. I had a big feeling he was going to come out okay. My confidence was also grounded by knowing all the dogs were sick this week; and they all got better. This puppy would get better too!! (Browne)

Soon it was lunch time, and Brian was home. He was upset. He came in saying the house smelled of dog. He said he was frustrated at work. He was trying to get a project done, and no one was helping him. He felt like he was all alone at work. He was mad because his boss was supposed to be sending him contacts, and people to help. No one showed up. There was still a high expectation for Brian to figure it out anyway. He was also very frustrated with our finances. He was finally verbalizing what I was feeling. We had done everything right; and we were experiencing failure. He basically wanted to go to sleep, and wake up when it was all fixed.

I listened. I knew his frustration, and was glad he was getting it out. It brought me hope that now it was out of him, progress would come. Brian went back to work and now I felt all of what he was feeling. I could not stand the barking dogs anymore or the mess in my house. I grabbed my library books and went to the library to drop them off. I had about two hours till I could pick up the kids. I hoped to find something to do outside of the house for those two hours. I had about 45 minutes left after the library. I grabbed my twenty from babysitting. I cashed it in for a soda and change for tithing. The drive helped; it cleared my head a little. I sat in my car at the gas station, and googled 'bankruptcy.' I was done worrying about money; I did not care anymore. This was not my fault, the renters were not paying, and I no longer felt guilty. I called Brian and asked him to do some 'bankruptcy' googling as well. He seemed in a much better mood. He said he would get back with me when he learned some info.

It was then the kids and me. I felt a lot better than earlier. We had a great afternoon doing homework. Soon Brian was home, and he was in the same mood that he was in at lunch time. I was mad that he was so 'shut off.' As I became more upset, it was harder to just 'let him be.' I was sitting with Aidan and the puppy, trying not to be upset at Brian. I was mad because I always seemed to be frustrated, I wanted him to hurry up and 'get over it' so we could move on. Obviously I was not as centered as I could have been.

Brian hears me talking with Aidan about how cold the puppy is. I was telling him that the puppy was sick, and might not make it. Brian runs in and is not okay with this decision. He made the puppy a bottle of "Almond Milk" and was forcing him to eat. We then gave the puppy a full body massage, trying to get his blood circulating. We were determined to not have this one die.

The puppy appeared to be getting better. There was hope! Then he seemed to fall again. Brian gave him CPR and mouth to mouth resuscitation. All of a sudden, the puppy looked at me and growled. I thought this was his frustration, him telling me, "Damn it, I don't want to live!" Instead it was his last breathe. The puppy died. I started to cry. I thought about my whole life, all of my stuff was dying. All of my achievements, my stuff, all of it was going away.

I called the agency lady and told her. She wasn't expecting this. She also told me about our pregnant dog, she needed an emergency C-section and her puppies died as well. I then called June. As I described what happened; I started to cry. The evening had a sad tone. We tried all we could do.

We soon went to bed.

Thursday morning was here. It was chaotic in the household. Dreana was sick the night before, and I was trying to find out if she was feeling better. I needed her at school because today was picture retake day. I thought it was funny, because I was back and forth on picture retakes. She had an 'owie' on her chin, and her hair was goofy in her first pictures. I would have preferred a better look; though these pictures were special because it was a moment between her and her teacher. Her teacher (on the first pictures) got her to smile when the photographer could not! I did not know if the moment was more important than a better looking picture, or if we should do re-takes.

Finally, Dreana decides she was going to school. She wanted make-up on and was very involved in her outfit. As she is getting dressed, I am taking sheets off of beds. The house is an overwhelming mess. I am also trying my best to get Aidan ready. He was running out of time, and was risking not being able to walk to school with his friend. Amidst all of this, I get a phone call from June. She called to tell me the foster home taking the seven extra dogs, backed out. She wanted to know if I would take them in. I sighed and said, "Of course I will be the back-up plan, but please try to find them fosters." I was instantly irritated with myself. I should have said "No", but didn't.

I also told June that another puppy was sick, and probably needed to go to the vet. Brian looked at me after he heard my conversation.

I looked at him and said, "I probably should have said 'No', huh?" He said, "Yes." We agreed I would call her back once Dreana was at school. I offered to bring Dreana because I wanted to talk with her teacher. I brought lipstick and asked her to help Dreana apply it when it was time for pictures. I also wanted to make sure Dreana made it to pictures because, I (in the past) had never sent in the form saying she was doing retakes.

I was still feeling the rush and frustration of the morning when I was home. I called June and told her I would not be able to be the back-up plan for the dogs. I also told her I was out of money, and now needed to be reimbursed every time I drove to 'the location.' I told her I felt horrible, though if she needed my help, she had to help me. She understood, and assured me she had plenty of money, and was happy to give it to me because I was such a large help to her. I was helping save all of these animals.

The next thirty minutes were spent on many phone calls back and forth between lots of people. Melinda had called and asked if I would take the dogs to the vet. I couldn't, because I needed gas money up front, instead of a reimbursement. My gas tank was empty. I then received a call from school. Dreana had to be picked up because she threw-up in the picture line.

I got all the dogs in from outside, and rushed to school. I asked Dreana if she still felt like taking her pictures. She said, "Yes." So we helped her prepare. Her picture turned out gorgeous! Earlier in the week, I was hoping for some insurance that she would take a good picture. Now I was able to make sure, as I was with her! This intention came true as well!

We soon were home, and she was on the couch with some movies. She was sick, and the sick puppy was on my mind. I checked my phone, noticing multiple text messages from people. June had texted and asked, "If she gave me 100 dollars, could I take the dogs to the vet?" I called her and told her "No." I then called back everyone who had called me. After a minute, I get a text message from another foster home saying she is coming for the dogs to take them to the vet. I was happy; stuff was getting done when I was honest, and said I could do no more.

The other foster mom was over and she was a good shoulder to cry on. It felt right for me to talk with her. I hate to talk about things that are 'bugging' me, because I do not want to give that energy, energy. Though it seems that by not talking about them, they stay in me. I felt 'safe' to tell her. After a while, she started telling me about her frustrations.

She was frustrated with her neighbor, frustrated with college; she had a week identical to mine. I then realized we were all attracted to each other because of our problems. This was not good. I was honest with her and told her this. Her body language changed, and she was no longer happy to be here. Funny, I am trying to solve the problem, and this conversation is no longer fun; only complaining is. She soon took the dogs. There were five puppies. Only one was sick; though while she was here, another one threw up. I knew this was the beginning of him being sick; she took that one too. She then decided to take four of the five, because the fifth one seemed healthy.

I was left with my three big dogs, Lexi and one puppy. I felt better after she left. I cleaned my house, mopped the floors and opened the windows. I wanted my outer world to reflect my inner. It felt good to feel the clean energy. Finally by me saying, "No," things were happening; things were clearing. God was hooking people up to do parts I no longer needed to do. I decided then, that being cleared felt a lot better than feeling frustrated. I wrote a list of everything I wanted, even the stuff I felt would be hard to obtain, and hard to believe.

While I was in my 'new energy,' I received another call! An old friend was on the phone asking me about my video blog's. I was surprised by this, but also recognized its progress from my now cleaner energy. She said they were inspiring, and wanted to know my intent with them. I told her they were a part of a big picture, along with my book, to help people grow into their journey. I said I wanted to dialog my journey so they could see my down's, and know the down's meant I was still on track. I wanted them to see the outcome, as well as the journey.

Her call was so 'on track.' I was feeling, 'in the flow' and of course she called with good things to say. I do not know who is watching my Vlog's; so it feels amazing when you get a comment like that! She was also very resourceful. She offered me contact info for publishers, and fellow authors. This was cool. This was a gift!

The afternoon was a mixture of sad and happy. I kind of just went with the flow; I guess I was feeling neutral. I later did another video blog. This Vlog was describing all the 'letting go and letting God.' I said, "When we do this; a neutral energy comes over us." At the end of the Vlog, I made a big ole apology (on the video) and sent off past hurts. This was intimidating; though I am glad I did it. I have tried a long time to forgive past hurts, I felt a lot better when I publicized my apology.

Moments later I received a phone call from my brother. This was ironic, I must have cleared something! We only talked about updates on our lives and our kids; and then my husband stole the phone and chit chatted with him.

This was good. I do not think my brother and I needed to "talk." I think we just needed to connect.

Soon it was dinner, and then I was off to our class. We were heading to class number ten. After tonight we are going to have two left. As I drove to class, I was still in that melancholy feeling. I was watching everything unfold. I wasn't happy or sad, anxious or nervous. I was an observer, just watching life. Kind of like when you get beat up; all your body wants to do is live, not excel, not complain; just live.

Our class began with the, "Daily Word." The message was about opening our mind to plenty, and receiving gratitude. I may think and see limits; this is because my mind will only hold what I will let it, and I am currently letting in limitations. I have to open up, God has plenty, and He wants to give. The Bible verse referenced was Isaiah 54:17; "All kids are taught by the Lord and all prosperity to all." (Paraphrased) (International Bible Society, 1984)

Next were our testimonies. One lady told of a twelve dollar find. Last summer she had a rummage sale, and collected all her money in a box. She put the box under her bed, and forgot about it. This week she was looking for a birth certificate that was also under her bed. She found her lost money! She laughed and said, "Twelve dollars may not seem like a lot, though the twelve dollars was all in quarters!" She felt incredibly prosperous! Blessings to her!

Another girl told of an opportunity to triple her income. She was beaming. Her story of the last few weeks, has been her newer business. As our class has progressed, her business is turning into something worth continuing! Blessings to her! Another member also spoke of finding ten dollars in change! Whoo hoo! Kind of curious what all this 'change' is about! Maybe we just found our answer from typing it! Lots of 'change' is within our awareness. This man also talked of some new colleagues he was meeting and working with. One of these colleagues helped him legalize his business, and created a free website for him. Awesome, prosperity his way!

Another member was creating a new calendar for her work schedule. She had to go to the school to do this. While she was there she realized that there was a new system for on-call teachers. She had to update her information, and now will probably be called for some teaching jobs. Prosperity is not always a direct answer, at times it is a process of getting us back on track! Here is a perfect example; our girl is now back-on track to receiving calls for teaching. Her teaching job is now inevitable! Another member received a ten-dollar jar of coconut oil as a gift. She also received five free lunches throughout the week. This lady seems to be cashing in. This week and last week, have been very prosperous for her!

Our discussion of our class than began. The question was: when we make amends how does it feel? Many people told stories of when they had done it. Many were positive. Another lady told a story of when she was making amends this week (with someone who had already passed away.) She really did not want to be doing it; she thought it was unfair that she had to be saying the 'sorry' when she felt it was not her fault. This made me feel better, because I did not want to make amends either. I am still hurt, and finding it unfair that I am the one who has to do the forgiving. I do not want to be the bigger person. I currently do not feel healed, though I have an idea many layers have fallen off and soon I will see.

More of the discussion continued with the topic of how certain choices have impacted large areas of our lives. One woman described her leaving her husband thirty years earlier. This was a big decision and looking back, it is still good, as she could see how many life alterations were possible because of it. Another man talked of his 'choice decision' he was currently experiencing. He has been remodeling his house for the duration of this class. His intention all along was to have it finished, as his result of our class. He said he ordered glass for his bathroom this week, and had to put it on a credit card. He talked of him being glad this was the final piece, and nervous because the amount was on his credit card. Though, after evaluation, the glass was definitely in line with his intentions. The seemingly 'bad choice' of the balance remaining on the credit card, was only one small hurtle he was ready to overcome. His intention was his remodel; he had to remind himself of that when the last purchase decision was being made. I feel he made the right one.

We had break, and then after our CD began again. We were listening to examples of four different kinds of imagination. *Spontaneous imagination* is in the subconscious; it has happened before. We can pull from this easily. Such as a memory that has been painful or happy. *Willed imagination* helps you own your story. With this imagination, you can see yourself in a future event, and create what it is you want to create. You can see yourself depositing a million dollar check. You can see yourself in Paris. You can see yourself marrying the person of your dreams. *Picture imagination* is used when we lose our keys. We can imagine what we did, or where a good place they would be. We could use this when buying a car. We could imagine what our friends will say, or what a road trip would look like with the new car. As we do this, we can decide if this is the best car for us. Our fourth imagination is *mime imagination*. This imagination is used to improve ourselves. I could use this to see myself speaking on stage. I could see what it feels like, as I glance at the audience, or hear the quietness of the room.

If I practice, at first I practice my fears of being there, soon after a few times of experiencing this, I become prepared and ready to be in front of many people. (Smith, 1992).

We (the class) were encouraged to practice the presence of God for the week. We were to practice being in the now, being in the flow. As I write this, I am experiencing this, I feel very melancholy. I feel like I have given up control, and am watching events happen. My bias is that I have already experienced the next week ahead. You have not, because it has not been written. As I look back, and type past events, I see my level of stress which correlated with future events. Though now, I am reading my story instead of living it, and seeing it in a different perspective. The new perspective is calm and alleviating control. This is good. I am currently not happy or sad, just here. Just here is good, it is better than being wound so tight.

A woman commented, she said, "Lack is only something we are currently getting wrong; we just have to open up a little more to learn the real definition. Currently we just have it twisted." The real definition is: there is no lack. When we learn this, we see nothing but peace.

What I took from her comment was that God wants to give us all the good. Though He can only give us what we ask for. We ask (on an energetic level, not necessarily the same as what we ask on a conscious level) for what we can perceive. What we perceive, may not be the best that we can have. An example of this is that every time I want to quit something, (upon reflection) all I can come up with is to create an argument; so all ties can be cut. I would like to leave something, and still enjoy the ties in other parts of my life. Though because this is all I see (a fight, an argument,) God keeps giving it to me. I ask God every time for it to be better. But asking is conscious; I have to clear my intent on an energetic level. I have to feel I can create a happy exit.

Next we were together in prayer groups. Our first prayer was for the spirit with in us all to remind us to be grateful for all we have. The spirit within us all helps us to forgive our debt, as we forgive our debtors. God within us all helps us shine through as our true selves. We asked for continued pursuits for academic excellence. And God within helps us be in line with our free-will, and serve our highest, holiest, purpose self. God brings us health. This or something much greater! There are many blessings with us now, and continuing to unfold for our good.

After our prayers, I began to talk. I told the group about the letting go I was doing for the week. I told them how I let go of feeling like I was the only one who could save the dogs. When I did this God found them all foster homes. This comment must have been vulnerable; it was followed up with another.

A girl in our group said her expenses from her divorce, are less than they were when she was married. Though she seems to be holding a belief that because she is a 'single mom,' she should be struggling. Logically she should not be. When she was offered the opportunity to increase her income three-fold, this scared her. This was creating a big shift for her. Submitting the button to say, "Yes" (to the increase in income) was the gold at the end of the rainbow. She was deciding to move forward from the beliefs that were holding her back. She mentioned that getting the job is only the icing on the cake, as shifting her belief is where the real excitement is.

As I was leaving class I was walking out with a friend. I ended up breaking down (again) and telling him how hard it was for me to forgive people in my life. I told him about all the stress from the renters, how my dad never cared, how my grandpa messed up my plans on a property. He told me I needed to let this go. He told me a story of him. Years ago he had been a drug attic. He caused many hurts. He said, "Let me say sorry for them; please move on." I thought a lot about that on my way home. I did want to forgive, for me. I did want to let go, for me. I knew I was, little by little.

I was home. Brian was watching a movie. I was glad he was occupied; I wanted to be by myself. I called my girlfriend. We had not talked in a week; there was lots of catching up to do. She told me she met a man. This man came into her life much unexpected. He was 'just there' one day. He is everything she had hoped for. He speaks and thinks on the same level as her. He is accomplished. He has plenty of money. He is a drummer. He is creative. He is good looking. He is perfect.

I am excited for her. She is an example of what happens in our lives when we finally let go of all the bad. Something so incredible, much better than we expected, shows up. Soon I was asleep.

Chapter 11
Humpty Dumpty finally fell

Friday morning was here. It was a good morning. Brian took the kids to school; everyone was okay even though there seemed to be so much stuff in a mess. We were low on food, but this was okay. The (foster) dogs were still here, but Saturday was coming. I had ten dollars left of my babysitting money. I asked Brian to bring me home some cigarettes after the kids were at school. He said, "Okay." We had ten dollars, this was good. We were still making it. We were okay. Brian brings me home one pack, because he bought himself a pack also. This is okay, I wanted two packs, but at least I had one.

I did some writing. Writing is therapy for me, it helps me breathe. I did a video blog. Then I called the rental company. This was something I was putting off. There were some issues that needed to be figured out; I just hoped they would take care of it. Today was the day it could not wait anymore. The rental company told me the new renters are only on month two of the contract, and have not paid rent (for this month) yet. I asked her what her next step was. She said, "I really don't know, I thought they were good, they looked good on paper." She said she gave them a five day notice, and the expiration was at the end of today. She said she was going to get ahold of the renter by Monday. She said she really did not want us to go through another eviction.

She also told me that according to the county website, the eviction (from the other property) has not been filed yet. She would get back with me on when that was to happen. I also asked about the status of one of the vacant properties; I had asked them to rent this one out. She did not know, and when the person that did know comes back, they would call me. I got off the phone with her, just baffled. I laughed. I realized I am a pretty good manifestor. I am manifesting a pretty 'crazy' story! I knew I could not do anything about it because it was all so odd. This all was for me. The only thing I could do was to manifest the opposite of all of this. I also realized I held a lot of guilt. Now that the rental company cannot collect rent from their own renter, I no longer thought I was a 'bad' landlord. These things are just happening. I do not have to feel guilty and think I am 'bad.' These are just situations, they are not happening to me because I deserve them or I am 'bad.' I had been feeling a lot of guilt, feeling like I deserved it. As I feel these feelings, more 'bad' things happen. It is a spiral.

After this, I intended to make me better. Within a half hour I was crying again. I gave up. I then called the doctor and asked for an appointment for depression.

I figured, I am so against drugs, but if drugs are going to have me not think depressive thoughts, then something should shift. I no longer am afraid of drugs; I am willing to do anything to relieve me of these lower feelings. I want to clear, I intend to clear and I give up all control of how that happens. I just want the end result. I want to feel better. The nurse told me I could have an appointment at three today, or I would have to wait till the next week. I called Brian and of course he did not answer his phone. I started crying, I can't even make the appointment to get better. I felt very lost, very unsupported, and very alone.

I wrote this next passage attempting to pass these feelings. "Why am I so sad? I am sad because my life is not happy. Maybe I miss my mom. Maybe I feel overwhelmed and that nobody loves me. Nobody wants to hire me; nobody wants to be my friend. Nobody cares to feed me. Nobody cares to clean my house. Nobody loves me. Nobody cares about my dreams. Nobody emails me back. I send an email and no response. Nobody cares that I am all alone. Just like when I lost all of my friends. Nobody cared then and nobody cares now. It feels good to have Cletus call 'out of the blue.' It felt horrible when I questioned myself about the puppies' death. It is sad to watch a dog die and not be able to save them. I feel inadequate. I feel like I can't save them because I can't save myself. I feel like there is no hope. I feel like I am too deep in the hole. I don't know what to do to get better. I don't know if I can be saved. I am loosing hope. I do not know what to do. I think I am going to go get some depression pills. Maybe chemicals will help. I do not know if this is the right decision. I am a healer. I should be able to heal myself. I do not want to get pills and then have them make me worse. All I can think of right now is to get on an exercise routine. I just do not know if that is enough. I want someone to swoop in and help. I have been battling with this for a while. Maybe if I do make an appointment, then it will be a start. Maybe by talking about it, it will get better. When I was a kid I was sad and self-conscious. A time I remember being really happy was when Brian was in Iraq for the first time and I had Aidan. I felt good. I felt great. I need direction. Maybe I need a counselor. Maybe they can listen to my stories and help. I just feel like such a fool to tell people about this stuff. I am supposed to know what to do. But now I do not know what else to do. I am scared to talk to them. Though I also feel everything I learned does not suggest anything non-metaphysical. I am mad that it is Friday and that it is 1:33. I maybe could have gone in and had it over with if the appointment would have been earlier.

I think I am scared to admit failure. I am scared someone will laugh at me. I logically know that is not the case; but I feel that.

When I was a kid they made us go to a therapy group for all kids whose parents were deployed. I could not talk then. I felt embarrassed when I accidently cried. I was sad then. Maybe all of this is about that. I never dealt with it. I clammed up. My dad was at war. I am an adult now; I should be able to get over it. I feel embarrassed talking about this stuff with a counselor.

I could use these writings for a therapist, though I am all by myself with them. Maybe a therapist will help move this stuff out of me faster. But what if I cry? What if I break-down? I guess I need to. I need to cry to get it all out. I am just so damn embarrassed. And what if I embarrass myself by crying and it does not go away? What do I do then? I need help. I am now willing to get help. God, I guess it's up to you. I trust you will bring me my answer.

Friday evening, I was in a 'defeated' mood. Brian took care of the kids and I watched a movie. The movie was sad, I cried. It was about a 'rich' kid who wanted to be his own person, though his father controlled a lot of his life. He ended up marrying a 'poor' girl and his father cut the money off. He still worked his way through law school and eventually made it. His wife got to quit her job and they were trying for their first baby. During this time he still missed his father. The wife ended up with cancer and died. Our character borrowed money from his father to ensure his wife died with no pain. He hired the best of the best for his wife's last days. After her death, the father and the son forgave each other for all the past hurts. It was a happy ending.

Brian had gone to the store to get dinner and gas. His credit card was declined, so he could only put 20 dollars in the tank. This sucked. We aren't even using credit anymore, just minimally until we figure out how to budget gas and cigarettes. This was just one more thing to set the mood.

Soon I was asleep.

....

Saturday morning was here. Here was a big day, are you ready? Warning, you might cry, I did.

I am writing this after the fact, so we are getting realizations as we dialog all of the events. Tithing has been a goal of mine; I am glad I am finally doing it. Tithing is asking God to restructure your life into what you prefer to grow into. Restructuring means some things have to be torn down. And just as a wall might go through pain, as nails are stripped from its skin, as we restructure we might also feel pain. Nevertheless, pain is a normal part of life. It does not mean you are 'bad' because you experience it, it means you are living and it is a part of experiencing. It means we are moving in the right direction and it is a necessary part of the process. With this said, here comes Saturday.

Saturday I had my morning to myself. Soon it was time to load up the dogs to take them to the puppy event. I was still feeling the vibration from yesterday, and the past weeks. I was feeling defeated. Brian had planned to go to Denver for the day to help Richard record his CD. I had an empty gas tank, and a lot of sad emotions.

Knowing all of this, I knew a shift had to be made. I had a realization; I had to let go and trust God. All of a sudden I decided to write some goals down. I asked for some big stuff, and for Brian to be able to go to Denver. I asked God for him to figure out where the gas money was coming from. I did not want to figure it out. I let my requests go, because I had no clue of how they were going to work out. I had no choice but to let them go. I did want Brian to go because it helped me that he was out of the house and clearing his own energy. I also prefer to drive my car and not Brian's truck. With all the dogs, there is more room in his truck. I started to ponder this question. My answer came. I would put two dogs in one kennel in the back of my jeep. I would fold up Oliver's kennel. I would let Oliver just sit in the back seat. I also had the small kennel that I could put the puppy and Lexi in. They would all fit. When Brian woke up I told him of my plans with the dogs. I also told him I wanted him to go to Denver this evening. I was trusting that this would happen. Some way, somehow, we were going to get the gas money. I asked him to trust and see what happened.

I get to the dog fair feeling down. The only thing I could do was remind myself that I was 'trusting God' and to keep moving. My vibration was low, but my body kept going in and out, as I got a dog kennel or another dog to add to the event. I attempted to socialize, though it seemed that everyone was distancing themselves from me. I went to move a dog into a different kennel, because a dog had peed in the first one. The agency lady looks at me, and in a mad rush yells, "Not that kennel (the one from my house) there is sickness in it." I did not react; I just watched this. I thought her distancing herself from me, and her reacting the way she did with the kennel, was because I had asked her for money each time I came to the event. I thought she was mad about that. So I just let all of this happen. I figured, 'This too shall pass.'

I saw Twiggy was back and was very happy. I held Twiggy and Lexi the entire event. I fell into the joy these two gave. After a while the puppies, which were at my house that had to go to the vet a few days ago, were at the event. They all three were sick; they had that 'look.' It was the same 'look' I saw in the puppies that had died. I knew this evening was their last evening. Someone eventually left and took them to the vet again.

Soon I saw different people than usual on the phone with June. I thought this was weird.

After a minute I told a foster mom (on the phone with June) to tell her I was taking Twiggy (also) home if she was not adopted. The foster mom (with this comment) quickly walked out of the room, almost as if either she needed somewhere quiet to talk, or she did not want me to overhear her conversation on the phone. I watched this.

The event got better. A lot of dogs were being adopted. Four new foster families filled out an application. Oliver was adopted! Then before the end a foster mom came up to me and suggested I clean my house with bleach to make sure my house did not carry germs of the puppy disease Parvo. I just looked at her. The thoughts running through my head were, "The dogs that died in my house were diagnosed with dehydration, not Parvo." The dogs were tested, and the tests came back negative. We knew this a few weeks ago. Why was this coming up again? Again not knowing what to do, I just watched.

The event was over; we left at three, not two. We left late because of the success at the end of the event. I think eight dogs were adopted! I was in a much better mood. I gave back a kennel, and took only one big dog home. The other dog went home with her new foster mom. My puppy was also adopted. I took home Lexi and Twiggy. I did not stick around to chit chat. It was a long week, and I chose to be quiet as my vibration was still not as high as I would have preferred. I drove home. I knew all of my 'stuff' from the last few weeks was clearing, and I just had to be patient instead of judging it, as it took its time to pass.

When I was home, the house was clean. Brian told me Richard's new girl was being dropped off, and she was paying for gas for Brian and her to get to Richard. This was cool. Brian got to go, and we received the financial help we needed. This was a vulnerable thing to ask for. I am usually the one always with enough. It was a little humiliating to ask for gas money; though when we did, Richard was more than willing to help. Our coffee maker also broke this morning. Brian said he was going to shower, than run to his office to give me his, so I had coffee for the morning. Brian left and I decided it was time to go through Dreana's toy box. I figured by cleaning it out, it would help push emotions out of me. We go through her toys every few months, and give her 'junk' to the thrift store.

I had taken a break for a minute and checked my phone. It was a busy day and knew there were some text messages to attend to. I had received a message delivered at noon (half way through the puppy event.) The message was from June. It said, "Michelle, I need you to go home now. If these three puppies die, it means you have killed five puppies within a month at your house. All the symptoms are the same. They were malnourished.

That means they all died a painful death. Words cannot describe how upset I am that you didn't take the time to check on these puppies and make sure they were healthy. Instead all I got from you was 'Maybe this or maybe that.'"

This message was unexpected. I sat for a minute with my mouth open. I was mad, hurt, confused; I was it all. I called my girlfriend. She was at the store. She took two minutes to listen to my story and told me to breathe; she promised she would call me back in twenty minutes when she was home. I was mad; I wanted to yell at June. I tried my hardest to stop. I called Brian. He had been waiting at the store (drop off location) for Jackie, she was stuck in traffic and not there yet. He thought June's message was messed up and told me not to worry about it. He said we did everything 'right,' and June was probably just upset and taking it out on us. He assured me everything would be better soon, and encouraged me not to 'blow up' on her. He told me he was coming home for a minute once Jackie was dropped off. He had forgotten to take the coffee maker out of his truck. This brought me comfort. He could give me a hug.

I was off the phone with him, and was mad again. I texted June, "I just received your message." I sat for a minute wanting to text more. I did. I was texting her how I was torn with what to do. I understood her rash comment because she herself was taking all of this hard (as was I.) I was also pissed off at her for even having these thoughts about me, none the less sending them my way. Before I could send the text message, my girlfriend called. Talk about intervention, God is good. It reminded me of a story I heard about Abraham Lincoln. He used to have a very flappy mouth to all of his oppressors, later in life he learned to write his aggressions in a letter, and promised to not send it until the next morning. He never sent these letters, and they were found after his death. It is a very good practice to write down your angry thoughts. As we write them down, the feelings have a way to get out, air out.

I talked with my friend. I cried. She listened. She told me that she read a Facebook post from the other day. It said, "When our heart gets broken over and over, it is because it needs that much breaking to get to the real, raw emotion again." Real, raw emotion is where we are able to be our authentic self. When our heart breaks, it is breaking off its mask, the mask that covers it up. Heart break hurts, though it is relevant to feeling happy. Throughout our conversation, I was mad and hurt; both, one after another. After all I had done, and this is the 'thank you' I get. The puppies died, it was not my fault. It was just my house that they died in. I cried a lot, because not only was it not my fault, it really hurts to have someone say and think thoughts like this about you. I thought this organization liked me.

I thought they knew I would never do anything to hurt these dogs. I thought they knew me. I trusted them; they betrayed me.

And then I came to acceptance. I understood June was overwhelmed. The stress I was under, her stress was ten times the amount. Also we (the organization) had a pregnant dog and she was rushed into the emergency room last week for an emergency C-section. Her puppies did not make it. (These dogs were at Melinda's, not my house). Melinda had also told me (this evening) that the mom dog had to be put down the hour prior. So there was a lot of death for June to be in charge of. I understood her grief, frustration, and feelings of out of control. I understood this, I accepted this. I felt a little better.

And then I cried again. And then I got mad again. This text message related to my renters. With my renters, I was a great land lord. I trusted them when they said they would reimburse me. I gave them time. I did the right thing. I always paid my mortgages. I committed to my commitments. I was the good one. Why were the renters not giving back what I gave to them? I then cried about having to ask for five dollars from the dog agency. How wrong was I that I couldn't afford to help these dogs? I then cried that we had to ask Richard for gas money. I then cried that we have been eating macaroni for three weeks. I cried and cried and cried.

My girlfriend listened. She told me she was honored to watch me as I cried; I was letting go. She said she was honored I trusted her to let her watch me. She said she was proud of me. She asked, If I could forgive myself for all of this. She asked, If I could forgive all of this death in my awareness. Can I forgive all of this heartache around me? If I could forgive myself enough to trust that all of this is growing me into whom I want to be. Who I want to be is more of who I am. I cried.

She and I ended our conversation. I thought about my Vlog's. My intent with this book and my video blog's was to go through my journey and have you watch what happens. I wanted you to see a down moment via me, and see it work out at a later date. I wanted you to know that a down moment was not the end in all. Tomorrow does come.

I was embarrassed to share my Vlog, but I knew it would be okay. It was my intent to show my vulnerability, and I was vulnerable. I cried on my video. I shared my video with the world.

I lay down for the night when Aidan came to cuddle with me. I told him what had happened, and my little man spoke the language of an adult. He said, "Mom, these dogs had been through a lot, their whole life has been a struggle. They could have gotten sick from any place along the way. They also could have been sick from the stress of living this life. We did nothing wrong, we loved them.

Some got sick and died; though we loved them anyway." He said it was not our fault, and I should never think anything else.

He is so sweet. I went to sleep.

Sunday morning was here. I was up early, feeling very different than the night before. I watched my Vlog from the night before and I cried. I watched it over and over, and all of a sudden it was not such a sting. It became an event. When you look at something enough, it no longer is the 'demon' or an obstacle; but something that can be moved through. I took a shower. I did another video and dialoged how 'clear' I felt. I spoke of how today did come. I spoke of the needing to be alive, to accomplish the tasks of today's to-do list. I felt so wise. I felt so appreciative of all the tears that helped bring me into the feelings of today. Without the tears I would still feel stuck. I was very grateful.

I received a phone call saying the realtor had an offer on my house. It was a good offer. I wanted an extra 2,000 dollars, though this was really good. This must mean a serious buyer. I was unsure of what to do, should I accept the offer or counter it? I was ok with not knowing the answer. I instead just allowed the day to unfold.

On the way to church, I was feeling neutral. The weight of the world was off my shoulders. Almost like the day after you are sick, you may not want to climb a mountain, but you are so happy to live and not be sick. I took the kiddos to Sunday school and I headed to church. I was looking forward to the meditation. I wanted to find answers for what I should do with the offer, and to keep me in this neutral energy. I considered asking a minister to pray with me after the service. They also were having an auction after church with lunch included. I considered allowing myself to socialize without my husband (he was still in Denver.) I was not sure; I figured I would find answers as the morning progressed.

The service was over and I was still considering lunch; I thought I would see what the kids thought. I went to Sunday school and as I was gathering my kiddos, Aidan decided to run and steal a cookie. He was laughing, so I was not sure if he was allowed to steal it or not. All of a sudden, the girl Sunday school teacher starts trying to get it out of his hand. The two are laughing as this encounter is happening. I just watched it, not knowing what to feel.

Then the guy Sunday school teacher grabs Aidan's body (in a very inappropriate way,) and chants over and over for him to give the cookie up and respect the female Sunday school teacher. Eventually Aidan gets up and says, "Sorry" to the teacher.

The male teacher looks at me as Aidan says his apology, his look was one of 'I do not know how the mom is going to take what she just saw; I guess I will wait for her to respond.' I did not know what to say. I know it did not feel right, but I had no words for what just happened. I took Aidan and Dreana out of the building. Aidan took our name tags and ran to church to drop them off. Dreana looks at me and tells me she forgot her toys, so we have to go back in. I take her in, and again I get that weird look from the teacher. I had found my answer. We were not having lunch with the church today. We drove home.

We were home and the kids occupied themselves with friends. I was in a really detached mood. I was not mad and not happy. I was in a wise vibration. Answers were coming from everywhere. I called my girlfriend. I let her know of my detached vibrations and wondered if she could assist with answers. I told her of the offer on the rental. She said to just keep waiting until I was pushed closer to accept or counter. I then told her of Sunday school. I told her from the moment I met the teacher, he seemed weird. I had a feeling that he thought thoughts of sexual abuse towards children. I also 'knew' until now, that my kids were safe there. It was okay for me to watch him the last few weeks until I knew more. And now I do not feel safe. Today was the breaking point. My kids were still safe, though the actions of our teacher became more physical than normal. I was beginning to think his thoughts were turning into actions. I made a decision that if we go back to that church; the kids were going into church with us and not Sunday school. We talked about everything I was feeling. The overall was to just keep watching. She told me more events of her new love life. All was good.

Soon Brian was home. He seemed relaxed; he had a good, needed weekend. He and I talked about the offer on the rental. We decided we were going to counter. We would do this after dinner, and after the kids were asleep. I also received a text message from Melinda. She said someone was coming to my house to hopefully adopt Bambino, my last big dog. They had texted and asked to come over at 4:30-5. I saw this as another sign of God, asking me to be more direct with my creations, my needs, my wants.

I texted back and said 4:30 would be good; 4:30-5 was not ok, 4:30 was. Brian and I then talked about Sunday school. I told him of my decision that I no longer felt comfortable with the kids going. He said the moment he met the male Sunday school teacher, he also had a 'funny' feeling about him. I asked what he meant. He said a few weeks ago the teacher had called and was wondering about the future attendance of Aidan.

He was creating a roster, and wanted to know who came to church regularly, and who came once in a while. Brian reminded him (then) that Dreana was also in the program. This confused the teacher. It confused Brian too. More than likely, their names would be together, since they both had the same last name. And there is only a max of twenty-five kids in the entire program. Two people with the same last name would usually trigger in most people's head. Though not our teacher, he was really thrown off when Dreana's name was mentioned. Brian said it seemed weird (at the time) that he was able to completely bypass Dreana's name because he was so (energetically) focused on Aidan's.

When Brian said this to me, every hair on my body stood up. I immediately called Aidan into our room and asked him question after question. I wanted to know everything that has happened in the last few weeks at Sunday school. His answers were comforting, as they led to nothing 'bad' that had occurred. I then questioned Dreana. Her answers were comforting as well. I told both kids that they no longer were going to that Sunday school. I said I did not feel comfortable with the teacher, and until we get a new teacher or new church, they are coming to the service with us. I let them know if next week they were upset, it was going to have to be okay. My decision was final, and all we could do from here was just 'go with it.'

Soon the neighbors came by and requested our kids to go play at their house. It was perfect timing because the couple that was coming to meet Bambino, were on their way. Well Bambino's couple was supposed to be on the way. Their baby was napping, and so they decided my time request of 4:30 was irrelevant, compared to the plans they currently found important. Usually I would understand this; no one wants to wake up a sleeping baby. Though now, I understand how important my requests are, and they too should not be ignored or bypassed.

As Brian and I sat and waited for them to show up at five instead of 4:30, we still found ourselves in that 'neutral' energy. We just watched, and did not judge our events. We talked about the text message (from June) the evening before. We decided that we loved the dogs, though the organization was not going to get better as it ran how it currently ran. We were only hurting the dogs by contributing to the organization. The dogs would eventually have a stronger organization when it was better run with better people. We decided if we let God take over, and we bow out, in the end the dogs would be better. If we stayed and allowed the disorganization to happen, we were not allowing the better to come in. We had to detach ourselves from it. I needed to walk away, and understand that my feelings for the dogs were being looked on by God. He knew how to help them, even if I no longer was with them.

I texted Melinda and told her my decision was to not be with the organization anymore. The people looking at Bambino were on their way over, and if they adopted him, that was awesome. If they did not, she needed to come get Bambino, Lexi and Twiggy this evening. She replied to my saying she needed a few days to find foster homes. I replied saying, "I am sorry for your troubles, though this is the evening you needed to be here to get the dogs." I asked her when I should expect her. She never replied back. My frustration continued. Now I was being taken advantage of again. I did not deserve the nasty text message, and now I also get to keep their troubles. I was mad.

I went to the grocery store and bought some spaghetti. We had dinner and the kids went to bed. Brian and I signed the offer for the rental and requested a counter offer for three thousand more than the offer price. We had to wait till the next morning because there was no counter offer in the email for us to fill out.

We went to bed.

....

Monday morning was here. I was still upset from the night before. I was trying to be patient and hoping to center myself as quickly as possible. I kept affirming, "God knows what to do." The kids were getting ready for school when I received an email from the realtor with a counter offer for us to sign. Brian and me rushed downstairs (where the printer and scanner are) to sign it and scan it off. Then Brian went to work and I took the kids to school.

When I was home I received a text message from the realtor saying she had not received the scanned counter offer. I thought this was funny. I took the time to ponder why this was happening. Was this God's way of telling me to just accept the offer? All of a sudden I get the urge to call my mom. I was upset with the business of the dogs, and the last thing I wanted to do was call her. I figured all we would do was complain about it, and that would help nothing. The urge was overwhelming; I fell into it. I called my mom, and we talked about the dogs. I then told her I had an offer that we just countered, though I wasn't sure if that is what we should have done. I told her if we countered two thousand dollars more, than we would have enough money to pay grandma back. My mom then said, "I talked to grandma last night, and she said she was going to waive the realtor fee. You would owe her less."

I then got mad. I screamed at her. I told her she had no business talking with the realtor about my transaction. Just because the realtor knows us both, they have no right to violate confidentiality. I told her Brian thought this was also weird the night before.

Why did the realtor tell my grandma she was writing an offer on our property over the weekend? We were mad last night, but decided to let it go. But it's happening again. She said, "Sorry." Then I screamed, "If you are going to talk behind my back, why would you not tell me about it before I submit a counter offer?" If I had known she was talking behind my back, then I would have known grandma was going to waive the realtor fee; and I would have accepted the offer and not countered it. Now I already countered it, and the buyer could walk away.

She said, "Sorry" over and over. She said she was just trying to help. Then I calmed down and said, "Well good thing the email did not go through yet to the realtor." My mom said she would call my grandma and ask her the specifics of what she was waiving, so I could move forward with accepting or countering. Soon the phone rang and it was my grandma. She clarified that she was not waiving any fees that were owed to her. Then she said she would do anything to make me happy. If I preferred, she would waive the remaining balance that I owed her anyway. Yep, all crazy; I know! I then told her that is not the answer. I enjoy paying back my debts, I just feel I can't right now. And I can't do anything about me not being able to fix it right now. We agreed that she would forgive me, and take the guilt off my shoulders. She said she understood I did the best I could to make good with her loan. We agreed that for the time being, there would be no remaining balance. And when I was back on my feet, and it was easy for me to pay back the remaining balance, at that time it would be received well. After I was off the phone with her, I felt better. I felt better because I could finally be honest with her. I wanted to pay her back; I was just having difficulty doing it right now. I could admit my hard times, and let her know I needed help. I was vulnerable with her. I felt a lot of weight come off my shoulders. I then called the realtor and let her know we were accepting the offer. That felt good. I could see the light at the end of the tunnel.

I wrote a lot this day. I was still very mad about the dogs. I was mad at feeling 'taken advantage' of by the dog organization. I wanted to get back at them; though I also knew I did not want the dogs hurt. My feelings of dropping the dogs off at Melinda's house and 'washing my hands of it' hurt me, because I would lose Lexi. I thought of taking the dogs to the pound, and telling her to pick them up from there. Though, this would put the dogs at risk. I felt helpless; I felt controlled. It was unfair. I had the 'unfair' emotion, the 'pity' emotion. I desired so much to gain forgiveness. I couldn't think of anything in the moment to make it better. I just sat with it. It currently was 'what it was.'

As I accepted this, I received inspiration. I Googled, "How to report a non-profit agency."

This was good, because truly the 'help' currently helping the dogs was not healthy. I felt 'right' about this. I know the agency is trying to help, though they need help 'helping.' I ended up getting the district attorney's office. They understood, and told me to call the pound and report the agency there. I sat with this for a minute, and decided I still wanted Lexi. So again I could not do anything. Then I got another idea. I made a complaint on the Better Business Bureau website. This made me feel better. Now there was proof that the agency needed help. They would be forced to reevaluate how they were helping the animals. So I did well. The complaint would go to someone who would assist a bigger and better agency. The dogs I had were safe and happy. In the future, because of my report, the agency would need to be restructured. They would be able to save a lot more animals then currently were being saved. I had made progress and I felt better. I still had some remnants of mad to deal with, though this was a great start.

After this, I thought about the properties. The original numbers that came back for another property I wanted to list, seemed impossible that I was going to be able to sell my house. But today I had the energy of mad and mad allows us to do things we are scared to do when we are sad. I called the realtor and asked if she thought we could get 41 thousand (This is the number we owed on the property) for the house. She said she thought 35. She said it would be tough for more. Today I was mad and was out of options. I asked her to 'try.' She sent over the papers and on Brian's lunch hour, we scanned the signed documents for both the accepted offer and the new listing back to her. The realtor texted back and said we were keeping her busy. She just finished listing my mom's other house. Again, there is that breach of confidentiality going back and forth. This was a trigger of mine. I just let it be.

I picked up the kids and we did homework. I knew my body was clearing; I felt numb and relief at the same time. We had a small dinner and the kids were soon in bed. Aidan spent the night with Bambino, and Dreana shared her bed with Lexi.

Later in the evening, I stopped being mad at the dog agency. I accepted Lexi leaving. Things again moved forward.
Soon we were all asleep.

....

Tuesday morning I was up making lunches, and encouraging the kids to move more quickly, as their pokiness was making them late. I was at school on time, and saw Dreana off to her class. I headed to the office with a checkbook, and picture order forms. I waited patiently in line, as I saw how cheery the staff was for a Tuesday morning. They were helping a new couple sign their kids up for school.

The wife stood behind the counter signing documents, while her military husband played with their two twins. They were nine month olds! They seemed so cute and loving. Soon it was my turn, and I told them that I called the picture corporation the night before, and have an address to send the order form. Though, I was hoping there still was time to turn them into the school. It would be easier if the school could be the middle person. They were so sweet and insinuated the request was small and easy to do. She collected my money and forms, and the process was complete! As I was leaving, I was full of relief and gratitude. I told them how thankful I was for them, and everything they have represented since we began school. I drove home feeling very thankful.

I checked my phone when I was home and saw the realtor texted; wanting to know which title company I wanted to choose for the property with the accepted offer. This was funny; I saw it as a manifestation coming true. This was one of my gripes when I listed the house! I wanted to choose the title company, and here I was being given the opportunity. I called an old friend and asked if he wanted to be my title company. I had to leave a voice mail. I assumed he would eventually say yes. I went ahead and let the realtor know he was our guy. She seemed pleased. She said, "Good choice," as she knew him very well. All the ladies seem to know him! He is a charmer and a very professional, successful business man.

I then went to shower. It felt good to make decisions. It felt good to start letting stuff go. I was moving forward, a lot was still in the works, but lots were moving forward. My shower was cleansing and comforting. I had a hard couple of weeks, and soon it would all reveal the 'new' me. I was changing, and it all is worth it. I was getting rid of the old and holding courage for the new. After my shower I poured some coffee as I texted the agency lady, saying I was going to need some dog food. Before I texted her, I had the fear if I contacted her she might take my Lexi. Though food was imperative; I needed to take the chance. After I pressed "send," my phone rang, it was my title company friend. He said, "I would love to be your title company."

He asked me what I had been up to, and what I was doing in Colorado. I let him know of my travels this year, and last. I updated him on my book. He told me I was an exceptional person, and I was one of those who could accomplish anything. He told me he loved how I took life by the edges, and made something of it. He told me I was a success. I was an inspiration. Oh did this feel good, considering my current feelings. What a nice thing to say. He is such a beautiful person. He told me he would take care of all the details for 'closing,' and keep me informed of anything he needed from me.

He made me feel he would take care of me; I needed this. Thank you again, I appreciate it! Our phone conversation was over, and I was feeling pretty good. Melinda had texted and told me she would get me food and wanted to know how I was doing. I was honest. I said, "I was still hurt, though okay with my decision in moving forward without the agency." She told me she was sorry for all that had happened. She thanked me for all of the dogs that I helped save. She also told me she was trying her hardest to find new foster homes, and asked if I could keep them until Saturday. I told her, "Thank you for saying 'sorry and thank you.'" All I could do was say, "Sure about Saturday," because, I still really wanted Lexi.

I then called my brother and asked him if he would drive to the rental company and give them a check for me. I would send him the reimbursement in the mail, but wanted the money to them today. I had decided to evict the tenant in the new property. More than likely she was good with her money, and would pay me back immediately; though she was the last string, I couldn't play anymore. This is unfortunate; this is how good people get screwed. They come at times when the bad have already been there. You know when you finally do one thing that is bad, and you get in big trouble. Well the reason this has happened, is because someone did a whole bunch of bad stuff, and the person on the receiving end has had enough. It just so happens, that the good person gets the brunt.

Cletus told me he would, but I should probably call Steve (my mom's husband) first. Because he was planning to go to the rental company, and inquire about why they still had not cashed his check. He then asked me if I would like to see him in the next few months. He was planning a trip to Wyoming with some buddies in January, and was considering having the boys drive while he flies. Wyoming is only four hours from me. He wondered if he should stop here in Colorado first. I thought it was a great idea! Cletus and I have a lot of healing to do. I would really enjoy him coming to visit! I only requested that he provide me with the gas money when I drive him to his friend's house, when our weekend was over. He smiled (I could hear it) and said he thought he could handle that part. Before getting off the phone with me, he told me his plans were not definite, apparently he was the fifth guy in a usual 4-man trip. He was still working himself in as the 'extra,' but was planning for all of this to be a go. I have a lot of confidence that he is going to make it to Wyoming; and on the way he and I will get to hang out.

I later became frustrated with the rental company, again. I was curious why it was taking them so long to file the eviction. It had been a week, a week further into my debt.

I was happy that Steve was on top of his check, (and checking to see if it cleared yet) so questions could be asked. I was also mad because Steve seemed to be invading my privacy. I had asked him for money, which he previously owed me. I did not ask him to be my property manager or manager of my property manager. He could have better handled it by letting me know his check was not cashed, and had me call the rental company to ask the questions. I decided (in this moment) to let it go. I was frustrated with him, though I did not know how voicing my frustration would help (currently.)

Steve had told me he was not planning on driving over there (to the rental company,) just calling. I said, "Okay" with the new info. I could now move forward with what to do next. He then asked me to keep him informed with when the eviction was to happen. He told me he thought the rental company was 'dragging their feet.' I was more frustrated with his input, but also saw it as relevant concerns. I just said, "Okay" and quickly ended our conversation.

I then called the rental company and inquired about the eviction. The lady on the phone said the person in charge of that was not in the office, but she would get back to me when they were. We also talked about the property they had not rented yet. She was informing me (19 days later) that the property was not rentable because a few things had to be done with it. I almost flipped, I told her we will not be renting it; we instead will be selling it. And the realtor would be by later to pick up the keys. We then talked about the missing rent check from one of the rentals. She told me she had not received the remaining money yet. I asked her what her opinion was on if, she thought the renter would be willing to change her lease to a month-to-month, if I choose not to evict her this month. I also wanted her opinion to see if the renter would be good to the realtor, if we put the house on the market. Again she told me the lady who knew the renter was not here today, and this is when I asked for the renters phone number, I wanted to call her myself. I was starting to see my role in this whole mess was to start acting more like the person in charge, instead of assuming everyone else was appropriately managing. She told me she was unsure of confidentiality if she gave me the renter's phone number. She told me she would let me know by the end of a day with a phone call.

After I was off the phone with her, I felt better again. I felt like things were going to be alright. I was moving into my role again of being in charge, and I tended to be successful in this area. I realized I did not need to be upset about the lack of other parties; I just needed to direct them. People appreciate when I take on the role of manager; this is when they respond to me best.

Brian picked up the kids, this was nice. Aidan had been writing a story at school in his free time for the last few months. He was excited to have me read it. I love this. I love connecting with him in this way. And not only did I like him writing; he is good at it. Dreana then read me her story she wrote. She recapped the, "Lady and the Tramp!" Her book was all pictures; it was clipped together and presented itself very well. My kids are awesome!

Melinda was supposed to be coming by with food and pills for the dogs; no Melinda yet. She was also supposed to be bringing pills because Twiggy started coughing and puking. This really would not have concerned me; it appeared just like a little cold. But after everything, I no longer was 'playing.' I had texted her that afternoon, and said she needed to bring medicine or take Twiggy to the vet. If she did not, it was not 'on me' if Twiggy got really sick. I soon had to leave and take Dreana to Girl scouts. We were going to the police station for her event. I was a little off with my emotions, though kept moving forward. Dreana was cranky; actually I think this is her new personality. She is a young woman who tells you what she wants, and she sticks to her guns. She is not crabby, just dominant.

We get to the police station and the officer behind the counter told us to go to the City Hall; we were at the wrong place. She was kind and dominant herself. I asked her for the address and she starts giving directions. I explain I was new to the area, and preferred an address for the GPS. She just laughs it off and says, "It is easy to find." I kind of just went with that. What could I do; all I do is move forward.

We did find the City hall. We walk in and were directed to go upstairs to the meeting room of the mayor. It was a big court room setting. We were late, so the presenter was already giving his speech. The Girl Scout lady came to us and gave us toys and cookies. She directed Dreana to the side table where her girlfriends were. Most of the parents there were sitting in the spots that the judge and council would sit. I thought this was cool to see. I wondered what their girls' thoughts of them up there were. I sat in the audience. The Girl Scout lady kept looking over at me. I think she is hoping we become friends, but is nervous as we move forward. She is the one that asked me to give a speech about the law of attraction.

Our speaker was this cool looking officer. He was Indian, and totally displayed the typical stereo type. He was good at what he did. He connected with the girls at their level, and was also able to educate them in all his job consisted of. He was patient and awesome. The girls had been given a speech, a movie, and a tour of the whole building.

It was a good night. One of the things I noticed on the tour, was the seven pictures that were displayed of the 'leaders' of the building. Three were women, our mayor was a woman, and our tour guide was a 'minority.' I found this cool; our society has changed a lot over the years; we are much more feminine in our leadership. I also noticed this with the kids' school. The two leaders of the school are woman, and I can guarantee you that their school is awesome! I am not saying that only woman can do this; but woman can do a lot. When I see them in charge, I am usually pleased.

Dreana and I then were in the car heading home. She still had her attitude and I was doing my best to maintain my happy mood from the evening. We spent an extra thirty minutes on the road; we were lost. It was still good. When I was home, I learned Melinda failed to show-up. She had texted me and asked if I could just use my dogs' food to feed the foster pups. She had to take one of her dogs to the vet because now she was really sick. There were a lot of sicknesses among all of these dogs. What could I do? Well I could do a lot of things, though the reasons I did not do them was because I truly love these dogs. So I just went along with my evening.

Another thought I had was Melinda's text seemed 'stressed.' She was going through all of this 'out of control,' and was trying her best to keep control. She didn't understand that her lesson was to 'let go.' All of this 'bad' stuff was going to keep happening, until she finally gave up. She needed to give up; this would let the project continue on a course that was much better. When we are no longer controlling something, we fear. Though, when we let go, we get something much better. When we go through this, loss is hard. Letting go is a hard thing to do. Our lesson is a daily practice of falling into the loss, so it can eventually die off, and turn into something much better.

This realization reminded me of when I quit real estate. This was the 'right' decision, though as I went through it, there were many layers as I let go. I remember in the beginning (when I quit) my girlfriend also quit. At that moment, quitting never even crossed my mind. In hindsight, it was the beginning of my inner self not wanting to be there anymore. She had quit, and went onto her new adventure. She just cut ties; she did not 'regret' her decision. She knew it was no longer where her heart was. When I began quitting real estate, I thought of her a lot. I instead tried to hold on. I ended up switching real estate companies, and prolonging the hurt of leaving. She didn't, she just knew it was no longer her journey, and left.

This makes me thankful about the puppy agency. I am 'being' my girlfriend right now. I am quitting, the moment it no longer feels right.

Melinda is 'being' me, she is trying to hold on and eventually she also will quit. Though with a lot of extra stuff to work through later. There are reasons that all of these dogs are dying. Something better needs to be done. Such as cleansing the diseased pound from where all of these dogs are coming from. Another option is giving all the dogs medicine before they leave the pound, prior to them all going to different houses, not after. Another option is being more careful and organized with their money. They throw twenty dollar bills to every problem. They purchase all their food at an expensive store. This store sells dog food more expensively than lots of other places. They could plan ahead, and buy the food from another store. They could buy multiple bags all at once, and probably get a discount. Another suggestion, all of these dogs had to go to the emergency vet. If they had proper medication prior to coming to all of the foster homes, the money spent on the emergency vet would not need to be spent. The emergency vet is a 500 dollar bill. Obviously if this agency would stop, breathe and re-center, much more good could come. Melinda is not 'seeing' this. She is stuck in the vibration of 'worry.' God is helping her 'stop,' by giving her problems until finally the problems are heavier than the need to fix them. When she gets to this point, she will throw her hands up, and a lot of awareness will come her way. The world will benefit from all of these good aware-nesses. With her clear head, a lot more animals will be saved. Our problems are good, and help create better creations in our world. With this awareness, I felt happy and calm. This felt good. I felt I could easily handle the holidays as they were soon approaching. I was becoming centered, and many of my aware-nesses were coming to me, to help me change.

The next thing I had on my list was the renter still owing money. I called the rental company when it was five (their time;) no answer. This frustrated me; they were supposed to let me know when the eviction was scheduled. I decided it was okay; I would call in the morning. I was happy with my new found 'role' in checking up on them. I could not check up on them now; tomorrow was good. Each day is progress. I just have to stay on them. I do not have to stress; just do my job at daily checkups.

The realtor then called and asked if we could turn on the power for the house with the accepted offer, it needed to be on for the home inspection. I did not know this answer; so I gave the question to Brian. He called, and had the power turned on. He told her the furnace would not work unless there was LP juice in it, and Brian did not want to pay for it. The buyer put his own money into the tank, and that was taken care of. No loss on our end.

As we were preparing dinner we heard the doorbell. It was only 5:30, but dark outside because of winter. We were surprised to see Aidan's friend. He wanted to play. He came in and the kids played Legos. Brian ran to the store. Soon he was home and it was time for dinner and Aidan's friend went home. We had spaghetti. This was a good dinner. It seemed like it was the best spaghetti we had in a while. It was full of vegetables! It was a very rich dinner. The beer was good. Dinner was good. Life is good.

As I lay in bed waiting to fall asleep, I remembered the clothes Aidan's friend's mom sent over. They no longer fit his friend. She gave them to Aidan. I am receiving, it feels good to receive. It was late, though I still texted her and said, "Thank you." We need to hear that even if the gifts seem small. The clothes were a very generous gift, thank you!

....

Wednesday morning was here. Brian had taken the kids to school. As I was about to begin my morning kid free, I received a text message from Brian. Dreana had received a cool pen from girl Scouts, and had taken it to school with her. As she was walking into class, she ran out of line and ran to Brian, and told him she thought her teacher might think her pen is a toy. She decided it was better that Brian kept it safe with him, at work. This was cute. It was cute to see Dreana getting big, so smart. I love it when I see her personality come out in her own decisive way.

My morning coupled with Dreana's comment, sent me in a frenzy of why I should love my life so much. There are so many happy moments. I have really experienced many of my dreams. I can actually say I had a successful business with rentals! I have done it. Yes it is going away, but to be able to have had it, is something worth being grateful for! I have been a realtor, and a successful one at that! I am now a stay at home mom! I am currently writing my first book! I do everything I want to do. Not many people do that. I instead choose me first, and go with it. This is a good feeling; I always wanted to be that three percent. I act as if I am every day. I am a pretty successful person. The business I am in is 'Me!' I grow more into it each day. I am a pretty lucky person. I am lucky to trust in me this much, and to succeeded with it. My current job is to get better at being me; to continue to become even more successful at it.

Continuing on with these awesome aware-nesses, I remembered a time when I was in the Army. I had a lot of money, and I continued to make more of it. I also felt bad about having it, and that other's needs were more important than mine. I had people always asking for my money, as I always gave it away. One particular experience was when a guy came to me and asked to borrow money. I gave him my room key, and said I had money laid out on my bed.

I had been counting it, as I was preparing to go on vacation to see my boyfriend at the time (my plane ticket money.) This man stole all my money and I had to hurry up and make more to go. I repressed this memory for a long time. I felt like a fool. I felt too timid to yell at him or stop others from taking from me. I was livid that I attracted all of this, and livid with myself that I couldn't stop it.

I realized today, that those people would always be doing what they were doing. A thief is always a thief, that is just who they are. I could stop them from taking from me, but I did not have to care if they continued to do it to anyone else. This is what they did; I could just stop them from doing it to me. And how this continues is, if I stop them from doing it to me; I lead by example, and then others stop people from doing it to them. Soon there is no one left to steal from. I did not have to feel guilty, that I let that happen to me. I just needed to let it go and not let it happen anymore. This realization helped. I stopped beating myself up for what I did in the past. I realized I no longer needed it to happen; so it wouldn't. Also the guilt I felt, that I let this happen, no longer needed to be there. I forgive myself. The guilt the guy could have felt, he could still feel it. I was no longer going to take his guilt from him. I am done; I forgive myself. The past is the past. I let it go.

This goes along with my renters. It is what it is. I have decided to forgive my perceived lack in my management of what happened. It is done. I am moving on. I no longer feel guilty about what I could have done better. I did what I did, and it is done. Same goes for past relationships. I forgive myself for how they fell apart. Currently I am moving on, and I am bringing more of today into my days. I forgive myself, in all that has been done. The past is the past, and I am moving forward.

I am also moving forward with my feelings of the dog agency. I no longer am feeling guilty for them. I have done my part. They now are in a mess. They have to find the way out. I was feeling guilty for not being able to help more. But guilt gets all of us nowhere. As I release my guilt, I trust that God knows the best way for all of us to move forward. I also remembered when the foster mom was here. She and I were doing well, until I started evaluating how we could change for the better. Then is when she became uncomfortable. The people the agency was attracting, were people who wanted to be in a mess. I no longer wanted to be in a mess. I want to move forward.

Brian was home for lunch, I was writing, and in a pretty good mood. Writing clears me. I had taken the last half hour to do the bills. I was in a great mood, and this is the best time to do them. Brian then tells me I also have to pay another credit card.

He was supposed to be paying this with some extra money he was getting in another account. He said he could not pay it this time, because the minimum balance was more than he had. I was a little irritated, but just saw the money and knew we had enough. He tells me he needs 150 dollars. I tell him to go pay it online. He then runs upstairs and tells me he actually needs three hundred dollars. I asked him why so much. I thought the balance was only five hundred dollars. He says, "I don't know." This irritated me. I hate when he doesn't know, or seems like he doesn't care.

I looked at the balance on his computer, and it is more than 5,000 dollars. I asked him how it got that high. He says, "I don't know." Then I got mad. We had just had this conversation the other day about our bank account in Colorado, and him spending money without checking the account balance first. I was livid. I asked how the heck it got that high, and why hasn't he been checking it to realize it was that high. I told him when it had gotten to 500; I would have seen that as a problem. I was confused that he wouldn't. Where was his check point? He had no answer.

I had to bring him to work because he came home with his truck, and then was picking his boss up with the government car. His boss would drop him off at the end of the work day. All the way to his work, I yelled and screamed and said I did not want any more surprises. If he did not have a limit, then he gets no more money. I said I understood that he was trying to provide for the family; but providing for the family involves my decisions too. As he thought he was just providing, he had no clue how any of it was going to be paid back, so really he was not providing for the family. He was causing me more stress, months down the road. I was mad because he thought he was 'handling it.' But really, it was not being handled because it ended up as a mess for the future.

As I was dropping him off, still miffed; I put my military I.D. back in my wallet, and noticed an extra forty dollars. Where did this money come from? This was cool. Still to this day (Sunday, a week later) I am still mystified of where that money came from! This is how it has been lately; something 'bad' happening, and also something good. It is hard to get excited, or really mad. I just ride the middle.

Another realization came my way. You know how they say in reference to business, the 80-20 rule? This rule applies to our lives as well. We need to take care of ourselves 80 percent of our time, and the other 20 percent goes to all the other stuff, all other people. As we are filled up, we have more energy and resources to take care of the rest. When we are depleted, and continue to take care of everyone else, this is where no one gets help.

Remember to remember you first, remember all others when you are over filled; Then it becomes a no-brainer to help and give.

I was home and the current theme lately has been something great and something bad at the same time. The other theme is realization and the next moment very angry. I had let Aidan walk home, as he promised to walk straight home, check in, and then continue to his friend's house. 45 minutes later he was not home, and I started to worry. I was back in my car and saw him hanging at his friend's house. He sees me, and I tell him to get home. He gets home and I inform him he is grounded. I have calmed down, so I can talk with him. I tell him he had me worried, and I currently do not know what to do. But for now, he needs to just be in his room. He understood. He actually went to his room without a fight, and played Legos.

Right after I received a ring at my door bell. The neighbor was over because his grandma wasn't home when he got home. Today was an early release so he thought his grandma had forgotten. Aidan asked if he could stay until his grandma figured out what was going on. I said, "No." I felt this was the right decision in the moment. I had an urge to 'help' in this situation, though I also knew it was imperative to just be alone as a family now. I had to let go and let God take care of the neighbor's situation.

Then I receive another knock on the door. When the knock at the door happened, I became frustrated. I was thinking, 'what next.' I run down stairs and it's Melinda. I was frustrated it was her. I have been frustrated for the last week (with her) and frustrated that she should have been here last night. My appearance is very angry. I see the dog food, and grab it. I say, "Thanks." She is very nervous and shaking, and she tells me she has pills for me as well. The only thing going through my head was, "What if Twiggy would have gotten sick yesterday, where were these pills yesterday?" I say, "Thanks for the pills." She then hands me a ten dollar bill. She tells me she felt bad that I had to feed her dogs with my dogs' food. I say thanks and walk away. I thought how funny it is that all you need shows up unexpected. I also thought how funny it was that I attracted money. I also thought how funny it was that I could accept money; though only when I was mad. There was no resistance to the money now; I felt like I deserved it. An affirmation I made then, was it was great I was able to receive when I was mad. But I also wanted to learn to receive when I was not mad. I gave eight dollars to God; one dollar from the ten, and four from the forty. I also had a whole slew of quarters sitting in my car that showed up miraculously. It could have come from Brian or Richard from last weekend, who knows. But there was some unexpected money sitting in my car.

Later I had been outside with the dogs. They started to bark at a lady walking by. At first, I told them to be quiet. This lady did not continue to walk away as most people do; she stopped, and talked with the dogs. She then grabs some treats out of her jacket, and throws them through the fence. I watched all of this, and thought about how sweet it was. She was not annoyed with my dogs; she instead loved them enough to reward them. I had never seen this lady before. Part of me thought she was an angel. See again, one moment I am angry, and then the next this angel walks into my life.

I then received a call from my mom. She was telling me, in the next few hours she was going to know if she was buying a house or not. All of this was weird because she originally wanted to move because she wanted to be closer to her sister. She felt alone at the house she currently was at. It was too far from my brother and her sister's house. So for the heck of it, she put her house on the market. She also started looking at houses for sale around her sister's house. A week later, she received an accepted offer on her house. She went and looked at the house she liked for a second time, and now was not too sure. Except now, she had to move within thirty days. In the meantime, her plans changed again.

My mom was considering purchasing a duplex, so she and her husband could live on one side, and her mother and father could live on the other. Though this is not what she wanted. She wanted to live near her mom, but not in a duplex. She was pulling at straws, trying to make it all work. As I type all of this, it reflects me, in how I have been trying to live life for a while. Where I see something I have wanted come in, in a way that almost fits. It almost fits; it is not perfect, it is only a version of what I want. For a few weeks I did not hear much of her decision. It appeared to be in limbo. I had told her she could move into my almost vacant rental; it would be vacant by the time she had to be out of her sold house. I told her it would give her a few months till spring, when she could make a well thought out decision. She told me she would think about it, and get back to me.

So you can imagine my surprise when I received her phone call. She said her husband was going over there now to negotiate a land contract with the seller. If the seller said yes, than this is what they were going to do. My mom's house is selling in ten days. This guy said he could be out in two. My mom and her husband can then move in. It all either seems like they are 'in the flow;' or this is all too much, and they should settle down and breathe a minute. Though, this is their thing. I do not belong in what they decide to do; though it is curious to watch. As I watch them, it helps me better understand myself and my decisions as I move forward.

I then receive an email from the church. Our minister was asking for donations for a cause. I was mad at this. Weeks ago I asked for a meeting with her, to discuss our prison project. I had also asked for her assistance in collecting donations for the dog agency. I did not receive anything back; not even a reply email. I tried to let this go, but it still bugged me. So here I was, mad again.

     The evening eventually ended.

....

Thursday morning was here. This was the day of my therapy appointment. Brian had said he would bring the kids to school, so I had extra energy for me. He made their lunches, and they were out the door. Soon it was me and the dogs alone in the house. I jumped in the shower. I looked at the clock, and realized I had a whole extra thirty minutes to get ready. Then the phone rings, it is Brian telling me I should probably leave now. He had left thirty minutes prior, and was still only half way to work. The snow had caused bad traffic, and it was taking 45 or more minutes to drive to post.

     I hurried up and was in the car within five. My car was frozen, and I had to wait for it to de-thaw. I probably had to sit for ten minutes. I really could not do anything at this point; so I reminded myself that all was fine, and I had no need to worry. I would make it on time. I had more than thirty minutes to be there. It was only a fifteen minute drive at most when the roads were good. I was also positive the hospital was expecting lots of late arrivals. I drove to post calmly; I enjoyed the traffic. I enjoyed the time to just be still. 25 minutes later, I still was not on post. I made the decision to cancel my appointment. I called Brian to tell him of my decision, and he said he was still in traffic, not at work. He had the phone number for the doctor; so I hung up with Brian and dialed the doctor. They told me everyone was late, and to just come in. I said I would be an hour late, and they said that that was still fine.

     I called Brian back and let him know, and told him my car was acting up. It was getting really warm, overheating. We decided for me to try to make it to the doctor, and after he would meet me to look at my car. I finally made it on post, and my car was really acting up now. I called Brian, and asked him to meet me at the gas station. He had just shut off his car, because he finally made it to work, and had to start it back up to meet me. At the gas station, he checked my car and it seemed as if it did not want to be healed. We finally decided he would follow me to the doctor, and we would think of our next step later.

     I had been nervous of my doctor meeting all morning. I wanted help, but I was feeling very embarrassed to ask for it. And I really did not know if they could help me. This was relating to my car.

I figured my car was acting up, because I was so blocked up. As I drove to the hospital, I was frustrated. I could not do this anymore; whatever needed to happen to make me happy again, I was going to do. I was not going to feel guilty, or think (anymore) that I did not deserve help. I then had a thought. What if the last two chapters of my book were only written with the positive things in my life? Maybe all of this was happening because I keep dialoging bad stuff. I decided, even if each chapter was only one thought, a happy thought; this was what you were going to read from now on. I then looked up and saw a plow truck pushing snow off the road. It was a very peaceful scene. The snow was so pretty; the plow truck was enjoying its seasonal job. Watching all of this happen, made me smile. I decided that would be what my chapter was about; how gorgeous the holidays are.

Soon we were at our destination. I parked my car, and Brian checked it. The temperature displaying on my thermostat returned to normal. Funny how that works; as I clear my anxiety, my car fixes it-self. My car was now fine. Brian offered me a ride to the door. He told me he loved me, and he hoped I had a good appointment. I walk inside and find the doctor's office easily. Everything seems calm. I am still a little nervous about my visit, but getting better. As I wait to be called, I see a girl from the dog agency. She is in scrubs, and walking by my clinic. I say, "Hey," and she stops and sits down. I did not know she was a nurse (she helps deliver babies.) We talk for a second, and I realize she is not getting up to leave; she also has an appointment in my clinic. It is such a small world.

She began telling me that her husband was the one that took all the dogs to the vet today. She was worried about his drive because of the snow storm. I told her I quit the organization and the reasons why. Her mouth dropped open as I told her my story. I was surprised she did not know; I figured everyone was talking about me. She then said she wondered why June was texting me (that day) when it should have been Melinda. At that moment I was called for my appointment. I said good bye to our friend, and followed the nurse down the hall.

I tried my best to release my nervousness. She took my vitals, and my weight. She told me the doctor was with one other patient, and would be with me as soon as they were finished up. I had about ten minutes in the room by myself. When the nurse had taken my weight, I weighed 141 pounds with my boots and all my clothes on. This surprised me. Weeks earlier, when I was at the gym I weighed 145 pounds. So I took off my boots, and sweater, and weighed myself. I was 137 pounds. This made me happy. How did I lose that weight in three weeks? I was not trying to diet; I was stressed. I thought it was funny when my focus finally was off weight, I lost it.

The doctor was finally in. He is a nice, go with the flow guy. He had seen me once before, and these were the only records he had of me. I had not yet transferred my medical records over from Wisconsin. He asked me what was going on. I told him I was going through some hard times. I told him I was not a believer in drugs, but I am willing to see if they help. He asked if I was still writing while I was feeling down. He seemed to know that writing was therapy for me. He then left the room for a minute, and came back and asked if I wanted to see the psychologist. It was all so sweet that someone was finally caring about me. I said, "Sure," we then walked to the waiting room where I filled out some 'depression' papers, and he scheduled me in for an appointment. They got me in to see her within the next few minutes.

Soon the psychologist comes to get me and we walk to her office. We sit down and she goes over the basics. She says, if I am planning on hurting myself or anyone else, she has to report it. Then she asked what was going on. I gave her a quick overview, and she starts probing me. She asked for more details about the dog agency. Here I start to cry. We talk about that, and she says, I'm probably not 'bad' if the dogs are still needed at my house. This made me smile. We talk about a lot of stuff. I told her about my goals and my book. I told her about my spiritual journey. I told her about the mess with the rentals. I told her about my overheated car. I said I think the big picture is, it is all good, but as it is all going on, it is very overwhelming and I'm feeling lost.

She told me I impressed her. She said I had done a lot in life, and she wished she had done some of the stuff I did. She also understood and agreed when I talked about my beliefs of past lives and the spirit world. She also said that there was probably a reason for my car overheating. With the traffic, it was probably God getting me off the road, before an accident would happen. She and I agreed on some pills, and we would see if they would help. She said all of this is probably situational, and not a long term depression. We would use the pills to help me get through it. She again complemented me on how much I believed in, and how much I do. She made me feel awesome to talk with. I told her it was all perception. She was proud of my accomplishments, and I am proud of hers. We all do what we love in life. I was thankful for her caring words, and am thankful for her choosing her line of work. We set up an appointment for the next two weeks to see her again.

She also told me during the meeting, that they do free vasectomies at the clinic. When she told me this it was so out of left field. This is the last thing I figured I would hear on this Thursday afternoon. When she told me, I said I don't want it now (pregnancy,) I wanted that for the last few years. I did not know what to think.

And how ironic, I thought, I am at my lowest at this appointment, and here she is telling me something so great; I can have my own babies again. The thoughts I left her with were, "Well at least I have choices now, and I now know I can have a baby." The rest will have to unfold.

I went downstairs to the pharmacy and waited in line for my medicine. I was now happy, it hit; I can have my own babies again! I texted Brian and asked if he was still on post, so we could do lunch. He said he was on his way to lunch with his boss, but he was going to drop him off and have lunch with me. I walked out to the parking lot and saw him. He was under the assumption, him, his boss and I, were going to have lunch. I said, "No, you only have your boss for today, go back with him." I asked him if he received my text message about the babies, and he said he had not yet. I told him the news. He did not have a response.

I drove home. I had an hour to myself. I sat in thought at how the whole afternoon went. I soon went to get the kids. They were home and finished up their homework. Then they were in and out of the house as they needed this or needed that so they could play in the snow. I spent my time googling stories about pregnancy. I was in awe. It was so cool to know this was really happening to me.

I texted Brian a grocery list and he texted back with a question. He asked how the whole reverse vasectomy procedure worked. He also asked if we were going to talk about his feelings with all of this. I said, "Yes." I then explained the procedure. He first had to go to his regular doctor, and then the doctor would refer him to a specialist. Then he would get his surgery. Then I would get my babies!

Finally Brian was home, and was immediately designated to help the kids with their current project. I patiently waited for our talk. I had to be patient for a while, so I got creative. I put a pillow in my shirt, and paraded around the house. Brian sees me and rolls his eyes. He soon comes up to talk with me, and I snap. I said, "I do not care for anything you want, when all you can do is roll your eyes at my dreams." He apologized, and did not realize he did it. I then said, "I have wanted this for three years, and now they (the doctors) are giving it to me. This is a dream come true. I wanted babies, and if he did not, then that was not good!" He just listened. I told him that years ago, I said, if this ever came true, (me getting prego with my own babies again,) then I could do anything in life. This dream was such a miracle. And now I am getting the opportunity. I think he finally got it, and he said, "Okay." He now saw what I saw; we were having babies!

I then received an email from church. They cancelled tonight's class because of the bad weather. I was excited for this!

I wanted to spend my time with pillows in my shirt, and talk all night about my coming babies! We had 'Daddy John's' for dinner. This was a treat. It was an expensive dinner. Brian brought home beer, and I had some. I had taken my pill about an hour before dinner. The evening had Brian and me having lots of awesome talk of babies, miracles and goals. I noticed that I was not thinking; I was only watching my thoughts; due to the pills. I was a little loopy, but happy.

I went to lay down hours later, and was asleep. The evening left me throwing up and feeling very sick.

....

☐

Chapter 12
Restructuring

Friday morning I woke up still puking. I was in and out of consciousness all day. Brian helped the kids get ready for school, and soon he was home for lunch, getting me my water that I had been chanting for in my sleep. He did not go back to work; he instead tended to me the entire evening. Dinner came, and I felt a little better. He made me a grilled cheese and hung out with the kids until I fell asleep again.

Friday was over.

Saturday was here. I woke up and moved very slow. I was happy to be able to move, and knew I was getting better each moment. I noticed I did not want to smoke as many cigarettes. Maybe the pills were helping me quit? I was scared to take the pills again. What if it was the pills that were making me sick? I did not know if I had the flu, if it was the beer I was warned against drinking with the pills, or if it was the pills that made me so sick.

Brian slept in the early parts of the morning. The kids were quiet and occupied. I decided to put up Christmas decorations. I usually wait until the day after Thanksgiving, though today was warm and I thought it was a good and safe day to put up Christmas lights outside. And why not mix up tradition once in a while? Change can be good! I cleaned the house a little. I moved very slow, still recovering from the sickness. I pondered a lot about where to put the tree, and where to move the furniture. I moved my couches and was happy with the arrangement. Soon Brian was up, and we drank coffee together. We talked about my plans with the decorations, and talked about spending the day cleaning. We cleaned the entire house, including laundry and mopped the floors. The house was clean; we were clean. He then put up our tree and brought up all the decorations. He decided to wait to put up the outside lights because there was snow and ice still on the roof. By Tuesday it was expected to all melt.

That morning I also received text message after text message, wondering where I was, and why I was not at the puppy fair. This annoyed me, but I let it go. Finally I get a message from June asking me my reason for not wanting to get the dogs adopted. I texted back, and said that I had quit the organization last week. I would not be at the puppy fair. I was under the assumption they were coming to get the dogs. By now, they must have room with empty foster homes. Yes, this is sarcasm.

The day was spent in peace. I had a beautiful view as I watched my dogs sleep the afternoon away.

The house was clean and all my decorations looked incredible. I only took a half a pill today. Yesterday I did not take any. I was hoping my sickness was not from the pills. I would not know my answer if I did not try again. It was soon night, I talked with my girlfriend. I told her about the pills I was taking, and she did not approve. Pills were not holistic, but to me, they were working.

....

Sunday morning was here. I was grumpy that I was thinking again. I enjoyed looking at my clean, decorated house; but was frustrated that I was still in the middle of the messes of my life. I want a shift so bad, but know I am still frustrated with it all. I kind of want to go away on vacation, and come back when it is fixed. Kind of like when you buy a property, and go away while the contractors fix it. Your roll is just to own the problem; they fix it. I liked watching my thoughts, instead of being in them. Though currently, this was not the case. Though, I was determined to work through it. Lexi then comes to cuddle; here comes my smile again. I had decided that we were not going to our original church this Sunday. I googled the other church, and found out their service was 9:30, not 10:30. We missed church. Well, all we can do is go with the flow. No reason to be mad.

Brian is sitting on the bed and I ask him how we should spend our day. He says he is worried about money. I am not really worried about money; just annoyed with it. I talk with him, and try to get him to stop worrying. He is not okay with this, but I am. I am not going to worry with him. I spend the afternoon writing. This is good for me.

Later I get an idea. Now, as we go through all of this stuff, our energy is focused on 'getting through.' I asked him if he wanted to research and start putting together our product that we are planning on bringing to the market. I said it was a good time to do it now, it was this or he instead had to think about worrying. We were going to wait until the year after his promotion to start preparing. But now seems good also. We do not have to bring it all out now, but we can begin the process. It is a way to use this bound up energy for something good. He agreed.

He also realized it was Sunday, without going to church we were kind of confused. Today was football day; he wanted to watch the games. He was happy, I was happy. Aidan's friend was over and all three kids were happy. We started a fire. The house smelled awesome, very Christmassy! The house was gorgeous. As I wrote all day, I would glance over at all the happy puppies; life was good!

I received a random text message from a friend from Wisconsin. She posted on my Facebook timeline, "I love you." I smiled and replied, "Love you too."

There was a recent post about how special friends are; I forwarded this to her. She them spent a few text messages with me, describing her current life. She is going through something large, and she is worried about it. She is feeling like a failure. This reminds me of my life, so now I get to be the wise one. I let her know that she was not a failure; instead this was a reconstructing of her life. Her life was in the process of becoming better. It is a filtering out of the old and into the new. She thanked me for my words, and for all of my video blog's. She told me I was a positive spirit, and through the internet, she was receiving all the good vibes I was sharing. So here, another compliment that I had no idea was coming.

I also checked the Craigslist ads, and saw a woman with a ten month old baby girl needing a babysitter. I texted her (as requested) and gave her some information about me. Later she texted back, and told me she was looking for Monday through Friday, 7 A.M. till 6 P.M. I texted her saying those hours would work. Then, I heard nothing back. It frustrated me that I was not getting any babysitting jobs.

Around 5 P.M. Aidan started to puke. I sent his friend home, and Aidan spent the evening sleeping in the bathroom. I am now thinking I was sick because of the FLU, instead of the pills.

Dreana, dad and me watched a Christmas movie and had some chili. I began to realize that I really love the smell of the fire place as it burns wood. Brian and I figured some numbers, seeing if we would save money if we would burn wood instead of using the furnace. We googled some ads of people selling wood. One of the ads said if we cut down their tree, then we could have the wood for free. Brian called them and they decided they would call us later in the week, after the snow storm. I also texted Melinda and told her we needed more dog food within the next two days. Bambino eats a lot! I did not receive anything from her. I talked about this with Brian; we agreed that by Wednesday night at 5 P.M., if we did not hear from her, we were going to text her saying, "We now are assuming responsibility for these dogs, because she (Melinda) is no longer doing it." Maybe this is how I get my Lexi?

Soon we were all asleep.

Monday morning was filled with a happy household. Brian was getting ready for work, and Dreana was being quiet and occupied as she was getting up for the day. Aidan was no longer sick, though was moving a little slow. I had gone outside, and saw the wind was really strong. I asked Brian to check the weather to make sure the post was not closed before he attempted to go to work. He checked and saw that everyone had a late start. An hour and a half later, Brian headed to work.

I checked my phone, and received an email from the Title Company (for the house being sold.) The closing coordinator was making contact with me, and wanted to make sure she had the correct email address.

I started to have thoughts of the job I still wanted. I really want to work for a property management company. I enjoy the role of creating projects, and making big money. I enjoy coordinating people, and I love how all of it fits perfectly into my life. I was frustrated that I still did not have that job. I worked through these frustrations, and realized they were on their way. Currently I had a book to finish.

Soon the doorbell rings. Aidan's friend comes in with lots of nervous energy. He tells Aidan to hurry up, because they have to be back at his house in fifteen minutes or he is grounded. Aidan starts to get ready. I alter their plans with conversation, and let them know Aidan is not going anywhere. I did not feel safe with the crazy weather outside. His friend is frustrated and doesn't want to stay here. He leaves my house in tears. I was okay with it. Aidan was surprisingly okay with it also. The house was calm again, and I started writing. I soon realized that today was Monday, and I needed to call the rental company and find out if our renter had paid the remaining rent. Also if the rental company had negotiated a new month to month lease with her. I called; she seemed irritated it was me. She told me the lady had not paid rent, and she began an eviction. That was that, looks like we are evicting her and the house is going on the market in a week. I texted the realtor and gave her heads up with the eviction. I told her within a week, she would be able to get in there to list the property.

I then had a realization. The dog agency and the renters are testing me. They want to know if I will actually do what I threaten I will do. Kind of like when you tell your kids, "If you do not clean your room, I will throw away your toys." The dog agency will wonder if I will actually take ownership of these dogs, if they do not show up. Will I, I do not know. I want to, but fear kicks in. I guess we will see how the next few days unfold.

Soon the doorbell rings again. It is Aidan's friend. His mom is waiting outside in the car. They came by to ask if Aidan wanted to go with them to run errands. I said, "No, I was not comfortable with the roads and did not want Aidan on them, on foot or in a car." I offered to have his friend stay here while his mom went to do her errands. He said he would go ask her out in the car. We sat for a minute and waited for him to return; he didn't, they drove off. I was okay with this, and again surprisingly Aidan was okay with this. I think I am finally getting it. It is not my concern if someone does not agree with me, and especially if they are mad. They can be mad, this is their stuff.

It felt right when I said Aidan could not go outside. This is enough, me, the way I feel. His friend and his mom can be mad, and when they are done being mad, I am sure his friend will be over again. They can feel and think what they choose. I am also allowed to feel and think what I choose. I do not have to feel guilty that I am not giving another what they want. I do what I want; I get to have my own thoughts.

I then saw a cool post on Facebook. It was a speaker speaking on the topic of depression. He said pills are not necessary. He says instead of pills, find out why your Serotonin levels are low, and concentrate there. He said most serotonin levels are low because of drugs, coffee, chips, and lots of processed gunk. He said if you want to be better, change your diet and within days you will be better. I thought about this. Though, I wasn't yet ready to give up cigarettes. I also realized I am a pretty healthy person. I eat mostly 'live' foods. I do not eat meat. I drink lots of water. I decided to be thankful for my progress, and not harp on myself about the cigarettes. I also am enjoying the progress of the pills right now, and am comfortable giving them a try. Here again I am deciding as we go. I do not have to follow a study or a speaker; I get to follow my decisions. And my decision now is that all is good, and I go from here.

Later that day I called Margie, she was my babysitter in Wisconsin. I love this woman. We put up our Christmas decorations and the most important of these are the little Knick knacks Margie gives each year. I called her and of course she was thinking of us.

We also received a call from the title company. She had forgotten that she had emailed me. She was just making contact. I confirmed I was doing all of my part. She asked if we held a mortgage with the property. I told her we had a land contract with grandma. She wanted us to get a letter from her to finalize that commitment. I told her that there was no legal agreement, just a paper between her and me. We decided to just go with that. It made me feel good to make that decision. I was deciding again. I started to appreciate selling the properties. Currently the money we have is going to the properties without receiving reimbursement. When the properties sell, we are going to have a lot more money than we currently have. This is a big blessing.

I also realized again, that I am learning to make decisions. I am getting back to the basics. To make large decisions, I have to get back to the basics. It makes me feel good when the realizations are coming. I then realized I was holding on to the properties. They were kind of like collateral or a down payment. I was thinking that for me to get my apartment building, I had to make these properties work first. But really these properties are not what I want. These properties are little money. I want big money. They are a liability. They are sucking me dry.

It is like playing high school football, when I want to be professional. I cannot spend my time playing with mediocre players. Even if I currently do not have the professionals to play with, I can spend my time visualizing what it's like to play with the big dogs. My properties are hurting me, and I have to let them go. I have to trust.

Later in the evening we needed more money for groceries. I checked the bank account and we had plenty. I wrote a check from the Wisconsin account to put it in the Colorado account. I thought that the check would need a couple days to clear. I asked Brian to deposit it, and shop with what we had, seventeen dollars. He usually does the grocery shopping and bank runs. Though after asking him, I decided to go; I needed to get out of the house. I went to the bank with my check and asked if it would clear right away. They said, "Yes," I was making progress. I then enjoyed my time in the store. I was getting rewarded by how good it all felt.

When I was home I received a text message from Melinda. She was nervous interacting with me; her text message was she left the dog food by the door. I began to forgive her more in this moment. I do want her to prosper; I want everyone to prosper. It was not all her. I wanted to be around different people and different vibrations. All of this happened to benefit us all; I do not need to be so mad, or hurt with the change.

Aidan went to his friend's for the evening. I texted his mom and asked if Aidan could eat over there. It was that or his friend waiting while Aidan ate here, and then Aidan waiting as his friend ate dinner there. His mom texted back saying she was confused. According to the friend, all day the boys could only play if they were at my house. I replied explaining that when he came here this morning, he expected to collect Aidan and go. I did not want Aidan outside in the ice; it was dangerous. And then when they came back and asked if Aidan could do errands, I still did not want Aidan driving around in the ice. I suggested the friend stay here while his mom did her errands, and then they were gone. This was my story; the friend instead heard, "Aidan couldn't play with him." She understood and all was good. The boys ended up spending the evening at their house.

Look what happens when we communicate, and when we are okay with our decisions. We have to be okay if we know we are following our heart. While another is mad, they eventually will come around. If we continue to feel guilt for someone else, the circle continues and no one ends up following their heart. Instead all are busy deciding if our decisions will be okay with the next person. The next person is doing the same thing. Nothing is progressing here, and this is where we find ourselves not moving forward.

The evening eventually ended. Tuesday morning began in our dreams.
....

Tuesday I woke up later than usual. The kids were still off from school; Aidan was at his friend's. Dreana was up and hanging out with dad. Brian had made the two of them eggs for breakfast. He was showered and in a very good mood. I woke up with a very peaceful presence. I went outside for my coffee and was happy. The temperature was a lot warmer than it had been, the snow looked beautiful. The sun was blazing and starting a beautiful day. I just felt happy. I recognized how happy I felt.

Ten minutes later I started to think. The thoughts were the same they have been for years, all of that old programming. I started to get irritated that my awesome mood was now being overtaken with these same old thoughts. Then I realized that this was a beginning. I chose to be thankful for the few minutes of bliss I did have. I realized that this only gets better; tomorrow I might get twice as much time with that bliss. The rest of the morning was happy as I realized my body was learning how to be happy again, one moment at a time.

I looked at Craigslist and saw ads of flipping houses again. I had many thoughts of property management, flipping and investing. I daydreamed what it was like to be able to be a part of it all. Then I realized that I was selling my properties and it seemed unlikely that I would get to be this investor. Then I realized that I will get to do that stuff because I like it so much! If I trust that it is coming, it is inevitable. I also daydreamed a lot about being pregnant. I googled many stories of post reverse vasectomies and signs of twin pregnancy. I engulfed myself in this world for many hours of the afternoon.

The day and the afternoon came and went. The evening hours brought the police department. There was a situation going on in the neighborhood which brought every cop in the town. The SWAT team was also here. We had a pool of neighbors standing outside with us, as we all attempted to understand the details. We got bits and pieces, and expected the rest to come out in the evening news. All the news reported was that it was a, "False Report." We kept the news on, hoping for more info as the night progressed. Dreana, the dogs and I all fell asleep on the couch in front of the TV, waiting. It never came.
....

Wednesday morning I woke up late again, though I seemed to not care anymore about eight A.M. verses five A.M. I felt relaxed as I awoke. It is as if I am getting some well needed sleep. My mood, as I had my coffee was a little dark. I did not experience the bliss that I did the morning before. I had a lot of thoughts of, "Poor me" and I was not liking the current events that were going through my head. I came inside, and realized it was a different morning. It was weird, the thoughts I was thinking were the same, but it really was a different morning I was experiencing. I decided to write and play with this new knowledge. The new knowledge that my mind was playing past stuff, and at the same time realizing it was a different morning. My mind can totally double focus; it can replay the old, and at the same time realize the now.

Brian during this time seemed to be frustrated. I decided to write and not get involved with his morning. I let him process for himself; this was cool to realize as well. He soon was out the door. A minute later he was back saying his truck needed time to defrost. We decided to have coffee together as his minutes passed. As he was telling me about his plans for the day, I had my moments of bliss. I realized I have a pretty cool life. I choose my work and where I do my work. Even though we are having money issues, I still get to do my work. I have a life I think many would like to have. I get to invest. I get to move forward with my ideas. I get to not have a job. I get to have all these dogs. I get to run my household. I have a pretty wealthy life. I have been able to do what I do for a very long time, and Brian supports it. Last week I found out I could have babies. Last year I wanted to homeschool my son. I owned rental properties. I know we are beginning to put our product in the 'getting out there' phase. All of this is good. I have the ability to keep moving forward. I have the ability to dream my dreams and think of them as a reality. I do what a lot of people would never consider. I go after what I want, and nine times out of ten, they come together. I have a pretty cool life. I think I forget this a-lot. Today I remember.

I think that I 'know' I have a pretty cool life. I also know I want to continue to grow my life. I now want my dreams to go further than they have. I am writing this book because I can. I also want to have this book be a NY best seller. This is what I am growing into; I want to increase what I have done. What I have done is 'know I can do it.' Now I want it to transfer into the goals I want. I want my forty thousand dollars per month (after taxes ;) I want to be a NY best-selling author. I am willing now to venture here; I am willing to learn how to attract this reality.

I am also growing into the reality that my story is significant as what I hope it to be. The reason for this book was for me to clear, as I wrote it.

It also was for you to see the day to day, and understand you are normal. I am sure that you go through a day to day that correlates with mine. I wanted you to see that your average life is what creates wealth. I wanted you to see that you did not have to begin as a billionaire to understand that your life and journey are worth it. Going along with this, I have been hoping for a big break through. I was hoping by the end of this book, that I would be a billionaire. I wanted to show you and me, that if we have the courage to do what is scary (go for what we want) that there would be that big financial reward. That it would all be worth it in the end. In the next few weeks, I may not be that billionaire I was hoping to be, though I am hoping I find value in what it is I have accomplished. Wealth is being created. My journey is continuing. My journey is worth everything. It is me, and me is what I desire to share with the world. The reward is in the process as well as the end result. I feel that when you read this, it will resonate with you. You will see that I am a normal person. You will see me having the courage to believe the worthiness of my story, before it has a price tag on it. The prize is me accepting my story. Once I accept my story; you will too.

How I accept my story is to finish it, and give it to an agent. I will hand my story over for you to study. Once I have the courage to do my part, believing the worthiness in my story; then you get to do your part. Your part is to see the correlations in my life with yours, and to realize that you have the courage to go after your story. Because, your story is worth billions; your dreams are worth billions. Though, it can never get paid, unless you get it out of you and in to those who need it. And the only way you can do that, is to face that fear. The fear, that no one will accept you for you. They will accept you for you. I accept you. My story is for me, but also for you. It is for you to be encouraged to love you, a little more than you did yesterday. It is courage for you to go for it. You can do this; I can do this.

The evening came to an end.
....

Thursday morning was here. The rest of yesterday was spent proofreading another chapter. We are over the fifty page mark with editing. This means we can send fifty pages to an agent. This was an accomplishment; not just in the work involved with editing, but on the energetic level. This means I am moving forward, and letting myself get to the next step.

I talked with Brian about what do we do when the book is finished. To me, writing the book is easy, getting it to you and getting it published is the hard part.

To me an agent is the easiest, though with an agent we have to wait for their approval. Self-publishing, I could get my book out immediately, though I have to do all the marketing. I am not as confident in this area, though each day I become more confident. In the beginning I would have not chosen self-publishing. Though as we get closer, it seems like a do-able option. Maybe I can do this. So far I have a friend who can help me with self-publishing. I also have a friend who called who has a contact with self-publishing. There are options; we will see where they lead.

Richard found a ride to Colorado Springs last night. He is here for Thanksgiving. He spent a few hours of the evening teaching the kids how to draw silhouettes. This was adorable to see. He is so good with kids. He also informed us he wants to move to Colorado. It would be nice to have him in Colorado. We will see if it actually happens. The boys spent last night playing pool out in town. Who knows how long they were there; but they are both back safe and a sleep this morning.

Today is Thanksgiving. I thought I would type what it is I am thankful for.

I am thankful that Colorado has been so prosperous. I took myself out of my comfort zone, and moved away from everyone I knew. I have found new friends and began building relationships. I am proud of myself for the progress in building these friendships. It takes a lot to build something. What I am building, feels good. I am thankful that I am gaining courage to be the real me, and attract people I want in my life. This part gets better every day. I am proud of myself for selling my properties. I am letting go and going for something else. I have been visualizing about flipping properties a lot this week; flipping ten or more at a time. I am starting to believe I can do this. I am happy that a lot of the stress is going away, so I can fill up with the new. The new shows a great, happy life. I feel successful and happy in my line of work. The clearer I get, the easier it is to see.

I am thankful so many pages have been written of this book. I have been writing for a long time, and this many pages, all at once, and all on the same subject, is an achievement.

I am happy that I am doing this. I have wanted this for a very long time, and now I am doing it. I am happy that I can have kids again. This, I never thought would happen. Having my own kids is a miracle. I am experiencing a miracle. This feels good. I am happy Brian is close to his SGT Major goal. He has come so far in his Army career, and this is huge. I am proud of him.

I am happy I can see my goals of my apartment building. It seems real now. This is a large dream and now it seems feasible instead of just a wish.

It is true we always get what we want; it just takes a longer time sometimes. Though, when we receive them, it is like night and day. It is just here.

I am thankful for Lexi and Twiggy. They make me smile. I would like to keep them forever, though I have them now, and that is what I choose to focus on. I love to watch them cuddle together. I am so happy they are together. Most puppies do not get to stay with their siblings; they do. They are beautiful and sweet.

I am thankful I slept through the night. I have not woken up in the middle of the night in a while. I am feeling safer, and less scared. This feeling is worth ten trillion dollars.

I am thankful that my house is gorgeous. It looks even more gorgeous with the Christmas decorations. I love waking up, and seeing all of the beauty. I am thankful for all of the growth. It has been hard, but the outcome is worth it. I have changed my beliefs. I am excited to live by a budget now. I am thankful that I am tithing. I am thankful that now, what I want is a car I can afford, instead of having to have a loan. It is no longer about perception; it is about what makes me feel good. I am now living.

I am thankful for my options with church. It took a long time to be able to go to the Unity church. I am thankful that I get to make my own decisions now. One more, I am thankful for my kids. They are the best thing, and I am blessed to be their mom. I am thankful for Brian. I am thankful for Cleo, Chevy and Dodger. I have a lot of love in my family, a lot of members. It makes me feel good that I attracted all of this. Aidan's friend told me the other day, that I am a nice mom, I am a fun mom. This feels awesome! Life is good! Happy Thanksgiving!

Feeling thankful, our day continued. We headed to a friend's house for the big day. We dressed up, but our friends wore jeans and football jerseys! They had cooked a lot of food and treats. The kids were excited to see all the cupcakes! My two were welcomed and loved. Our friends have a teenager, so for them, they enjoy having little's over.

Richard, Brian and Aidan decided they were eating all the meat they wanted this day. We are vegetarians, but the boys take the day off here and there to eat food with the rest of the population.

In the past, I had borrowed two books to their teenager. She is an avid reader and writer. I love this girl! One of the books I borrowed to her was the one my girlfriend had written. I had been missing that book and was excited to get it back. The other book I borrowed, I had two of, so I let our friend have it and keep for her book shelf. It was nice that she enjoyed them. It is nice when you can connect with others on interests that are similar to yours.

Different stories were told throughout our dinner.

Our friends were moving out of their rented house in a few weeks. They arrived in Colorado this summer, like us. Their experience with renting was not as great as ours. They had quite a few problems with the rental company, and this month was the icing on the cake. They were done. They wrote a letter to the company saying they are moving out prior to the end of their lease. They are forging their security deposit. They figured the loss of their security deposit was small, compared to the foreseen problems they would incur if they stayed for the whole lease. They went to the bank and applied for a loan. Their loan was approved, and now they are moving into a brand new house. They are happy and hoping to be in prior to Christmas.

The evening was filled with excitement of their future move, and lots of interesting conversations as we were all like-minded people. The husband was going to school for his doctorate, and talking with us about his thesis. He wanted to write about being honest and playing with the golden rule. The wife recently received a new job at the YMCA, and she loves it. She was telling us of her plans as her career progressed. He was getting out of the Army and going to teach three days a week. She was going to be working for the YMCA.

Richard played music, and told us all of his progression with the treatments. We all got a chuckle as he had another date this evening. He is a total ladies' man. After hours of a really good time, it was time to leave. Soon the kids and I were in bed. Richard was on a date, and Brian was doing whatever it is he does, when he doesn't sleep!

Happy Thanksgiving!

Our prosperity class was cancelled this evening due to the holiday!

Chapter 13:
New Beginnings

Friday morning was here, and I was up early to help Richard pack and get back to Denver. Later I was in a great mood with my morning to myself. I checked online for different jobs that I could do from home. Brian slept in all morning. As he slept, my nice thoughts gained a darker cover. I was frustrated that it seemed like I was never going to get a job. I was thinking my book may not go anywhere. I was thinking I would not get my foster kids because of our rental issues. I was mad the rentals were not gone yet. I was frustrated with life. These feelings built for a lot of the morning as I anxiously waited for Brian to wake up. Later he was up and I blew. I told him I needed help with figuring out how to get a job. I was mad at me, but also mad at him because he did not seem to care. We fought for a long time. Well it was really me that did the screaming. Finally it was all out of me, and he offered to help me find a job.

I looked at the ad on Craigslist again about the company that was flipping homes. This is what I want to do. Though I also want this to be successful with money; and I do not want to pay any start-up costs. I really wanted to do this, but was scared because I wanted to be sure I could be successful at it. I am done with companies that I seem to fail at. I am turning over a new leaf in my life, and I choose to be successful and committed to the ventures I now go into. So I wanted to be sure, before I just 'signed-up.' Brian emailed the company and asked if it was a program we sign up for, or if they were a local company that I could start making money right away with. This made me feel good that he was being involved, and helping us make 'right' decisions.

We then talked about our product that we will be bringing to the market place. When we had looked into the cost of a paten (in the past) it was a little expensive. Though now, as we wait for our finances to get better, we have plenty of time to be preparing our patent application. We started our research; this felt good. It felt like we were moving in the right direction.

We also found a work from home opportunity on Craigslist. Again, I was unsure because I did not want to 'mess up.' We went into the process slowly, and one step at a time. We only considered information that was relevant, information that we currently knew in each moment. I called about the ad, and the lady was very informative. She told me what it was they did, and it left me with a lot of confidence. We scheduled an orientation for Sunday at 2:45. This is the only information I had, a scheduled orientation. I decided this was perfect for the now, and I let it go until Sunday. This felt good.

After all of our successes from the afternoon, Brian and I watched a movie. As the movie was playing, I received a random phone call from a mom who wanted me to babysit. Isn't it funny, when you are in an awesome mood, how everything else starts coming your way? She was coming over tomorrow morning for an interview. Tonight was Lexi, Bambino and Twiggy's last night with us. Bambino and Aidan cuddled together, and Twiggy and Dreana cuddled in her bed.

All were asleep.

Saturday morning was here. I was up early because the dogs were supposed to be picked up at seven. Instead, I received a text message saying the time would be 9:30. I was happy about this; I had my ladies for a little longer. The babysitting lady would be here at noon.

We had some cleaning to do. All morning I cuddled with the dogs and cleaned the house with Brian. Soon the doorbell rang, and a guy was here to get Bambino. We loaded the kennels and Bambino in his truck. We were about to give him the ladies, instead he told us another foster mom would be here in a minute to get them. We had a few more moments to cuddle.

Soon the doorbell rang and it was the foster mom. I asked her to come in as we all were (almost in tears) saying our last goodbyes. We let her know if she still needed us that we were open for these dogs to come back. As the dogs left, I repeated my affirmation that, if it is our highest and best good, that they would be back. Dreana was upset; she cried for 45 minutes until the doorbell rang again.

It was our landlord. He came by to say, "Hi" and to give the kids some apples! We chit chatted with him for a minute. I told him of our rental mess and let him know I was thinking of him as each of my decisions were being made in reference to the renters. He (in the past) had told us a story of how he had to take a renter to court, because they stole windows out of his house. As I was going through what I was going through, I thought about how victorious he was in his end. We love our landlord, and I think he loves to be loved. He is a mentor to us in many factors, he proves as a father figure to Brian, he is a successful business man, and he is a retired pastor. All in all, he is an awesome guy. We are lucky to get to interact with him.

As we are talking with him, the doorbell rings again. It is the lady I am to babysit for! Our landlord leaves, as now we have more company. My kids and her kids started playing right away. It was as if they have known each other for years. I really liked their mom, and she liked me too. We were a perfect fit.

My babysitting job is for her kindergartener and third grader, every day after school, and on days off of school.

Later they were gone, and the kids went to their friends' house. It was warm that afternoon, and Brian and I sat outside trying to find something fun to do. All of a sudden, the idea came to me that we could have a roommate. The room down stairs is perfect for that. We googled Craigslist and looked for people to choose from. After a minute, we decided we really did not want to do this. And then, at that moment, Brian found an ad of an army officer moving to Colorado. He needed a room to stay for a month, until his family could get here. This was perfect. Our guy was an officer, and only needed a room short term. This way we could help. We understand his situation, since we have considered it many times with all of our moves. We could also meet a new friend, and help him out in the meantime. We emailed him.

Next I called my neighbor and asked if she wanted to go on a walk. It would be just the two of us, and we would leave all the kids with the husbands! The walk was great; she is awesome and we have the same interests. I can openly talk about energy healing with her, and she gets it. We had so much fun, and also enjoyed our exercise. She is also a runner; she runs each day and enters herself in marathons multiple times per year. I always wanted to run in a marathon; maybe by knowing her, I will actually do it.

Later it was time for dinner, and bed for the kids. I called my girlfriend and told her about the officer roommate. I mentioned this is how God works. When I woke up this morning, I did not have any interest in a roommate. Then out of the blue, I was excited to share my house with a stranger! Maybe, my induced idea, was because this guy had an intention to get himself a room. God talks to us all, and lets us know who to call and what to expect. He has it all under control; really there is no need to worry. Our officer friend may have been worrying, though God had a plan, and that plan comes in unexpected sources! That unexpected resource may be us! They are unexpected, because we may not know, but God always does.

Our evening was almost over when a knock at the door came again. The lady I was to be babysitting for came by with the entire year's schedule for her kids. She is very organized!

We then were asleep with another very prosperous evening!

....

Sunday morning was here. It was a good morning. As I enjoyed my coffee, I kept seeing Lexi everywhere. She was in my awareness; I kept getting confused if it was my imagination, or really her. I do not know what this means.

She may have been visiting me, as she was sleeping. Or my visualizations may have been so strong, that it was inevitable she will be coming back. I do not know.

Soon it was time for church. We decided to go to a different church because of how uncomfortable I felt about Sunday school at the other church. We thought we were on time, then when we punched the address into the GPS, it said we were going to be fifteen minutes late. We all laughed and said, "Well, at least we tried." We decided to still drive to church, and be late anyway!

When we were there, we were exactly on time. I do not know how time stopped; but it did! We have been to this church once before and really enjoyed it. The kids ran upstairs to Sunday school, and the morning was off to a great start. It was a beautiful service. I really like how large the church is. I really like how awesome and large the Sunday school is. The church has lots of bright colors, and seems to attract people that are like me; I feel comfortable here. The culture fits! The first Sunday of every month, the church purchases many cakes to say, "Happy birthday" to all with a birthday in that month. So of course we went to church on cake Sunday! We enjoyed conversation with lots of people. Our conversations were as if we had been going to that church for a while; I loved it!

We were later home, and the kids went to play. Brian chopped fire wood, and I waited patiently for my 2:45 phone call (for the at-home business.) I asked Brian if he wanted to be with me during the call, and to my surprise he said, "Yes!" How much better does all of this get! The phone call was awesome. The business still seemed easy, and Brian was involved!

After the call, our next step was internet training. I listened to the training while Brian watched football. Soon it was another prosperous evening, and we all went to sleep.

....

Monday morning was here. Oh was this a good morning. Everyone was excited to get back to work and school. I was already feeling like it was going to be an exciting week!

Soon the kids were at school, and I recorded a Video blog. I wanted to hold off, and not tell everyone about the reverse vasectomy; but then today felt right to share the news. I set up my phone camera in front of the Christmas tree, and let everyone know about my awaited three year miracle. I could have my own babies again!

I later spent time in front of the computer, listening to training with my brand new work-from-home business! I had to set up a Google phone, and a PayPal account.

This is stuff that is usually hard (for me,) and I usually wait for Brian to do it. Not today, today was too good. I was going to learn it this time. I then get to a part of the training where I had to create links on the computer, this was above my head. I called the guy who told me about the business, and hoped he would help. I received a text message from him saying he will call this evening when he had more time. I was okay with this answer. I knew I was on the right track. He would call when the time was right.

Brian was home for lunch and not feeling well. He slept for his hour. I decided to do the grocery shopping for him. While I was at the grocery store, the guy stocking the shelves was flirting with me. Here was proof I must have been having a pretty good day!

I was soon home to unload groceries, when I was back in the car, and on my way to my counselor appointment. I was excited to go. The pills really seem to be working. I went to my appointment in a great mood. I was very happy that I did not have to pick the kids up from school, it was a nice break. It was almost like 'alone time' for me. Some people go out to the club; I go out for a doctor appointment. Life is good!

I get to my appointment, and I am flying high. The doctor is surprised at how good I am doing. I explain to her all the good that has happened over the week. I have an accepted offer on one of the properties, I can get pregnant, I am not thinking about the bills, and I actually can see the light at the end of the tunnel. She talks with me and says my levels are getting a lot better. She scheduled me for future appointments with an outside therapist that could see me for a few months. She also scheduled one more follow up with her. She renewed my pills, and suggested I go to Toast Masters (A public speaking course.) As I was leaving, she reminded me I have done a lot, and the only one who does not see it, is me. She says the continual therapist sessions and Toast Masters will help with my confidence. She says I am doing great, more than a lot of people would do. She said it would be good if I start recognizing it for myself.

I get home at 4:30, and my kids are playing with the two kids that I am babysitting for (Brian picked them all up from school.) It is a very happy house hold. I soon sit with the oldest child, and help her with her homework. I am in a very good mood. Before we know it, it is five and their mom comes by. She gets to witnesses this great evening. She is happy that she has found us. Life is good!

Later Richard calls. The connection was bad. All Brian could hear was that he was upset, and was leaving the treatment early. He asked Brian if he could pick him up the next day. Brian agreed, though was worried about Richard, because he did not have the whole story due to the excitement and the bad phone connection.

We ate take-out pizza since the kids received personal pans for their reading for the month. Aidan and Grand-dad talked about what Christmas gifts Aidan wanted. Then the phone beeped in, it was my girlfriend with the toddler. She told me her daughter was sick, and asked if I would go with her to the pharmacy. She wanted me to wait in the car so she did not have to get our little princess out in the cold. Soon the girls were parked outside, and I left my pizza and phone with Aidan, as he continued his conversation with Grand Dad.

As I waited in the car, minutes later the mom was back after the pharmacy. She looked exhausted. I offered to take her daughter overnight. She was stressed; her husband was coming home (from Iraq) soon. Her job was Chaotic, and her daughter now was sick. She needed a break. She reluctantly agreed.

After, we were at my house, giving our friend her medicine when the mom tells us her shower nozzle had broken that morning. She was telling us of her plans to wash her hair in the sink. We had to convince her to let us help. She felt guilty about me taking her daughter and her being okay with it. We had an extra shower nozzle, and Brian and her went to her house and replaced the broken piece.

Soon all were asleep! Our toddler in our crib, the kids in their beds, and me in lots of gratitude!
....
The next morning (Tuesday) my friend told me she did not sleep all night. She felt guilty handing over her sick child. All I wanted to do was help her; and give her a break. I told her over and over, I did not feel taken advantage of. I begged her to let her guilty feelings go, and to please use the day to get a well needed haircut. She needed to de-stress and recuperate.

I also recorded a Video blog in the morning. It was about learning how to receive. It seems easier for us to give, then to receive. But if we do not receive, the circle is broken. It would have broken my heart, if my friend would not have let me help her. It makes me feel good to be able to give, and I also love hanging out with her daughter. When we have trouble receiving, try to receive in the giver's eyes. Try not to think about how hard it is to receive, instead think about how good the giver feels by giving. Just use their feelings, until our skills of receiving improve. It is just like my pills, they are helping add happy thoughts, until my body starts creating them by themselves again. Use the giver's thoughts, until your body learns how to receive on its own.

Later that morning I watched more training videos for the business. The videos were exciting. They were referencing the training as a multi-level marketing company.

This excites me because this business is easy, and I can succeed at it. It is even better now, that the training referenced multi-level marketing; even though it is not. I have always wanted to succeed at a multi-level marketing company; this was a dream coming true! I did have to keep reminding myself to slow down, as I was daydreaming. I had to keep bringing myself back to the present moment. Yes, it was exciting, but I wanted the excitement to continue, so I had to bring myself back to the current step and enjoy that!

Brian did not come home for lunch; instead he headed to Denver to get Richard. Later it was time to get my kids, and then the kids that I babysit. When we were home, Brian and Richard were already there to surprise us! As I was letting the kids play, Brian reminds us of our closing papers for the house that we were selling, that needed to get notarized before five o'clock. I had almost forgotten; I was tired from the long day with our toddler, and all of the excitement. We quickly printed the closing papers. We had to go to the bank to get them notarized. I called the mom we babysit for and asked if we could take her kids to the bank with us; she said yes. When we get there, I realize I do not have my purse. Brian and the kids go back to the house, while I make an appointment with the loan officer and wait. I had to wait a long time. The security guard is older and funny. You can totally tell he loves his life, and lives each moment 'in the moment.' I tried to steal his energy, and relax and patiently wait. Soon Brian is back, and we get our documents notarized.

We get home, and the lady I babysit for is waiting for us. Her and her kiddos go home. We go inside and try to sign the rest of the documents (the ones that did not need to be notarized.) They are done. Brian takes Aidan to the Fed Ex office to mail the papers, while I take Dreana to Girl Scouts.

We get to class and I am anxious about the documents, and trying to let it all go. I sit there talking with the other moms. Soon I receive a phone call from the Title Company. They wanted to go over the documents (the ones we already signed) with me. They are already mailed! I let her know we were not positive about everything we were signing, but we were confident all would go well.

Later we were home eating chili for dinner. We listened to Richard playing his guitar. It was a good evening. Soon we were all asleep.

Wednesday morning I woke up and realized Richard's girlfriend had spent the night; her car was outside. Richard, who is usually up early, was still sleeping. I had my morning to myself. Brian was also awake.

Last night the news reported the Army post was going to have a snow day. Though, this morning, the weather did not seem that bad. Brian checked the weather channel, and it was confirmed, it was indeed a snow day! The kids still had to go to school.

The kids were very loud, and Brian and I kept asking them to be quiet, because Richard was still sleeping. Then the doorbell rings, and the dogs start barking again! Aidan's friend was here to get Aidan. I was not going to let Aidan walk in the cold, so Brian and I drove the three of them to school.

Soon it was just Brian and me. We talked about my car, and me wanting to trade it in. I called the bank to ask for the payoff, and they told me after a few days, they would call to tell us what the underwriter said. Richard and his friend were then up. They said they did hear the kiddos being loud, though they thought their excitement was cute. They left and had a day to themselves. I did bills, and talked with my girlfriend.

As the day progressed, Brian and Richard went to get the kids from school. After, the boys took off for the evening to do some shopping. They were gone for a long time. I watched a movie while the kids occupied themselves.

Later the boys were back with gifts. Richard bought Aidan and Dreana each a guitar! There was lots of excitement in our home after that surprise! He also brought home groceries and pizza. All evening the kids, Richard and Brian played beautiful music. We had a concert going on. With them occupied, I took advantage and went to sleep early.

Thursday morning brought lots of snow and cold weather. Richard was up early, making omelets. Brian was up earlier than his alarm clock to share in the excitement of breakfast. We ate as Richard watched. I asked him why he was not eating. He said he had Burger king earlier.

Whatever, he is a character!

As the early hours progressed, I received a text message from my friend; day care was closed for the day because of weather. I was getting my toddler for the day! We then checked the weather report and learned the kids had a two hour delay also! I texted Aidan's friend's mom, and asked if her son wanted to come over for the two hours. Good thing I did, because she had no clue of the delay. As we awaited our friend to come over, I received a call from his mom saying school was cancelled!

Soon Brian was off to work, and I had a whole bunch of happy kids in my house! All the kids played! They played Lego's and guitars, and did lots of running throughout the house. Our toddler enjoyed them all. I think she loves being around big kids! I talked with my girlfriend on the phone a little; it was a very good, energetic day.

Also during the day, I received a call from the guy with the home-based business. I was having trouble with some of the computer stuff, and was confused. He walked me through my last step, and told me it was time for the Craigslist ad to start making money. I was shocked. I told him there was still more training to do. He told me I knew everything I needed to know. I could just jump in, and learn as I go. I was very happy that we were finally to this step. The last bit was things I was going to go over with Brian, and then we were scheduled to do our ad. This was actually working!

The rest of the afternoon Richard was teaching Dreana the guitar, and my toddler went home with her mom. Dreana cried, and begged to let her stay. Though, our afternoon was over. The mom and I talked about her husband coming home. This summer they are being transferred to Georgia. She was excited and also nervous.

I was a little impatient. I wanted to finish up everything for the business, but I had to wait for Brian. He came home, though had to go back to work again because of an unfinished project. I found myself waiting longer. I later received an email from the foster agency, saying they are now ready for me to schedule a home visit. I was shocked. This was happening! They wanted to know if I wanted my home check in December or January. I scheduled if for December! This is awesome, not only am I getting my own babies; I'm finally eligible to get foster babies!

I was in a great mood after all of this. I realized what a great story, this story we are writing is. There have been a lot of events that have happened. It almost seems like fiction, a made up story. But you know and I know that all of this did happen. There is a lot that went on in the last few months. I love it; I really appreciate dialoging all of these events! I feel really good!

The things I am thankful for are: my money appears good. It is do-able, and we are holding on. I have an online business, and it seems to be working. I am very excited for this. I can get pregnant again! I am getting foster babies! I have a really cool house that I live in! I am getting my new car! I am getting rid of all of my debt! I am writing my own book! A lot of really cool things are happening. I am happy!

All evening I was floating. I was trying to figure out what kids I wanted from the foster agency. I decided, if I still have my current car when the kids come, I will get one baby. If I have my new car by then; I can have two babies! I currently have the two I babysit for, so I no longer need to get another five and nine year old; I have them already. I can still get a teenager who is pregnant, because she can have the room down stairs and her own car.

The night was awesome.

There were more guitars and good times with Richard's visit! Life is good. It was now time for class. I left the good stuff at home, and went to get some more from church!

This week was our last class. The class began with all of us in excitement. We talked about how cool this experience has been. How we were nervous, yet excited to do this.

Testimonial time! Our first testimony was prompted by our leader, to another lady in the class. The leader had suggested for this lady to get a 0% credit card to pay for her new car. She did, and received approval back with no interest until September 2014. She mentioned she had received these offers before, but had thrown them away, as she was afraid of debt. This time she was able to see this answer was safe and an available option. God speaks through others at times, when certain messages need to get to us!

Another story came from a member and her puppy. Apparently, she has been having difficulty training her dog. She signed him up for puppy classes, and this week the dog received a reward for, "Most improved dog!" Blessings to the both of them!

Another lady received a call to be a substitute teacher! Before she knew it (that day) she was running late. She started to worry, then she noticed the school had a two hour delay; she relaxed again. She then drove to school later, and realized school was cancelled for the day because of the snow. She was happy though, she 'almost' got to work. The rest is on its way! She spent the rest of her day-off, going to a doctor's appointment. This appointment needed to be done, and now she had the time. Her thoughts as the evening ended were, "I almost worked today!" She is seeing all of her blessings, good for her!

Here is another story; a lady left her purse in a shopping cart at a store parking lot. She did not realize it was missing until she was home. She first began to worry, and then started to affirm, "I am prosperous, no matter what this looks like." Her purse (when she got to it) was still there, as well as everything in it! This lady is very prosperous, blessings to her.

Another lady spoke of feeling very warm and safe. She is enjoying the beautiful snow, and wanted to send blessings to the rest of us! And right back at you, thank you. Blessings to you and all of us! Another lady put a spin on our testimonies. She shared with us her forgiveness! She chose to apologize to each of her three children, as well as her X-husband, for the hurt caused during her divorce, thirty years prior. She also thanked her children for their understanding, and never ending support for each other. She thanked her X-husband for his and his wife's understanding, and friendship over the years. Wow this is beautiful.

Another testimony came in from one of my favorite members of our class. He mentioned how he feels blessed to live such a prosperous life. He leaves on Friday for Atlanta, to visit his brother and family. He previously had stayed with them for two and a half months, during a summer while he was going through a liver transplant. He is going back to thank them again, for all they had done for him. He will also be visiting two doctors who worked very hard at keeping him alive during that time. He is looking forward to showing them what great things he has done with his life! He is feeling lots of gratitude. I want to thank him for his message; I am feeling his gratitude as well! Thank you for being such an awesome friend! Blessings to you!

Soon our class was over, and it was time for our last prayer circle. On the way to class, my car had started to act up again. I was anxious to have the group pray for my safe ride home. Our next prayer asked God to always express, most beneficially, to those He serves. Our third prayer was for God to show us our correct paths, and always show us how to serve. Our fourth prayer was continual guidance of our highest good, now and forever. We have a fifth ongoing prayer for a member no longer in our class, which is: may all that occurs, be in line with her free will and serve her highest, holiest, and purposeful good. May the God within her, also bring her health! These prayers are for the individuals, and also for all of us. May all of this come to each and every one of us; this or something much better. Blessings to us all!

After our prayers, I was giddy and happy. I was happy to see everyone again. I told the class about being able to have babies again. Everyone wanted to know what happened; well God happened! We said our good byes, and promised to keep in touch. This was, and is a beautiful class. I recommend this to any, and all who want to continue to prosper in their lives!

I drove home. My car was still acting up. Though, I knew the prayers were working. I did not worry too much about it. When I was home I had Brian check it and he thought maybe it just needed to be cooled off. Soon we were inside, and I was in a great mood. I was also hungry! I made myself a very elegant breakfast meal, and enjoyed my current vibration. I talked with my girlfriend for a bit, and shared my bliss with her. Soon Brian and I were asleep. Thursday faded away in our dreams!

Chapter 14:
The Finale

Friday morning was here. I woke up in a very good mood. I felt accomplished. I was excited the class was over. I was excited because this period of my journey was moving along; and I was succeeding with it. The kids were at school. I was home, and did not want to do anything productive. There were a lot of writings to catch up on. Though, now was not 'that time.' I was excited about all the current events happening. I wanted them to hurry up and happen.

I called my girlfriend and she did not answer. I began slowly with my to-do-list. The foster (foster for the kids, not dogs) agency lady was coming this evening, and we had to prepare our house to pass her inspection. I rearranged my kitchen because I needed a cupboard that locked for all of the cleaning supplies. I then collected all the medicine into a basket; this too needed a spot that could be locked. I had to wait for Brian to get home to help me create that spot. While I waited, the medicine hung out on the counter. I listened to my prosperity CD, and played solitaire. I relaxed into my game; knowing a break was A-Okay because the work could not continue until Brian was home.

It was now noon. Brian was home. He found all the locks, and helped secure our medicine. We cleaned out the storage area, and then mopped the floors. We had a good time, and everything looked amazing. Before we knew it, it was time to get the kids, and then it was time to get the next set of kids. I was creative with keeping the floors clean by having the kids dance in their socks. This fashioned an outlet for their rambunctious energy, and gave a reason for no shoes!

Five o'clock was finally here. The kids' mom was here. She paid me for the week and took her kids home. Moments later the foster lady was to be here. She wasn't; she was late! Un-patient minutes passed, they turned into three fourths of an hour; and she finally arrived. We talked small talk, and she met the kids and dogs. We did a tour of the house, as she went through her inspection list. We had two things to improve. We had to get a guard gate for our fire place, and a lock for the unfinished area of the lower level. She told us we can do all of that, as she continues to come by for her visits. This is good. I had worried that everything would stop until these two things were fixed. I was happy everything was able to continue.

She also mentioned that the kid's bathroom was the cleanest she had ever seen. This made me feel awesome! I think she liked us. We were prepared for the inspection. We were also prepared with every bit of baby gear you can think of.

Well, we still need baby gates; though I am positive this intention is on its way! Before she left, we scheduled the next five visits. The next visits were a lot of interviews to see how we do as a foster family. It was cool that we were at this step in the process!

The evening was good! Soon we all were asleep!

Saturday morning we all slept in. The house was still clean; the kids were in great moods. Dad made everyone eggs and toast. Everyone was smiling. This was the day I was hoping to get a new car!

After breakfast we drove to the dealership. Brian drove, as I was the passenger. He removed my totem I had hanging from my mirror. It was the part of my car that broke last year, when I was driving to Indiana. When he was taking it down, at first I was mad. And then I understood he did not want the dealership to wonder if there was something wrong with my car. I remembered my group prayer for church the other day. I had asked the group to pray for my car, because it kept overheating. Maybe my car was messing up because my totem was hanging this whole time? Yes, I was proud of my car part hanging from my mirror; it reminded me of how blessed I am. Though my car, instead may have felt the energy of the broken part, and this is why it still acted as if it was 'broken.' Maybe if Brian removed the totem, my car would fix itself! I now keep the totem in my purse, not my car. It is for me, not my car!

We had decided to only go to one dealership that morning. Previously we had picked out two cars from two different dealerships we wanted to see; though both dealerships were far apart from each other. We hoped the car we were going to see was going to be the perfect one. And the car search would be over by the end of the day. As we were driving, I was nervous. I think I was nervous because of the change. I closed my eyes, and repeated over and over, "I am guided to my highest good, and I am remaining centered all day." We get to the dealership, and the van we are there to see is parked by the door. We go in, and the person we are working with is not there. Instead a new person is the one they decided would be helping us. It felt a little off, almost discriminatory. We were purchasing a five thousand dollar car, and it seemed this was the treatment that we were to expect. Though I knew I was calm and centered, and all would be okay. I let their vibration go, and continued to let the day unfold.

We test drove the car, and it was good. The only issues I had was that there was a leak. I wanted it fixed, and I wished the van had a few more seats. But all in all it was a good car. I was ready to talk numbers. We get inside, and things again seem weird.

The sales woman asked what the pay off on my car was, without telling me what she would buy my car for first. This felt weird, but I went with it. Maybe all of this extra information was a way of making this transaction go smoother. I gave her what she wanted to know. Soon she comes to me with a credit application. I reminded her we were not financing. My car is worth a lot more than what I was taking her car for. There was no need to finance. She insisted, and I soon decided we were not supposed to make a deal with this dealership. I kindly let her know that we were going to leave, and possibly come back later in the week.

Then a 'more experienced' car sales man came to talk with us. He brought me a paper that said they would buy my car for twelve thousand dollars. This would pay off my nine thousand dollar loan, and I would also bring them a check for fifteen hundred dollars to finish the transaction. I started to laugh. I know my car would sell for at least seventeen thousand. If I sold it myself, I could get 18,500 for it. He asked what it would take for this deal to go through. I said, "17,000 dollars." He proceeded to tell me twelve thousand is the most I could get, and when I go to another dealership, I should remember that he was the first person to be honest with me. We kindly said, "Okay," and were out the door. Both Brian and I felt they were treating us like we were very young and ignorant. We tried to brush it off and continue on with our day. I called my brother and asked him his opinion. He confirmed seventeen thousand was the only number I should take from a dealership. He encouraged me to tell each dealership that did not honor that price to, "Go screw themselves!"

Soon we were at the other dealership that had the other van we wanted to see. This van had fifteen seats. When I saw the van, I was excited. It looked pretty, and it was very functional! Prior to seeing it I had horror images going through my head. Though in person, it was awesome. This dealership was very small, but the sales people seemed to be really cool people. They had cool bobble-heads and loud music playing. They were busy with ten million customers, but having fun with them! We had to wait fifteen minutes, but we were okay with it. We were having fun. As we waited, the other dealership called back and offered us fourteen thousand. Brian told them we would think about it.

Soon we had a car sales man, and he informed us the vehicle we wanted to see had sold earlier in the week. The one I was looking at was a newer version, and did not fall in the five thousand dollar range we were after. A little irritated, I continued to move forward and asked him to look at my car and tell me how much he would buy it back for. With his numbers we could come up with a new plan.

While they were evaluating my car, they also looked on-line and found a few more five thousand dollar vans. They told me they would buy my car for $14,500, and I told them I would take seventeen. They agreed, and said we would make a deal once I found a five thousand dollar van to purchase. They would look all week, and let us know what there was to choose from. Later we were home; we were pleased with their offer. We decided to keep that in our awareness, but to also put my truck up on Craigslist, and see which sale came first.

Before long it was time for our party (we were having a Christmas/Birthday get-together at the house.) The house was clean, and the doorbell started ringing. Our neighbors were here with some good looking dip, and lots of energy and excitement. We were going to have a fun evening. Their three kids and my two, ram-shacked the house and celebrated together. Brianna and me sat at the table with wine and enjoyed some long overdue girl talk! Brian and Chris were outside by the campfire doing the guy thing! It was a good time. They eventually brought their puppy over, and she added to the excitement with our three dogs.

Later we had a few more couples over and also Aidan's friend. The evening was a success. As I was reminiscing about the night, the doorbell rang again. This time it was two fire men all geared up. Their fire truck sat outside, announcing to all the neighbors, that there was an emergency at our house! Apparently, a neighbor called about our camp fire outside. They came to check it out. Colorado is not big on camp fires; though we thought we were doing everything right via the code. The fire men ended up saying we had to get a store bought pit, instead of an in-ground one. Tonight we had to put our fire out. Even though the situation seemed 'bad;' it was good. The firemen hung out with the kids, and hooked them up with stickers and autographs! They sat, and let the kids ask question after question about what it was like to be a fire man! These men became an inspiration for my three! This was so sweet of them!

There is always awesomeness in a perceived bad!

Now we were all asleep.

....

Sunday morning was here. We were up early and soon on our way to church. The kids went inside and headed to Sunday school, as Brian and I went into the service. On our way in we saw some familiar faces. This was cool; we are starting to find this church a home church, as we are beginning to make friends! I was excited about tithing; this would be the first time I tithed in church, instead of class. The service was nice. I really like the culture here; it is very upbeat and fun. Everyone seems happy here. It was easy to give hugs, it felt right.

At the end of the service, all the kids come to the front of church to tell the congregation what they learned for the day. I love this part. Aidan walked in holding Dreana's hand; oh I love my kids! After, we had hot cocoa and talked to a few people. We then were in the car, and on our way to the grocery store. Richard had given us a fifteen dollar prepaid-grocery card. We purchased dinner and a cake. Blessings what fifteen dollars gets you!

We then were on our way to another store. I had my 45 dollars from babysitting, and I was hoping it was plenty to get Aidan's friend a Christmas gift, the Angel gift (gift for charity,) and new shoe laces for Brian. I reminded myself to trust that we would be guided with our purchase. And we did; we had three dollars left over! We purchased two whole gifts, and shoe laces for less than 45 bucks! Life is good!

We later were home and had new friends over. Some kids down the street wanted to play. I enjoyed watching the kids with their new friends. I realized we are really beginning to connect with this neighborhood. Brian cleaned out my car, and put it up for sale on Craigslist. I spent my time watching the movie, "The Secret." Soon Aidan was off to his friend's house. There, they had home-made tacos! Dreana stayed home, as the neighbor girl came over!

Later we had dinner, and then the kids were asleep. Brian and I watched a movie with the fire going. He then headed to the store, and bought some movie snacks. I started to feel a little sick, and wondered if the flu was on the way. I began to affirm, "If I am sick, it will pass by morning!" Soon we fell asleep on the couch, and Sunday was over.

....

Monday morning was here, and I was no longer sick. It was a good day; it was Brian's birthday! We all said, "Happy birthday" a million times! The kids were off to school with lots of smiles and excitement for their days. I was feeling a little overwhelmed. I felt like there was a lot to do, and that I was slacking on time. I wrote down everything I needed to do, and decided to make the day a to-do-list day. I emailed everyone back who had called over the weekend for the business. Then I prepared directions for where to drop the 'angel gift' off, and then where to go for my doctor appointment.

I was going to the new counselor, referred by the Army counselor. The list was working; I found myself a lot calmer than when I began. I was shortly in the car, and headed to the Salvation Army. My GPS took me straight there, and the lady I gave the gift to was very cheery and grateful. It felt good giving that gift. I was finally apart of something I never realized I wanted to be. I was a part of a community of people that do neat things for the public.

I then was back in the car, and my GPS was right on track with the therapist office. It was a large building, and seemed to be a successful organization. The reception desk was warm and a good place to be. I fill out my papers, and before I know it the therapist is ready to see me. Our talk was an overview of why I wanted to see a therapist in the first place. I told her, now I was much better, though I feel it is good to be seeing someone regularly anyway. The pills I was taking seemed to be working. I talked about myself, and answered her questions. At the end, we decided her role would be more of a coach than a therapist. We would see each other every three weeks.

I thought it was funny that she used the word 'coach.' I have been affirming for over a year that I would be able to be coached by some big names. Though as God always provides, I got myself a coach in the best way it could currently come! She showed me how my self-talk could be improved. I enjoyed our talk. She encouraged me to realize when to let things go, and let them unfold. She advised me to affirm, "I may have done this (a perceived 'bad,') though now, I currently accept it and am making better choices every day." Basically to admit to myself it was not the preferred outcome, but to also realize it is getting more and more perfect every day.

Also in the session I mentioned that I had not started my Christmas shopping yet. I felt like I was running out of time. I really wanted to find time to do it with Brian, and while the kids were in school. As I was driving home, Brian called and told me he had the afternoon off! The perfect time to Christmas shop showed up! We later were at the store with a very detailed list of gifts to purchase. I needed gifts for the kids, gift cards, Christmas cards, and a few groceries. I think these to-do lists are helping me. I am excelling in them. We only had an hour, though we handled it all. We had plenty of money, and I was feeling great. We were short on time, so I dropped Brian off at school to walk with the kids, as I unloaded the car at home.

When Brian and the kids were home, we jumped back in the car to take Brian back to work. He had brought his truck home for lunch because he was going to let his boss use his government car, while he was here for a few days. Brian needed to be dropped off, so he was not juggling two cars when he picked up his boss from the airport.

After we left Brian, the kids and I headed to the grocery store to pick up another box of school snacks. During this time I received a text message from Aidan's friend's mom. She asked if we wanted a bag of toys she was going to give to the donation store. After the store, we headed to her house. She gave us some really nice toys; some of them Dreana also enjoyed! We are lucky and blessed to receive so much, thank you.

When we were home Brian and his boss were there! We sat outside and chit chatted for a minute. It was nice to talk with him. The two of them seem to connect. It is good to see this.

Later Brian and the kids made cupcakes for his birthday. It was fun to watch them all have so much fun. Soon dad and Aidan were ready for Cub Scouts. Dreana and I were getting the evening to ourselves. We girls were hanging out for thirty minutes when I remembered today was the Cub Scout Christmas party. All families were invited. Dreana and me got ready, and headed to school. As we were walking in, we saw Santa and Mrs. Clause in the parking lot! The party was good, all the kids had the opportunity to sit on Santa's lap and tell him what they wanted for Christmas. Brian also sat on Santa's lap. He said he was a very good boy, and asked for his nine thousand dollar gun that was on his wish list! Everyone had a chuckle!

The Cub scouts received their derby cars as gifts. We had lots of cookies and snacks. Dreana also told the moms that daddy had a crush on one of the teachers. This was an unexpected comment. Everyone had a laugh! After the party we came home to Brian's birthday party! We sang "Happy birthday" to daddy and had our cupcakes! Soon the kiddos were in bed, and Brian and I were downstairs hanging by the fire. We all went to sleep happy!

....

Tuesday morning was here, and the kids were off to school. I spent the majority of my morning wrapping gifts. I then went back to the store to get the remaining gift cards I needed. Then I was on my way to drop off two bags for donation. I was home, and wrote out my cards, and wrapped the two gifts I had; one for Dreana's friend (a boy) and one for Aidan's girlfriend. I wanted to go to the post office to send out the Christmas cards, though was short on time for the kiddos.

I headed to school, and when Dreana gave her gift to her 'friend,' he was so excited. He walked with his mom to their car in utter astonishment! I am sure him and his mom had a big ole conversation about why a girl was giving him a Christmas gift! I also found Aidan, and gave him his gift for his girlfriend, though she was already on the bus. Later when we were in the car, away from earshot of any of his friends, Aidan told me his concerns. He told me giving a girl a necklace (which was what the gift was) was like being in college, and giving a girl an engagement ring. He said he wasn't sure if he was ready for that kind of commitment. I smiled; my boy is so mature. I reassured him that all girls like jewelry: friends, teachers, and girlfriends. He had nothing to worry about. Then we planned how he should give her the gift the next day.

A good time would be when it was just the two of them, when no friends could see or hear!

After, we went to the post office. As we waited in line, we had a really nice conversation with an older lady. She reminded me of how important the current moment is. She was not stressed in the long line; she was enjoying it. I really liked talking with her. It was because of her that our wait was peaceful. When we were at the counter, we received really good customer service! Blessings to our friend, thank you.

We were then home, and so was Brian. In the mail we received an unexpected twenty-five hundred dollar check! Brian quickly reminded me this was to pay property taxes. Even though the money was already accounted for; it still felt good receiving it! As the evening continued, Brian and I were on the couch, exhausted. I dreaded having to still go to Girl Scouts. As we waited to leave, my girlfriend called. We then were out the door. We get to Girl Scouts, and there are lots of cookies that the girls will be decorating for their activity. I had a big ole smile on my face, and I think everyone there was responding to my high vibration!

Later our leader told me her electricity for her kitchen was out; also one of her daughters was home sick. I think she is feeling overwhelmed, and this is why her power is out. Another woman there gave her a phone number for an electrician that would be available the next day. I offered for Brian to help her. She said, "Thanks, but I can wait till tomorrow." As the girls were doing their cookies, some moms and I went into the library to help with projects the school was doing. This was nice, lots of ladies with no kids; just putting Christmas Frisbees together!

Soon we girls were home. The kids had macaroni, and Brian and I had chili. The kids were in bed, and Brian and I were also asleep.

....

Wednesday morning I was awake at three A.M. I had not woken up this early in a long time; I was surprised. I reminded myself that I was done with getting scared at night, and I was safe to go back to sleep. I went back to sleep! I dreamed quite a bit over the night. My dreams were very vivid. I had a feeling that lots of other stuff is clearing out. I am improving without even knowing!

It was then seven and I was up again. This was later than usual, though it still was a good morning. Brian did not have to be at work until noon. He and his buddies have half days for the holidays; so I let him sleep in. I have been noticing that I am very good with the pills I am taking. And it is Brian who seems to being having a hard time all of a sudden. I think I am not processing for him anymore, and now it is affecting him. He mentioned the other day that he would like to go get pills also.

When he had returned from war (years ago,) he had a very hard time. He was nervous and jumpy every day. For a year, he took pills and it helped him a lot. Well the other day, he said he was feeling nervous again. We decided it might be good to check into them again. I think I am clearing, and so therefore Brian is going to have the opportunity also. This is important to mention. As we improve, everyone around us has to improve; this is law. Sometimes we are scared to improve, because we think we will lose certain individuals if we do. Though what really happens is that those individuals also improve. It is a win-win. This is why we should never be reluctant to improve, and get better.

I spent a lot of the afternoon writing and catching up to where we are now. This feels good; it feels good to be caught up. I received a call from my neighbor asking to borrow eggs. This was cool; I finally have a neighbor I can borrow eggs to! I am really enjoying Colorado! I went over to her house, and she gave me a tour. She was making cookies, as I played with her puppy and three-year old. It was fun; I enjoy having a friend!

Later Brian was up, and we were outside talking. I kept hearing a whole bunch of sirens. Sirens to me mean that something good is going to happen, and I should be ready! Brian then asks me if I had seen the lottery numbers. He said last night the numbers were 636 million. My affirmation is that I will win 656 million in the lottery. When I had made this affirmation years ago, Brian did not think we would see it for at least ten years. The numbers had never been that high. Well, ever since I made my affirmation, the numbers had been getting higher and higher. I told him I had been noticing the lottery a lot lately. It kept jumping out at me; though all I saw was fifty million. I did not understand why it kept jumping out at me. We realized this was good. All I was seeing was the fifty million so I could realize my affirmation was on its way. It was not now, but getting really close! When it is 'the day,' I will notice more than fifty million; I will notice my number and know exactly what to do! Life is so blessed!

We then walked back over to the neighbor's house with a few desks. When we moved here, we had picked up thirteen desks from a school that no longer needed them. With me being creative, I was considering decorating the kids' living room with them. Though after a while of living here, we were only using four. I gave the extras to the kids I babysit for, and our neighbors. On the way to their house I almost stepped on a garden snake. I ran and screamed, and Brian laughed. I do not think I will ever get used to how 'okay' it is that snakes are around (here in Colorado.) I found it significant a snake was on my path. A snake means I am growing very deep into myself. I think our friend was a reminder that I was doing a very good job. I was learning!

We had little time left before Brian went to work for the day. The dealership that offered me twelve thousand and then fourteen thousand for my car, called again. This time they said they will take sixteen thousand if we buy their van. We said we would think about it. Then another dealership called. This lady saw our ad on Craigslist, and was asking for details. She asked us how much we owe on it. Because of prior experience, we told her the information she was looking for was not necessary. What we were concerned with was what they would buy our truck for. There was no grumpiness in our energy, just straight forward facts. We will see how the car unfolds!

Finally Brian was out the door to work. I spent a few more hours writing our story. I received a text message from our neighbor asking for the phone number of another neighbor. I thought it was cool that I was a connector for these two ladies. I remembered (in the past) I was the connector to friends that are no longer my friends. After I connected them, they wanted to be friends and ditched me. I was scared this might happen again. I then chose to take a chance. I was going to be the connector again. I was going to trust this time would be okay. I enjoy connecting people and was not going to choose fear instead of doing what I enjoy.

The rest of the afternoon was filled with getting my kids from school. Dreana received a Christmas present from the boy she gave a gift to; she was very excited! The whole family enjoyed her joy! We soon were at the high school, and watched as Aidan was on stage for his Christmas school program. It was an African theme, and a very good concert. My kids had so much fun. This school is awesome, and I am blessed that we are a part of it!

We later were home and had dinner. The kids were in bed, and I talked with my girlfriend for a minute. She was crying; a lot of things in her life seemed to come to the surface. She kept repeating over and over, that she knew her heart-ache was for a reason. Her reason was a chance to grow; but it still currently sucked. Soon her phone beeped in, and she asked me to stay on hold. I was on hold for twenty minutes! I was not frustrated; I knew it was for a reason. I was holding the space for her, while she was having her 'hard' conversation on the other line.

The evening ended with Brian and me watching a movie. I ate a lot during the movie. I have been eating a lot lately, and I have been craving meat (I am a vegetarian.) I think my body is anxious with all the changes. I am loading up on the calories to keep me going!

....

Today is Thursday! Our last day of writing is today. Our time period is over. Wow, a lot has happened! This morning I woke up remembering a lot of my dreams.

Again, I feel a lot of stuff is subconsciously leaving me through my dreams. I also have been having bouts of fear again. Though now I talk with myself, as it is happening. It seems as I let the fear happen, without judgment or a need to make it go away, it leaves quickly.

The morning was good. The kids were happy; Aidan was off to school with his friend. Brian offered to take Dreana to school. She was extra happy as she had lipstick on! I have been feeling very excited today. I kept wrestling with the dogs! This afternoon the foster lady is coming over. I am very excited for that. I am in a great mood. Life is good. I feel cleared, and in anticipation for what is next. It is good to be here. I love it! There are things not finished yet, like the fire place wood. Obviously the wood is not yet here for a reason; I am just not sure of the 'why.' When I do not know the 'why,' I get frustrated! I am centering myself. When I finally let go, I am positive our delivery will show up. Also I am picking up my two at 2:40, and the other two kids at 3:30. I scheduled the foster appointment from two to four. I feel goofy for the over-book, though I trust this was done for a reason. I am letting this go every moment of the day as well.

The afternoon was here. Our foster lady was twenty minutes late. How we figured out the schedule conflict was, Brian and she were to start interviewing first; and then he would go get our kids. While he was gone, my interview would begin, and then I would go get the second set of kids. Soon all the kids were here, and all were being exceptionally good! She stayed until five, and this was the same time the mom of the babysat kids came by. Everyone was here to meet each other.

After, Aidan went to his friend's house. His mom was driving the boys to go swimming. Dad, Dreana and I prepared ourselves to go swimming as well, but in our own car.

The pool was nice. They had a Santa movie playing, and ginormous cookies to offer the party! The kids had fun; we had fun. The three of us came home and Dreana prepared for bed. Aidan came home an hour later. Immediately he jumped in the shower. Apparently Aidan's friend was sick on the way home, and used Aidan as a sounding board!

Brian and I watched a movie. Before I knew it, we were all asleep.
....

This is the end of our day, and our story. Before we end, I would like to thank you for being on my journey. I am excited that I was able to dialog every part of my day, as I tithed. I wanted to know if tithing would work. As you can see, I had ups and downs. Though in the end, a lot of progress was made. I did make it. Tithing did work. As of now, you can see that I was able to continue to pay the things I needed to pay. This was happening before I was tithing.

Though with tithing, the same things are being paid, but with only two thirds of my income. The extra blessing was yes, all of that was getting paid; but also a lot of other stuff was clearing up. As things were clearing, I went through a lot of emotions. Emotions are good, even the hard ones. In the end, I have proved to myself that God does care, and has helped transform my financials. Does tithing work? Yes it does. I believe.

I am glad I was able to dialog my fears when I was testing this. A lot of time, when we have fears, or things seem to be messing up, we think we are doing something wrong. As things mess up, it only means things are changing. Change messes things up. Change gets us to the next step. I hope you see, through me, that you are normal. Your journey is normal. Your journey is getting you where you want to be. In the meantime, you will overcome the change. We realize our demons are really not demons, but misguided bouts of fear. Fear just shows us we do not know the answer yet. As change shakes things up, we soon learn the answer. So fear was good all along. It warned us that we were changing into what it is we wanted.

I am thankful for you. Blessings to you as you continue to thrive.

Chapter 15:
After thought: April 2014

I wrote this book for many reasons. 1: I always wanted to write a book. 2: This book showed up as one inspired idea after another, from beginning to end. The rest of my writings never were able to come together before this time. It must be 'right' that this book has been written. 3: I wanted to become perfect from writing all of my secrets down; I felt by me writing it, I was being honest, and so naturally my world would change overnight. This reason was worth the 'pain and fears' I endured, as I encouraged myself to keep going. 4: I wanted you to be able to learn from me. I wanted you to be able to have the courage to do something, something huge, because you were inspired by my courage.

It is now April 7, 2014, as I type this passage. Our time line for this book ended at the end of December 2013. It did take some time to finish writing, as well as time to edit what was written. I still have a to-do list of at least another read-through; and to name our chapters. I have to create our cover, and then format it for publishing. I have the option of submitting our book to a publisher, or to self-publish.

This is my to-do-list. A list is easy to overcome; you just do it. The other stuff, the stuff that has made my to-do list take a very long time to complete, I am still battling with. I am nervous that people will find my book irrelevant, a waste of time. I fear my 'secrets' will be out. All the things I think in my head are now out on paper for the world to read. I am scared to face this. I am scared of what people will think. This is what I fight against. I have been fighting my whole life to feel significant. I want to be a part of a cause, to help embrace and change humanity for the better. I want to be worth it. This is what I fear most, that I am not. I fear you will finally know the real me, the "Me" I am afraid to be.

After all this said; this is why it is taking me so long to publish this book. I hope that once I do face my fears, and publish this book, that I will learn I was significant all along. I will learn my fears were just an illusion. I hope this is what I learn. I do not know what the answer is. I am curious of the feedback, of what the events in my life over these months, looked like to you.

I wonder if I look like an achiever or a go-getter. I wonder if I look like someone with no fear. I wonder if I look like a busy body, or one who 'does it all.' I guess this question matters a lot to me. Because I think you think that. Everyone tells me that all the time. They tell me I achieve this, and I am always doing that. And honestly, I think it is 'normal' to live life like I do. I think it is normal to always be doing something.

It is hard for me to understand when someone only does one project at a time. I appreciate that person who only has one focus, one project at a time. I appreciate them, but I do not understand them. It is like my husband and me. I can clean the whole house, and he is given one task (in that time frame) which is to scrub the shower. It takes me a few hours to clean multiple areas, and he a few hours to clean one area. But that one area is cleaned well. I get it; though I do not understand it.

It matters, because if you did not think of me as the over achiever, then you must think of me, as I think of me. At times, I think of me as a waste of time, insignificant. I think of me as a person who causes havoc. I think of me as a person who is not worthy to have others do things for me. I feel I should not 'not make' money while my husband does. I feel I should be a great mom and home maker, and also make money. I also feel that all of the things I preach and believe are wealth and abundance. I feel I have to make more money than the average, so I can teach others to do it too. If I am not making that, then I must have failed at what I try so hard to teach.

Though, ironically, this book actually was written. I feel God wants me to publish it. I feel He knows this writing will help someone. I need to do what I am told to do, and just get it out there. Once I do, I will see what the rest of the world sees. I will see I am significant. I am worth it.

And another thought. Maybe all is good, and life is just a process. I heard something really good the other day. A lot of life is filled with very high highs and very low lows. The 'not so average' do not have very low low's; they have more of a flow in all of life. The suggestion was that when something in your life is triggered, we have a tendency to try to understand the trigger, and work with it. Instead, a better practice is to not make the trigger better; make you better. Instead of trying to find the 'good' in a money issue, make your-self feel good. Do anything to get you in a better mood. Once we are in a better mood, answers will come for how to solve the problems.

Also life is just a process. Maybe the answer is not, "What have I achieved," instead, "Who have I become to allow myself to achieve this." This is what I have accomplished since our book was finished. I have quit smoking; I have made it a month now. I have stopped taking my depression pills. I am here now (in this current moment) finishing this book; even though the world may judge me. I have become licensed as a foster mom; though I am still waiting on our first placement. I have hired my mom's husband as the property manager of the remaining properties. I am still tithing.

My husband is taking his P.T. test this month, and his reverse vasectomy will finally be scheduled thirty days later. I have fallen in love with Colorado. My goals of moving to different states are changing, as now I just want to build a huge life here. I have been putting up farms in Colorado on my goal board. I have also found my full-bred mastiff, and as an added bonus she came with breeding papers! We are waiting on Anabel to go into heat in the next few months, so we can finally breed puppies. I have found my huge dining room table with two leafs! This was a goal I had for a while, now I have finally manifested it! I have also manifested my two baby gates that are now installed for my stairs.

I have achieved a bigger and better version of myself. This is good. These manifestations came because I had the courage to want them. Here is another manifestation, I am going to be jogging a few miles today. A week ago, I put up on my goal board a picture of two women running together. I chose this picture because I wanted a girlfriend to run with instead of my husband. Yesterday, as I was picking the kids up from school, my neighbor (a runner) asked me to run with her today. I am hoping to keep up with her; she runs at-least four miles at a time. Maybe I will be better then I think.

I think recognizing your achievements more and more is how you do not fall into the really low lows. Instead you just keep moving forward. For instance, getting this book past where it is has been a challenge for me. I am busting through a lot of fears. This week I have been recognizing the comment we spoke about a few paragraphs up. To be better, we do not have to make the problem seem better; instead all we have to do is make us better in that moment. How I have done this is each time I sit down to write, I write until it is no longer fun. Then I go on a walk or do something else I enjoy. I focus on how I, not my problems, can be better. This instantly raises my vibration.

Years ago I heard the comment, "A writer writes at least one hour a day." This is what makes a writer; a consistent hour each day turns into a book. I now write at least one hour a day. This makes me feel good. It is all just a mind trick! It is finding ways to understand how to continue to be good at what it is you do. As I write my one hour a day, I feel like a published author. Feeling like a published author makes me feel good.

The bills are better also. Currently I have six months of our two years and a half, of our debt consolidation finished! Seriously, you were here when I started that, one fifth is now done! This is on track. All of that time we have also been able to live with cash only. Our bills here in Colorado are rocking! We are not accruing any debt, and our budget is awesome!

Our rentals are also moving along.

I am proud of myself for as far as we have come. We have sold one property and this is good. I think the end goal is to sell the rest. We are still deciding on this decision. The one property that took forever to get vacant is now vacant. It now looks beautiful after a replaced window, carpet cleaning, and a good scrubbing. A lot of our money from our tax check went into fixing this property, and getting its mortgage up to date. My mom's husband is renting it out; this is nice to have my mom involved in one of my projects. Maybe we will end up keeping this property for thirty years, maybe we will not. I am okay with both.

My mother's husband is also taking over all the properties. The rental company's contract is over this summer. They have been very expensive for us. It will be nice when this transition comes.

Two other properties are in the same situation, they seem like they will be rentals for a little bit. The last property, the bank wants me to refinance. I have decided when they call, that I am not refinancing it. I am not stressing about it. If they want to take that property because of foreclosure, I am A-Okay with it. I just want my nine hundred dollars per month back. It currently is not rented. I do not know the future of this property, but I wouldn't be upset if it would go away.

So as you can see, I still have issues. I still have stuff I want to be better. Though, many things have already gotten better.

I think tithing has taught me that no matter what, I would have been safe. I am always safe. There is a passage in the Bible talking about how God always takes care of the birds; so why would He not take care of us! (International Bible Society, 1984) We will always be safe, though tithing brings finances to that next level. I want to prosper, and tithing teaches me how. Since I started, I have learned what it really means to trust. I remember in the beginning I was crying and terrified to tithe my first check. I knew I did not have enough money to be doing this. I did anyway, and viola, God gave me what I was missing. Now, since then, I still get nervous about giving my money; but now it is just nervous instead of the gut wrenching fear that it started out as. As this process continues, I think I will grow more into it each day. A year from now, I am positive my life will look very different. I also am positive that the differences will be in my favor.

Tithing is like learning to swim for the first time. We are so scared, but we want more, so we decide to jump. When we jump, we learn we are safe. This lesson is worth a billion bucks. We learn we will not die. We learn it is natural to swim; our bodies are equipped and know what to do. The water does not want to hurt us; it just wants to be a part of us. It wants to help us grow. God wants to help us.

He will always take care of us, though when we want more, He wants to show us how to get it. He wants to show us how to grow. How we grow, is to trust that we can and we will. We grow when we are courageous enough to jump. We then jump, and learn we knew how to swim all along.

I do not think I will ever stop tithing. I jumped and learned I wouldn't die. Now that I know I won't die, I am learning how to really live.

I am thankful for you. This book has helped me open up. It has helped me be courageous to tell you who I really am. It has helped me ask for what I really want. I am still scared, but I also feel like God is holding my hand as I walk through my fears. I am not sure of the future; but I am sure I am moving in the right direction. I hope because of me, you saw that it was okay to be scared. I hope that you saw that it is normal to be scared. I hope I have given you the courage to jump.

-Thanks for being my friend-

Chapter 16:
After thought 2: A Year or so later since we began...
October 2014

After our first Afterthought, I finished editing this book and put it down. I was not ready to publish it yet. I had foster kids during this time, and when they left, mid-October 2014, I picked up this book and began editing it again. I was ready. Here is what has happened since.

I affirmed all last year that I was going to write a book. I did. This year I affirm I am going to publish a book. The progress I have made is, I have met a best-selling, self-published author, who offered to help me self-publish my book. Though over this time, I have decided I want it published. My dream publisher is Hay House, though I am open to the process. I have also learned to look through my favorite books, in the Acknowledgement sections, to find my Literary Agent. I have also published over one hundred video blogs during this time. One of my videos has 2,321 views. I wanted my videos to be more of a success. Though, I am already a success. I am successful because I created my Vlog's. I shared with the world. The people who have seen my videos have prospered. This is enough. I am proud of me.

I am feeling better about my religious views. I do not feel I have to hide them anymore. Well, a little still, but very little. I am comfortable with the subject, and am now getting positive feedback. I picked up my son from a sleep over one day, on the way to church. At the house, the older sister asked what church I go to. I told her; and she says she has the same beliefs as I do. This was cool. I just told her what I believe, and not only did she not shun me, she believed the same things I did. The ironic part is that our outer world reflects what are inner world is telling us. My outer world finally produced a person with my same beliefs. This is cool.

I had a family of eight this past year. I had four foster children, my children, my husband and I. The range of children in my family were: age 1, age 2, age 3, age 6, age 7, and age 9. We had a very energetic household for a while! I am not sure if I will do it again; for now we are taking a break. We will see where this leads.

I have a fish, her name is Rose! I have always wanted fish. As a kid I wanted to have a fish tank the size of a big screen T.V. I wanted to look at that instead of the television. I held on to this dream for a while. When we moved to Colorado I began checking ads every day for fish tanks for sale. A few months ago, my son came home asking me if we could have fish. His friend was giving what he had away. Immediately I said yes! Not only did we get fish, we received a fish tank, pump and food! Just like that, fish were handed to me! And it was all free!

My husband did not make his E8 this year. It was a disappointment, though we are going for it this next year! The board is in February 2015. We were told in September that my husband's job is phasing out. They are replacing the people in this position into new jobs. They will let us know by September 2015, if he still works in Colorado or if we move again. I was excited about moving as I was writing this book; ironically, now, I am not sure if I want to. I like it in Colorado. I have made friends, I like the weather, and I like the school. I am still open to moving, and we will see what happens!

We have paid off Brian's mom from when she loaned us the three thousand dollars. We then paid off one of the credit cards. We now are working on our second card. This one will only have five hundred dollars left as a balance by next week. Our next payoff will be the debt company. All of our extra will go to pay that off, as it has a normal monthly payment coming out. After that we will pay off our car. Next we will begin paying one of our two houses off. Then we will pay the second one off. This is all complete within only a few years. Ironically what we knew in the past, was a mortgage needed thirty years to be paid off. Now I am paying off two mortgages within a few years. It is better now. If I would not have fallen, I would not have learned this new lesson. I sheathed off everything I knew, and now I know better. What I had was good, but now I have better.

This last year we sold a house, and then last week we sold another one. In the next two weeks we will be selling number three. We have two left, and we are keeping these. The two are rented. My mom's husband is managing them. I told my son the other day that we sold another house. His response was, "Why would we do that, don't houses, rentals, make us wealthy?" I love how smart my kids are! I told him the ones we were selling were actually liabilities, because each month they were costing us money. I explained an asset could be a rental as long as it is making money; if not, it is a liability. It was good that we were letting the old go, and focusing on what was working.

My car is very near on the list as a paid off item. Before I know it, I will be collecting close to a thousand dollars a month into an account all on its own. I am excited to see this account grow each month. It is neat to see an account grow monthly, instead of a loan reducing what is owed each month. When I pay all my other debts off, ending with my two mortgages, the money will be able to collect until we have another use for it. Until then, it will all be extra. This is a good feeling.

It is crazy what one year can do. Just like that, no million dollar job; just using money already being used, and keeping the habit.

When my car is paid off, within ten months from then, I will have ten thousand dollars sitting in my bank account. It is the same money. You either pay a car payment your whole life, or every year you get the choice to purchase a car in cash. If you choose this route, you pay less for your car because it is not an ongoing payment; it is a one stop purchase. You save so much money when you decide to become your own bank, and loan from yourself. It is the same money, just a different perspective on the money. The lessons I have learned this year are priceless.

I now am involved with Girl Scouts. I see it for what it truly is. It is a way to have life-long friends. It is a way to be a part of the community. It is an ongoing organization. I love all the different activities we get to do. I love the friends we have made. This is not a three month sport. Girl Scouts is a life style; and I am blessed we are a part of it.

I now am focusing on publishing my book. I think it is a great book that shows tithing works. You truly can be a millionaire, billionaire, via this process. What this process teaches you to do, is let go of what you have already known. It teaches you how to open up to a different way of thinking. It teaches you change is good. It shows you how to go through change. My book shows a real life example of a huge change. It shows my vulnerability. It shows my fears. It shows that all of these feelings are okay, they are normal. It shows how I changed; I changed because I trusted. It shows that we do get out after we go into the tunnel. It shows reality. It shows us that change is scary, but it is not the end for us. My next big change will be when my book is published. I will show myself that this is possible. I will show myself another dream of mine is possible. I will become an even stronger person, not because I am a published NY Best Selling author; but because I allowed myself to be that. I allowed myself to grow into the person I wanted to be. Change is scary, though change is imperative.

-Thankyou for being on my journey; I am forever grateful for you-

Chapter 17
Final After Thought 3, December 3, 2014

I began this chapter in bullet points, to show you the changes I have made in the last year. I think I will list them now to show you. I then will describe the last bit of this current journey in paragraphs, as I end our time together. Our time began 19 September 2013. Then it continued in Mid-October 2014. It finalized today, December 3, 2014.
Here is what has happened in the last year for me.

- I am worth Multi-Millions
- I have had my four foster children
- I had 3 babies
- I started my second book
- I have a business, making seventy thousand per year
- I have decided I want to live in Colorado
- I have begun looking at properties in Colorado. I am looking for my 5 acre farm and 25 rentals here in Colorado
- We have pinpointed an E8 slot here in Colorado that we have added to our Goal Board
- I have a kitten
- I have asked a friend to read our book
- I have a full-bred Mastiff with breeding papers; she will be a mamma!
- I manifested free vacuums that I affirmed for over three months
- I have had flowers on my table all year long. This is something I have intended for years
- I now, always have a clean house
- I am involved with Girl Scouts. We now see this as a life-long accomplishment
- Aidan is now in an "Army" Cub Scouts like dad and he wanted
- I have created a large office in my house like I have always wanted
- My father is coming here for Christmas, this is awesome!
- I respect my brother. I now see all he has gone through
- My dog Anabel has received Reiki. Her red in her eye is now almost nonexistent. Magic is Real
- I hear with my ears. I no longer only hear words through my forehead; I hear the spirit world with my ears
- I am losing weight, not by diet and exercise; instead with telling food I love it. It works! I now eat all that I want!
- I have recorded more than 100 Vlog's and have more than two thousand viewers

- I accomplished Rhonda Byrnes' gratitude list, "The Magic"
- My coffee maker is fixed; this was not talked about in the book; long story, but it is fixed now!
- I have received an abundance of jeans like I asked for; all free
- Received many pairs of free shoes for Aidan, as I asked for them
- I have found a cheap veterinarian
- I finally have my fish, Rose!
- I successfully bought and sold all year; I find many deals and fix items to sell at a higher price
- Made money off babysitting
- Got my truck, I have this with no car payment and it is large enough for all the kids I want to drive around with!
- My bills are awesome now
- I learned a different version of tithing
- Had a session with Christie Marie Sheldon
- My mom has visited three times!
- I manifested a dog door! I wanted this ALOT!!
- I now take care of me. I treat myself to a manicure once a month!
- Learned I was on the five house plan, and now I am on the 25 house plan!
- Learned how to be a, "hard money investor"
- Manifested free wood to heat the entire house all winter long!
- Both of my kids are top readers and popular!
- Both my kids have a wealth consciousness, like I had always hoped!
- I have learned how to ask for mentors in the Spirit World!
- I attracted free Reiki sessions!
- I received my, "The Silva Method" books that I wanted!
- I manifested all of my baby gear I wanted; including my triple stroller!
- Manifested family photos
- Brian is awesome as a business owner! I am proud how natural he is with this!
- Chevy has a professional groomer now!
- I am a successful coupon-er! I love price checking
- Brian manifested himself a gorgeous new leather jacket
- I love my neighbors; I love our community!
- I love my girlfriend's success! I loved watching her prosper this year!

The general has been listed. All of these amazing things have happened as I had hoped for. Here is a more detailed explanation of a few more details.

As I was editing this book a few months back, I was taking a break, to decide if I wanted to have more foster kids. I was also evaluating if there were other things I wanted to do that took me out of the house. It was also Mercury Retrograde. During Mercury Retrograde it is an awesome time for re-evaluation, and definitely not a time to commit to anything. It was break time. This time was perfect to wait, and see if I was done with the foster life. It was great to re-evaluate my book. It was great to research different positions, and see if I had any current interest. During this time I also did Rhonda Byrnes' Magic practice. This practice I highly recommend. Get her book, read it, and do the practice. Her book is called, "The Magic." I instantaneously felt the benefits as my vibration skyrocketed. I began writing my second book.

As I was editing, I made it to only a few chapters. I was not sure if my book was good, or if the vibration of my first book was as good a vibration as my second one. I put my first book aside and continued to write my second one. This is why the second 'After thought' is so short. I was writing it when I stopped with that book.

These are the things that happened during this period, coincidently while I was doing, "The Magic Practice." Within a few days of doing the practice, I started writing my second book. I had been googling testimonies for the practice when I came across information about property. I learned a lot from these videos. I learned how to own 25 rentals. Currently my only knowledge was how to own five. With five properties, you can purchase each one with only five thousand as a down payment. When you have six or more, you need to bring in twenty percent. This is twenty thousand, and I had no clue, in the past, how to do this consistently. Now I learned how to not have to bring in twenty thousand. I can have all of these properties, all for only five thousand down. This is cool. I also learned I can be a, "Hard money lender." In the past I had tried to borrow money from theses lenders to get more properties. Now I realized I could be the lender and make money off interest from those borrowing from me. There are so many ways to succeed; here I learned a whole new one. I spent a lot of time engulfing this new info.

I have critiqued my tithing since I began. I have grown. This summer God reminded me I am a version of Him. I was tithing to the church. At this time I was not attending church regularly. Where we went was great, though not, "the one" yet. Where you are supposed to tithe is where you gain your most (current) spiritual growth. Since I began, I tithed to church.

I then grew into tithing to something else I believed in. I spent my tithings on a few clearings with Christie Marie Sheldon. This has been a goal of mine for a while, I finally experienced it. It was good. I highly recommend it. Then, a few times, I was guided to give my tithings to a friend. One time I felt it was right to take my tithings to Toys R Us and splurge on my kids. I was opening up to the true meaning of a tithe. This summer God told me to tithe to me. He told me to believe in me. One of my biggest things for a while now, has been to feel safe. I tithed to feel more of this safety. Each month, I still collect ever thing I earn and take the ten percent out. It is a ritual. Currently I used that money to pay off all of my debt. A lot of that debt was from renters. As I paid each of these bills per month, I forgave my renters. I was going to give this money to church; instead I am giving it to them. I forgive them. I also forgive me each time I pay this tithe. As one more debt goes away, I forgive myself more. Now our debt is almost gone.

What I have learned is that my debt is disappearing. I no longer hate so much. I have forgiven. As the debt is going away, I realized (within the next twelve months) that money will not be paying off debt. What it is paying currently is the remaining credit card, than the debt company, and then the car. In this time I decided I did not want to pay off the next two rentals quite yet. Instead, I realized a large chunk, after this next twelve months, can go into investments. I calculated the money we would be saving each year, and it is over thirty-one thousand dollars. I had this money all along and did not realize it. I did numbers one day, and mixed this money with my interests, and by doing nothing, only tithing, I am a multi-millionaire as I continue to live my years. This is doing nothing more than tithing. This is money that already existed. This answer was here all along; I just never saw it. I am a multi-millionaire like I have always dreamed of being. It was here all along. We have always been as great as we hoped one day we would be.

I also thought it was funny that I affirmed all summer to be working with flipping houses. I wanted a coach I did not have to pay for. As I researched more and more, I was finding all of these dreams coming true. As a, "hard money lender," I am working with many mentors. As an investor with over thirty-one thousand per year to spend, I can flip as many houses as I want. Holy cow, where did this come from?! God.

Then, as if there is any reason for it to get any better, it did. I found an opportunity online. Someone had a handyman business they were selling. The opportunity felt awesome. We went moment by moment, and became comfortable with this new destination. We bought this business. This is what we do already. We have been fixing properties for years.

This opportunity came out of no-where. We have had this business for a few weeks now, and have made a lot of money with it. It is good work. We enjoy our customers and the projects we get to be a part of. Each customer I send a thank-you card to. I get so many reasons to be thankful lately!

The moment we pushed the submit button to purchase our business name, which is, "Integrity Maintenance and Repair LLC," we received a phone call. A lady called to ask if we could update her newly purchased six-plex. She then said she hoped to get to know us so we could offer names of good apartment managers. My husband told her all about me. She was to fly into Colorado in a week, and then is when we would finalize everything. How much better does that get? I have wanted that job forever! This is the job I spent my Mercury Retrograde trying to get. And she just calls! I called every job on Craigslist; no answer. Instead, she just calls me? This is cool.

Then, a Sunday afternoon we received a knock on our door. Three teenagers were holding a four week old kitten, and asked us if she was ours. She had been hanging out in our front bush. We decided to keep her. We are not cat people, but she was cute! Her name was Mykah. She brought us a lot of joy. Each day we did something new for her. We were deciding this whole week if we were cat people! The first day she settled into our home from out of the cold; she ate dog food! The second day we bought her cat food. The third day we bought her a collar and decided to name her. The fourth day we bought a litter box. We had tried very hard to have her go potty outside, but she wasn't having it! She won, day four she got her own indoor potty! She became a Finlayson!

As the week continued, the six-plex lady never called. This was okay. We were sure something even better was on the way. The business was booming. We also received an unexpected inheritance from Brian's grandma. She passed away this year and remembered us in her will. This was nice to be loved this much. The financials were a beautiful gift. We appreciate it. It is funny when we needed the money, we never received. And when we can only be thankful for the money, is when it comes in, in abundance. We are blessed. We are blessed we were remembered; as were those who will also miss Grandma.

During these weeks another amazing thing happened. This was a miracle in my world, as a friend was excited to read my book. This day while I was getting my kids from school, I was talking with a mom about my progress with editing, again. I think I was on Chapter three at the time. When I was home later, I realized she is the person I was looking for. She is someone I respect. She knows and talks to God all the time. She is who I am writing to. She is my audience.

I had wanted the courage to get this book to you. I needed someone's approval. I asked her if she would read this book, and give me feedback. I wanted to know if this book was worth reading. I wanted to know if it was inspirational. I wanted to know what she thought. I wanted to know what all of you would think. She said she would, and I gave myself a two week time limit to finish the editing. Today is two weeks and three days. Tomorrow I am handing her this book. This is not the easiest thing to do; her opinion in not something I can predict. It is scary to walk through these doors, but I'm doing it anyway. It is just like tithing. Either it works or it doesn't. But there comes many times in each of our lives where, finally, knowing the outcome is more important than fearing the outcome. Just like tithing, I decided I would rather chance God not existing, then go any more moments in life wondering if I should tithe or not. I would rather chance knowing my book is not great, than going any more moments wondering if it was or not. I spent the next days editing as fast as I could, and preparing myself to actually hand over one of my largest dreams. I was ready for anything, even if it was failure. Because knowing I could be great, was more important than hiding in-case I was a failure.

This reminds me of a story. It is a story of a prison guard in charge of a prison. He is in charge of the final days of his prisoners. On the day for each prisoner to die, he offers a choice. No one knows of this choice until the final moment. He says to the prisoner, "Today you have a choice, you can go through door number one or door number two. Door number one is the fenced-in area where a group of soldiers will shoot you to your death. You know this outcome; you have known it for months." The prisoner then asks what the second option is. The guard explains that no one knows. It is or is not the shooting range. The guard then says, "All I can tell you is that it is an outcome you are not sure of. And the first door is an option you are positive you do not like. You can be 100% sure of your future, or you can take a chance that your future may change."

Most people choose door number one. They find comfort in knowing what door number one offers. They do not like door number one, though they like knowing what door number one is. Door number two is an escape back to the prisoner's home. It is a door that comes with a bus ticket, dinner, and freedom. Most prisoners never experience door number two.

The days continued and were filled with lots of excitement as all of the new kept being injected! One thing we did not have was plans for Thanksgiving. This bugged me. It was a reminder of us not being near family, they were all in Wisconsin.

We were new to this area, which was good, though gaining friends that are loved like family, is a skill we still were learning. All I could do was continue our days and hope that we would learn this skill quickly. I trusted all would be good. Each day we learned to trust more. We accepted the current, though hoped for more. On the Friday before Thanksgiving, I picked the kids up from school, and went shopping! We were going to buy snails for Mrs. Rose. Snails are what keep her tank cleaned. We went to the store and were feeling really good. It felt good to be the shopper. I have grown so much over the year. Our money was so much more manageable. I could easily buy the essentials. We picked up what we needed for groceries for the evening. As I was leaving the store, I (spontaneously) checked my phone and noticed a missed call. It was a lady looking for an apartment manager. This was a few weeks later than when I sent out my application, my hundreds of applications. This was unexpected. I called her back. I told her I was shopping and not around my calendar. I hoped to be home before 5:30 to call her back and schedule an interview.

Then we went to the snake store. There we were helped in picking out our second fish, Jack. He is a different color than Rose, but still a Gold fish. We also purchased two snails. They are white and black; their names are Angel and Thunder. We also bought a plant. This plant floats in the water. The fish can snack on it and it purifies the water; his name is Dufus! After, I treated the kids with milk shakes from McDonalds! It is so nice to afford these little treats!

We get home, four minutes till 5:30. I call our lady; she answers and my interview is scheduled for the next Tuesday! I could not believe all this awesomeness was happening! Brian was not home till later, he had a job to do for the business. This evening was spent with our new family members and thoughts of my possible new job. Brian was home and we had lots to talk about. I was nervous for the new job. I wanted it; it was a dream coming true; though currently I was occupied with staying home to answer business calls. I also put myself back on the foster list, and was writing a second book. I also had a dead line to finish the first one. This was all good, all the things coming. They all seemed overwhelming, but they were all what I wanted. I trusted balance would eventually show itself, and just went with it all. This night we also received a call from an old friend. He used to work the same job Brian did while we were in Wisconsin. He is now moving to Arizona. On his way, he is traveling through Colorado. As we talked with him, we realized he will be here for Thanksgiving! He had no plans, we had no plans; we planned to spend the holiday together! We were so happy!

Saturday I spent my morning researching ways to take pet dander out of my house. The reason was our guest is allergic to pets. There is a plant called Peace Lilly that does this. I called every plant nursery in town and finally found one that has our plants! I also saw an ad for a gorgeous fifty gallon fish tank that was for sale. Rose and her new friend Jack were going to love it! We went to get our tank and then to the plant store! It is so nice to spend money! I love the opportunity! It is not as if I am spending ridiculous money. I got Rose's tank for 40 bucks, when its value was 1000! I still get every deal there is! It is just nice to be able to spend money when I want to. This year is so much different than last. I love it. I am thankful. We later took all the dogs to the vet. It is the same vet that we took them to last year. It is a discount traveling veterinarian. They are happy; they found a cool niche to make money. We are happy we get our dogs their shots, and at a discount! Later, we went to the snake store again on the way home. We purchased two more fish, Fate and Snowflake. Four fish was our limit as we only had fifty gallons! Brian later in the evening had another job. I love this business.

Sunday I wanted to fill my empty fish tank. As rose had moved to the bigger one, I needed a new renter. We added a new member to our family this day. His name is SGM (Sergeant Major) Fin! He is a very tiny turtle. I love him! Boy we have become an exotic family! Now we have four dogs, one kitten, two snails, four fish, Dufus our water plant, two peace Lilly's, and a turtle!

Monday, the kids and I were veg'ing as Brian prepared to go purchase his business shirts. He had made them with his logo of the business, and was about to drive to their location to finalize the details. At that moment, he decided to check his government cell phone. He was not planning on doing this for a week, because he was on leave, vacation. On his work emails, was an email stating we were moving to Utah on February 23, 2015. Oh, we wanted to stay in Colorado so bad! He called the guy in charge of submitting orders; he was on leave for a week. Brian then called his boss. They noticed they were not official orders, and maybe they could be changed. Though nothing could be done till next week. We researched our business and learned it was easy to transfer to Utah. We all then decided to get in Brian's truck, and went to order the Business shirts as a family. Later we went to the store for dinner, then ate, and enjoyed our evening as a family. If we had to go, we were going to miss Colorado. Colorado was real good to us. We knew we would not know any answers till next week. We had to be okay with both. We had emailed the orders guy, and asked to stay here as there was a position opening up here this summer. Whichever way the decision went, we were okay with both.

If it was not Colorado, there must be a reason. We were going to trust this reason.

Tuesday was my interview. Brian left the house early because a call for the business came in at eight A.M. I was expecting him back within a few hours. He was gone a long time. I used a lot of my morning editing. Before I knew it the doorbell rang. It was our friend from Wisconsin. Brian invited them over today to visit. They brought their laundry since they spent the prior week in hotels. Brian was not here yet. We chit chatted and caught up on all the good. They started their laundry as I noticed the time for my interview was fast approaching. Soon it was apparent that Brian was not going to be home in time for me to go. Our guests offered to watch the kids. I went and my interview was great. She told me I had the job. It was a dream job. I then learned she was looking for a full time candidate. Oh no! I told her I needed to think about it. I was torn. This was a dream job, but I did not want to be working full time. When I was home, Brian was home. He was talking with our guests. They were leaving, his allergies were acting up. We had a good visit. We planned for Thanksgiving dinner to be at a Restaurant. Wednesday morning our new kitten was sick. She was very sick. Within a few hours she died. We all cried. We did not understand what happened. She was fine the night before. We said our goodbyes. We were very sad. Later Brian remembered a memory from child hood. He said when he was at his grandma's farm; there was a litter of kittens. There was always this one that was separate from the rest. Brian kept bringing that kitten back to its brothers and sisters. And then the next day she would be separate again. Eventually Brian's grandma told him to stop. She said the kitten was sick. Brian said it did not look sick. The grandma said she agreed, but the mamma cat knew better. She separates this sick kitten from the rest so the others do not get sick. This sick kitten was going to die. Now, in our case I always found it weird how this tiny little kitten was just dropped off. She was too little to travel the town herself. I always felt she must have been dropped off; though I thought it was by an angel. In hindsight, our kitten was really little, and she did not have a voice. She would "meow," but no voice ever came from her. She was sick all along. She came here to die. I am honored that she chose us. I am sad she left, but honored I was able to spend those two weeks with her.

Thanksgiving we had planned dinner at a restaurant. In the morning our friends called to cancel. They decided to spend the holiday driving the rest of the way to Arizona. We were heart-broken. We then decided we were enough. We were enough to spend Thanksgiving with! We showered and dressed-up and then headed to the store to buy food for Thanksgiving.

The kids were awarded a toy for being the best kids ever; ones we enjoyed spending our holiday with! We stopped at the gas station for treats on the way home. We wanted fast food, though all were closed. Gas station food was our lunch, as Brian would be cooking dinner all day. When we were home, we saw kittens posted on craigslist and called the ad. Dreana and I drove to pick up our new seven week old kitten! She does not have a name yet, though she is awesome! Thanksgiving ended up being awesome. We even had two sets of kiddos come and hang out for the day. Our day was amazing!

Friday we decorated our house for Christmas. Christmas is going to be awesome this year!

Sunday evening we received an email. We have official orders for July 13th and/or prior to move to Utah. The orders guy, because of our email, extended our move till the summer; though was firm on the official move. We are moving to Utah, unless things change between now and then. Brian has his E8 board in February. Results should be out by March. If he gets his E8, all of these plans change. But until then, we are moving to Utah! It is funny; Utah is only eight hours from here. We love here, and there is only eight hours from here. Also, one of the only gripes we have with Colorado is that it has no grass. In all of the pictures of Utah, all we see is grass. Maybe this intention has wanted to happen all this time. Maybe Utah is a dream coming true?

Monday, the kids went back to school and Brian went back to work. I edited a lot this day. I was getting closer; this book is destined to come out! Brian learned that there are certain licenses that are going to need to be done for the business. He brought home lots of homework and study material.

Tuesday evening we went to a tree lighting ceremony put on by the community. Last year, a mom and her daughters skipped Girl Scouts and went to this ceremony. I wondered the entire year what the ceremony was. This year when the brochure came home about it, I immediately marked it on the calendar. When we were at the festivities, this year, I saw that same mom. I told her all about us coming because of her story from the year prior. She was surprised I would circle my entire year around something she suggested. This made her feel good. She was this good, that I would intend to go to this event, because she mentioned it the year prior. We are more important than we think. We are more special than we think. We mean something, to many.

This brings us to today. Today I am finishing this book. Tomorrow I am letting a friend read it. I am allowing myself to feel significant. I am allowing myself to matter. I remember, about this time last year, I had bills stacked up on a shelf.

I was scared with which one to choose first. One year later, I can buy groceries, I can buy a business, and I can buy milk shakes. I am way beyond that. I am worth multi-millions. I was all along. I just never realized it. Does tithing work? Yes.

I am honored to have gotten to know myself. I found my courage again. I found myself back. I am a pretty awesome person. I thank you for being with me. You have been a real friend. I am blessed by you. You know you are worth whatever it is you desire, right? You are worth it all. It actually already exists; you just have not noticed it yet. Let it un-camouflage for you. You are worth it. I have wanted to write to you since I was a little girl. This is how important you are.

I wanted that big bang from writing this story. Look at that, I accomplished it. I am a multi-millionaire. I wrote a book! What big goals I have finally accomplished! What a big bang this is. Funny though, I was this already and didn't even realize it. It was here all along. I just needed to see how cool I already was. You are cool too, just see it.

P.S. In one year my world changed 100%. In one year this happened. Miracles do happen. Believe this, believe in you. I am honored to have shared my story with you. I am honored I was able to document it, and prove to myself that God does care. God is real. Magic is real. Love is real. I challenge you to grow into that person you want to be. Here is how you do it. Every day make the time to write a gratitude list. Write ten reasons of why you are thankful. Do this every day, for the rest of your life. Let gratitude transform your desires into reality. This is the key. This is what my second book is all about. Really, all you have to do is make the time each day, to write ten reasons of why you are thankful. When you do this, God takes over. My second year has been so much more exponential than my first. The reason is simple; I am thankful now. Gratitude changes everything. I think it was Napoleon Hill that said (paraphrased,) "Just do what I say, believe it as truth, and watch what happens."

As always, Michelle

-I am forever grateful you are in my world-

References:

- The online group spoke about throughout the book is, "Attracting Abundance" found on Facebook. The creator of the group is Shanae Tomlin. Or check out her website attractingabundanceeasily.com

- Byrne, R. (2012). The magic. New York: Atria Books

- Byrne, R. (2006). The secret. New York: Atria Books.

- Gutierrez, D. (2014, October). How to Attract Money [Interview]. Retrieved from http://youtu.be/SJlm5_vPQC4.

- Harrington, P., Heriot, D., Byrne, R., Prime Time Productions., Nine Network., & TS Production, LLC. (2006). The Secret. Melbourne, Australia: TS Production, LLC.

- International Bible Society. (1984). The Holy Bible: New international version: containing the Old Testament and the New Testament. Colorado Springs, Colorado: International Bible Society. Print.

- Jason Emery is the music star talked about throughout the book. You can also find him on YouTube.

- Secret Stories. Website. Available at www.thesecret.tv/stories. Numerous testimonies of, "The Secret."

- Smith, S. (1992). Stretton Smith's 4T prosperity program: Tithing of time, talent and treasure for prosperity and the fullness of life. Carmel, CA: 4T Pub. Co.

- Sylvia Browne. Website. Available at www.novus.org/home/prayerchainform.cfm. Here is how you can be on her prayer chain and learn a lot of neat info.